Investigating Social Problems

Using MicroCase® *ExplorIt*

David J. Ayers

GROVE CITY COLLEGE

THOMSON

WADSWORTH

Australia • Canada • Mexico • Singapore • Spain • United Kingdom • United States

D0082285

Printed in the United States of America
1 2 3 4 5 6 7 08 07 06 05 04

Printer: West Group

ISBN: 0-534-60984-8

For more information about our products, contact us at:
Thomson Learning Academic Resource Center
1-800-423-0563

For permission to use material from this text or product, submit a request online at
http://www.thomsonrights.com.
Any additional questions about permissions can be submitted by email to **thomsonrights@thomson.com.**

Thomson Wadsworth
10 Davis Drive
Belmont, CA 94002-3098
USA

Asia
Thomson Learning
5 Shenton Way #01-01
UIC Building
Singapore 068808

Australia/New Zealand
Thomson Learning
102 Dodds Street
Southbank, Victoria 3006
Australia

Canada
Nelson
1120 Birchmount Road
Toronto, Ontario M1K 5G4
Canada

Europe/Middle East/South Africa
Thomson Learning
High Holborn House
50/51 Bedford Row
London WC1R 4LR
United Kingdom

Latin America
Thomson Learning
Seneca, 53
Colonia Polanco
11560 Mexico D.F.
Mexico

Spain/Portugal
Paraninfo
Calle/Magallanes, 25
28015 Madrid, Spain

CONTENTS

ABOUT THE AUTHOR

David J. Ayers grew up in Washington D.C., Athens, Greece, and Frankfurt, Germany. He received his Ph.D. from New York University, his MA from American University, and his BA from Edinboro University of Pennsylvania. He is currently Professor of Sociology, Chairperson of the Department of Sociology, and Assistant Dean of the Calderwood School of Arts and Letters at Grove City College. Dr. Ayers' research experience includes serving as Special Research Affiliate at the Office of Policy Studies, Department of Housing and Urban Development, as well as medical cost containment studies and other corporate research and writing projects for numerous companies. The latter work included authoring a complete K–11 environmental educational curriculum for Anhauser-Busch/Seaworld with his wife Kathleen, titled Kids Can Change the World. He is author of *Experiencing Social Research: An Introduction Using MicroCase*, and also of the test bank and instructor's manual for Rodney Stark's *Sociology*, 9th edition.

PREFACE

This workbook helps instructors to impart an understanding of sociological methods, concepts, and creativity in asking and answering specific questions about social reality, within the context of a Social Problems course. It ought to enhance students' sociological skills, increase their understanding of major social problems, and enliven classroom discussion and debate. At least, this is my hope; that this workbook will help to stir up students' "sociological imaginations" with regards to social problems.

Investigating Social Problems can be easily used along with just about any major Social Problems main text. To help the instructor do so, a table is provided immediately following this preface that shows, for most major Social Problems texts, which chapters correspond to each exercise in this workbook.

Major concepts and skills are unfolded in Exercises 1 through 3. All exercises following these introductory ones assume mastery of the material in these first three exercises. *Thus, it is important that instructors assign and cover Exercises 1 through 3 at the beginning of their courses,* before moving on to subsequent exercises. Content in those exercises is designed to fit in well with typical introductory discussions in Social Problems courses. However, once these first three exercises are dealt with, the *other exercises can be covered in any order* that the instructor finds convenient.

It would not be fair for me to let this opportunity pass without recognizing the excellent oversight of Wadsworth/International Thomson editor Robert Jucha. Eve Howard and Lin Marshall played a major role in helping me to work through my initial proposal for this project, and to sharpen its focus. Julie Aguilar and Jodi Gleason provided cheerful, invaluable assistance and guidance on this project.

Too often, we social scientists forget how impossible much of our work would be if not for the labors of those who design and conduct so many critical data-collection efforts. These include James A. Davis and Tom W. Smith of the National Opinion Research Center (NORC) (General Social Survey), along with many of the staff at NORC, the various supervisors and staff at the Center for Political Studies, Institute for Social Research and the Survey Research Center who have done the National Election Studies for many years, and those at the Centers for Disease Control and Prevention (CDC) who conducted the Youth Risk Behavior Surveillance System Surveys and made the data available to all of us at no cost. But of course, this list does not even begin to scratch the surface of these important data providers, as even a cursory glance at the source list for the COUNTRIES and STATES data sets used in this workbook will show.

I wish to thank my superiors here at Grove City College, who have always provided an environment and encouragement which has enabled me to complete projects like this while carrying a significant teaching load and (increasingly) administrative duties. Throughout writing this book, these have especially included Dean Charles W. Dunn and my Provost and fellow sociologist, William P. Anderson.

My eldest daughter, Leah Marie Ayers, was also my research and editorial assistant on this book. There were no mistakes too small for her to detect and point out to me, and I am sure I didn't always make it easy for her to do so! Thank you, Leah. This book is much better for your painstaking labors in going over every line and exercise twice.

Finally, I must thank the other members of my family, who gave me the freedom to spend the time I needed to get this project done. At the top of this list is my wife, Kathy, whose counsel and love enables me not only to get through jobs like this, but through life.

David J. Ayers
Grove City, Pennsylvania

Correspondence between Exercises in this Workbook and Chapters in Major Social Problems Textbooks, Part A

AYERS Investigating Social Problems	Mooney, Knox, & Schacht 4/e[1]	Kornblum & Julian 11/e[2]	Henslin 6/e[3]	Macionis[4]
Exercise 1	Chapter 1	Chapter 1	Chapter 1	Chapter 1
Exercise 2	Chapter 1	Chapter 1	Chapter 2	Chapter 1
Exercise 3	Chapter 1	Chapter 1	Chapter 2	Chapter 1
Exercise 4	Chapter 8	Chapter 8	Chapter 3	Chapter 8
Exercise 5	Chapter 3	Chapter 4	Chapter 4	Chapter 9
Exercise 6	Chapter 4	Chapter 5	Chapters 5 & 6	Chapters 6 & 7
Exercise 7	Chapter 2	Chapter 3	Chapter 10	Chapter 10
Exercise 8	Chapter 10	Chapter 6	Chapter 7	Chapter 2
Exercise 9	Chapter 6	Chapter 7	Chapter 8	Chapter 3
Exercise 10	Chapter 7	Chapter 8	Chapter 9	Chapter 4
Exercise 11	Chapter 9	Chapter 9	Chapter 2	Chapter 5
Exercise 12	Chapter 5	Chapter 10	Chapters 5 & 11	Chapter 7
Exercise 13	Chapter 13	Chapter 14	Chapter 13	Chapter 16
Exercise 14	Chapter 2	Chapter 2	Chapter 10	Chapter 10
Exercise 15	Chapter 14	Chapter 15	Chapter 14	Chapter 17

Correspondence between Exercises in this Workbook and Chapters in Major Social Problems Textbooks, Part B

AYERS Investigating Social Problems	Zastrow 5/e[5]	Curran & Renzetti 5/e[6]	Eitzen & Baca Zinn 9/e[7]	Kendall 3/e[8]
Exercise 1	Chapter 1	Chapter 1	Chapter 1	Chapter 1
Exercise 2	Chapter 1	Chapters 1 & 2	Chapters 1 & 2	Chapter 1
Exercise 3	Chapter 1	Chapters 1 & 2	Chapters 1 & 2	Chapter 1
Exercise 4	Chapter 5	Chapter 6	Chapter 10	Chapter 6
Exercise 5	Chapter 4	N/A	Chapter 13	Chapter 8
Exercise 6	Chapter 2	Chapter 3	Chapter 12	Chapter 9
Exercise 7	Chapter 3	Chapter 10	Chapter 17	Chapter 10
Exercise 8	Chapter 9	Chapter 4	Chapter 7	Chapter 2
Exercise 9	Chapter 6	Chapter 5	Chapter 8	Chapter 3
Exercise 10	Chapter 7	Chapter 6	Chapter 9	Chapter 4
Exercise 11	Chapter 8	Chapter 8	Chapter 5	Chapter 5
Exercise 12	Chapter 10	Chapter 7	Chapter 15	Chapter 11
Exercise 13	Chapter 16	Chapter 12	Chapter 3	Chapter 15
Exercise 14	Chapter 11	Chapter 10	Chapter 17	Chapter 10
Exercise 15	Chapter 17	Chapter 15	Chapter 4	Chapter 15

[1] Linda A. Mooney, David Knox, and Caroline Schacht, 2005, *Understanding Social Problems*, 4th ed., Belmont, Calif.: Wadsworth.

[2] William Kornblum and Joseph Julian, 2004, *Social Problems*, 11th ed., Upper Saddle River, N.J.: Prentice Hall.

[3] James M Henslin., 2003. *Social Problems*, 6th ed., Upper Saddle River, N.J.: Prentice Hall.

[4] John J. Macionis, 2002, *Social Problems*, Upper Saddle River, N.J.: Prentice Hall.

[5] Charles Zastrow, 2000, *Social Problems: Issues and Solutions*, 5th ed., Belmont, Calif.: Wadsworth.

[6] Daniel J. Curran and Claire M. Renzetti, 2000, *Social Problems: Society in Crisis*, 5th ed., Boston: Allyn and Bacon.

[7] D. Stanley Eitzen and Maxine Baca Zinn, 2003, *Social Problems*, 9th ed., Boston: Allyn and Bacon.

[8] Diane Kendall, 2004, *Social Problems in a Diverse Society*, 3rd ed., Boston: Allyn and Bacon.

Correspondence between Exercises in this Workbook and Chapters in Major Social Problems Textbooks, Part C

AYERS Investigating Social Problems	Sullivan 6/e[9]	Coleman & Kerbo 2/e[10]	Coleman & Kerbo 8/e[11]
Exercise 1	Chapter 1	Chapter 1	Chapter 1
Exercise 2	Chapter 1	Chapter 1	Chapter 1
Exercise 3	Chapter 1	Chapter 1	Chapter 1
Exercise 4	Chapter 8	Chapter 8	Chapter 11
Exercise 5	Chapter 10	Chapter 9	Chapter 12
Exercise 6	Chapter 9	Chapter 10	Chapter 13
Exercise 7	Chapter 4	Chapter 5	Chapter 6
Exercise 8	Chapter 5	Chapter 6	Chapters 7 & 17
Exercise 9	Chapter 6	Chapter 7	Chapter 8
Exercise 10	Chapter 7	Chapter 8	Chapter 10
Exercise 11	Chapter 8	N/A	Chapter 9
Exercise 12	Chapter 2	Chapter 3	Chapter 2
Exercise 13	Chapter 12	Chapter 12	Chapter 15
Exercise 14	Chapter 4	Chapter 5	Chapter 6
Exercise 15	Chapter 13	Chapter 12	Chapter 16

Correspondence between Exercises in this Workbook and Chapters in Major Social Problems Textbooks, Part D

AYERS Investigating Social Problems	Parillo 5/e[12]	Lauer & Lauer 9/e[13]	Palen[14]
Exercise 1	Chapter 1	Chapter 1	Chapter 1
Exercise 2	Chapter 2	Chapter 1	Chapter 1
Exercise 3	Chapter 2	Chapter 1	Chapter 1
Exercise 4	Chapters 7 & 14	Chapter 2	Chapter 15
Exercise 5	Chapter 13	Chapter 3	Chapter 13
Exercise 6	Chapter 9	Chapters 4 & 5	Chapter 12
Exercise 7	Chapter 11	Chapter 13	Chapter 14
Exercise 8	Chapter 5	Chapter 6	Chapter 2
Exercise 9	Chapter 8	Chapter 8	Chapters 3 & 4
Exercise 10	Chapter 7	Chapter 7	Chapter 5
Exercise 11	N/A	N/A	Chapter 11
Exercise 12	Chapter 10	Chapter 12	Chapter 10
Exercise 13	Chapter 3	Chapter 15	Chapter 6
Exercise 14	Chapter 11	Chapter 13	Chapter 14
Exercise 15	Chapter 3	Chapter 15	Chapter 6

---

[9] Thomas J. Sullivan, 2003, *Introduction to Social Problems*, 6th ed., Boston: Allyn and Bacon.

[10] James William Coleman and Harold R. Kerbo, 2003, *Social Problems: A Brief Introduction*, 2nd ed., Upper Saddle River, N.J.: Prentice Hall.

[11] James William Coleman and Harold R. Kerbo, 2002, *Social Problems*, 8th ed., Upper Saddle River, N.J.: Prentice Hall.

[12] Vincent N. Parillo, 2002, *Contemporary Social Problems*, 5th ed., Boston: Allyn and Bacon.

[13] Robert Lauer and Jeanette C. Lauer, 2004, *Social Problems and the Quality of Life*, 9th ed., Boston: McGraw-Hill.

[14] J. John Palen, 2001, *Social Problems for the 21st Century*, Boston: McGraw-Hill.

GETTING STARTED

INTRODUCTION

This workbook is part of a fully integrated package using the Student ExplorIt software, a powerful statistical analysis program developed specifically to introduce students to social science quantitative analysis.

Each exercise in this workbook examines a topic of the Social Problems course. The preliminary section of each chapter uses data provided with the workbook to illustrate key issues related to the topic in question. You can easily create all the graphics in this part of the exercise by following the ExplorIt Guides you'll be seeing. Doing so will take just a few clicks of your computer mouse and will help you become familiar with ExplorIt. The ExplorIt Guides are described in more detail below.

Each exercise also has a worksheet section where you'll do your own data analysis to further explore the topic. This section usually contains about a dozen questions that will either follow up on examples from the preliminary section or have you explore some new issues. You'll use the Student ExplorIt software to answer these questions.

SYSTEM REQUIREMENTS

- Windows 98 (or higher)

- 64 MB RAM (minimum)

- 20 MB of hard drive space

- Internet Access (broadband recommended)

Macintosh Note: This software was designed for use with a PC. To run the software on a Macintosh, you will need PC emulation software or hardware installed. Many Macintosh computers in the past few years come with PC emulation software or hardware. For more information about PC emulation software or hardware, review the documentation that came with your computer or check with your local Macintosh retailer.

NETWORK VERSIONS OF STUDENT EXPLORIT

A network version of Student ExplorIt is available at no charge to instructors who adopt this book for their course. We strongly recommend installing the network version if students may be using this software on lab computers. The network version is available from the Instructor Companion page for this book at http://sociology.wadsworth.com.

INSTALLING STUDENT EXPLORIT

A card has been packaged with this book. This card contains a PIN code and a website address from which you can download the Student ExplorIt software needed to complete the exercises in this book. You must have this card to obtain the software. Only one person may use this card.

To install Student ExplorIt to a hard drive, you will need to follow the instructions on the card to register for access. Once you are on the download screen, follow these steps in order:

1. Select DOWNLOAD to begin downloading the software.

2. You will then be selected with a choice:

   a. Run this program from its current location. <u>This is the recommended option</u>, and this option will allow the installation to begin as soon as the file is downloaded to your computer.

   b. Save this program to disk. This option will allow you to save the downloaded file to your computer for later installation. This option also provides you a file that will reinstall the software in the event this is needed. If you select this option, you will then need to specify where to save the file. Be sure to select a location where you can easily find the file. This file is named STU519113.exe. Once the file has downloaded, locate the downloaded file and open or double-click the file name.

3. A security warning may appear next. Select [Yes].

4. The next screen will display the name of this book. Click [OK] to continue.

5. The next screen shows where the files needed for the installation will be placed. We strongly recommend you accept the default location, but if desired, you can specify a new location. Click [Unzip] to begin the install.

6. During the installation, you will be presented with several screens, as described below. In most cases you will be required to make a selection or an entry and then click [Next] to continue.

   The first screen that appears is the **License Name** screen. Here you are asked to type your name. It is important to type your name correctly, because it cannot be changed after this point. Your name will appear on all printouts, so make sure you spell it completely and correctly! Then click [Next] to continue.

   A **Welcome** screen now appears. This provides some introductory information and suggests that you shut down any other programs that may be running. Click [Next] to continue.

   You are next presented with a **Software License Agreement**. Read this screen and click [Yes] if you accept the terms of the software license.

   The next screen has you Choose the Destination for the program files. You are strongly advised to use the destination directory that is shown on the screen. Click [Next] to continue.

7. The Student ExplorIt program will now be installed. At the end of the installation, you will be asked if you would like a shortcut icon placed on the Windows desktop. We recommend that you select [Yes]. You are now informed that the installation of Student ExplorIt is finished. Click the [Finish] button and you will be returned to the opening Welcome Screen. To exit completely, click the option "Exit Welcome Screen."

STARTING STUDENT EXPLORIT

There are two ways to run Student ExplorIt: (1) from a hard drive installation or (2) from a network installation. Both methods are described below.

Starting Student ExplorIt from a Hard Drive Installation

If Student ExplorIt is installed to the hard drive of your computer (see earlier section "Installing Student ExplorIt"), locate the Student ExplorIt "shortcut" icon on the Windows desktop, which looks something like this:

To start Student ExplorIt, position your mouse pointer over the shortcut icon and double-click (that is, click it twice in rapid succession). If you did not permit the shortcut icon to be placed on the desktop during the install process (or if the icon was accidentally deleted), you can follow these directions to start the software:

Click [Start] from the Windows desktop.

Click [Programs].

Click MicroCase.

Click Student ExplorIt - SR.

After a few seconds, Student ExplorIt will appear on your screen.

Starting Student ExplorIt from a Network

If the network version of Student ExplorIt has been installed to a computer network, double-click the Student ExplorIt icon that appears on the Windows desktop to start the program. You will need to enter your name each time you start the network version. Anything you print from software will display the name you enter and the current date. (Note: Your instructor may provide additional information that is unique to your computer network.)

MAIN MENU OF STUDENT EXPLORIT

Student ExplorIt is extremely easy to use. All you do is point and click your way through the program. That is, use your mouse arrow to point at the selection you want, and then click the left button on the mouse.

The main menu is the starting point for everything you will do in Student ExplorIt. Look at how it works. Notice that not all options on the menu are always available. You will know which options are available at any given time by looking at the colors of the options. For example, when you first start the software, only the Open File option is immediately available. As you can see, the colors for this option are brighter than those for the other tasks shown on the screen. Also, when you move your mouse pointer over this option, it becomes highlighted.

ExplorIt Guides

Throughout this workbook, "ExplorIt Guides" provide the basic information needed to carry out each task. Here is an example:

> ➤ Data File: **STATES**
> ➤ Task: **Mapping**
> ➤ Variable 1: **2) POP 2002**
> ➤ View: **Map**

Each line of the ExplorIt Guide is actually an instruction. Let's follow the simple steps to carry out this task.

Step 1: Select a Data File

Before you can do anything in Student ExplorIt, you need to open a data file. To open a data file, click the Open File task. A list of data files will appear in a window (e.g., COUNTRIES, ELECTION, GSS). If you click on a file name once, a description of the highlighted file is shown in the window next to this list. In the ExplorIt Guide shown above, the ➤ symbol to the left of the Data File step indicates that you should open the STATES data file. To do so, click STATES and then click the [Open] button (or just double-click STATES). The next window that appears (labeled File Settings) provides additional information about the data file, including a file description, the number of cases in the file, and the number of variables, among other things. To continue, click the [OK] button. You are now returned to the main menu of Student ExplorIt. (You won't need to repeat this step until you want to open a different data file.) Notice that you can always see which data file is currently open by looking at the file name shown on the top line of the screen.

Step 2: Select a Task

Once you open a data file, the next step is to select a program task. Six analysis tasks are offered in this version of Student ExplorIt. Not all tasks are available for each data file, because some tasks are appropriate only for certain kinds of data. Mapping, for example, is a task that applies only to ecological data, and thus cannot be used with survey data files.

In the ExplorIt Guide we're following, the ➤ symbol on the second line indicates that the MAPPING task should be selected, so click the Mapping option with your left mouse button.

Step 3: Select a Variable

After a task is selected, you will be shown a list of the variables in the open data file. Notice that the first variable is highlighted and a description of that variable is shown in the Variable Description window at the lower right. You can move this highlight through the list of variables by using the up and down cursor keys (as well as the <Page Up> and <Page Down> keys). You can also click once on a variable name to move the highlight and update the variable description. Go ahead—move the highlight to a few other variables and read their descriptions.

If the variable you want to select is not showing in the variable window, click on the scroll bars located on the right side of the variable list window to move through the list. See the following figure:

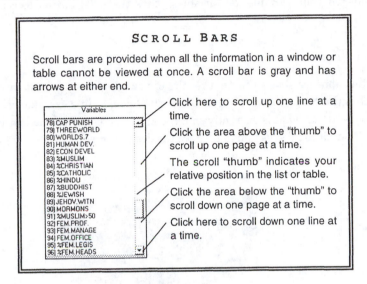

By the way, you will find an appendix at the back of this workbook that contains a list of the variable names for key data files provided in this package.

Each task requires the selection of one or more variables, and the ExplorIt Guides indicate which variables should be selected. The ExplorIt Guide example indicates that you should select 2) POP 2002 as Variable 1. On the screen, there is a box labeled Variable 1. Inside this box, there is a vertical cursor that indicates this box is currently an active option. When you select a variable, it will be placed in this box. Before selecting a variable, be sure that the cursor is in the appropriate box. If it is not, place the cursor inside the appropriate box by clicking the box with your mouse. This is important because in some tasks the ExplorIt Guide will require more than one variable to be selected, and you want to be sure that you put each selected variable in the right place.

To select a variable, use any one of the methods shown below. (Note: If the name of a previously selected variable is in the box, use the <Delete> or <Backspace> key to remove it—or click the [Clear All] button.)

- Type the **number** of the variable and press <Enter>.

- Type the **name** of the variable and press <Enter>. Or you can type just enough of the name to distinguish it from other variables in the data—POP would be sufficient for this example.

- Double-click the desired variable in the Variable List window. This selection will then appear in the variable selection box. (If the name of a previously selected variable is in the box, the newly selected variable will replace it.)

- Highlight the desired variable in the variable list, and then click the arrow that appears to the left of the variable selection box. The variable you selected will now appear in the box. (If the name of a previously selected variable is in the box, the newly selected variable will replace it.)

Once you have selected your variable (or variables), click the [OK] button to continue to the final results screen.

Step 4: Select a View

The next screen that appears shows the final results of your analysis. In most cases, the screen that first appears matches the "view" indicated in the ExplorIt Guide. In this example, you are instructed to look at the Map view—that's what is currently showing on the screen. In some instances, however, you may need to make an additional selection to produce the desired screen.

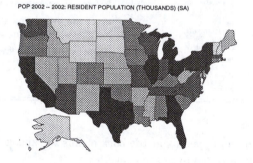

POP 2002 -- 2002: RESIDENT POPULATION (THOUSANDS) (SA)

(OPTIONAL) Step 5: Select an Additional Display

Some ExplorIt Guides will indicate that an additional "Display" should be selected. In that case, simply click on the option indicated for that additional display. For example, this ExplorIt Guide may have included an additional line that required you to select the Legend display.

Step 6: Continuing to the Next ExplorIt Guide

Some instructions in the ExplorIt Guide may be the same for at least two examples in a row. For instance, after you display the map for population in the example above, the following ExplorIt Guide may be given:

> Data File: **STATES**
> Task: **Mapping**
> ➤ Variable 1: **48) %POOR00**
> ➤ View: **Map**

Notice that the first two lines in the ExplorIt Guide do not have the ➤ symbol located in front of the items. That's because you already have the data file STATES open and you have already selected the MAPPING task. With the results of your first analysis showing on the screen, there is no need to return to the main menu to complete this next analysis. Instead, all you need to do is select %POOR00 as your new variable. Click the [[↺]] button located in the top left corner of your screen and the variable selection screen for the MAPPING task appears again. Replace the variable with 48) %POOR00 and click [OK].

To repeat: You need to do only those items in the ExplorIt Guide that have the ➤ symbol in front of them. If you start from the top of the ExplorIt Guide, you're simply wasting your time.

If the ExplorIt Guide instructs you to select an entirely new task or data file, you will need to return to the main menu. To return to the main menu, simply click the [Menu] button located at the top left corner of the screen. At this point, select the new data file and/or task that is indicated in the ExplorIt Guide.

That's all there is to the basic operation of Student ExplorIt. Just follow the instructions given in the ExplorIt Guide and point and click your way through the program.

ADDITIONAL SHORTCUTS

There are some additional ways to navigate through the software that you may find helpful.

- If you are frequently switching between two to four data files, you can quickly change files from any screen by clicking [File] on the drop-down menu. The last four files opened will appear at the bottom of the drop-down list. You can select the desired file from this list, the file will open automatically, and you will be returned to the main menu to select the desired task.

- Again, by clicking [File] on the drop-down menu, you can select [Open] to open any data file from any screen. When you open a new file, you will automatically return to the main menu.

- To switch to a different statistical task, instead of returning to the main menu, select [Statistics] from the drop-down menu and select the desired task. NOTE: If you select a task that is not enabled on the main menu, a message box will open alerting you that this task is not available. •

- You can open a list of variables in the open file at any time by pressing the <F3> key.

ONLINE HELP

Student ExplorIt offers extensive online help. You can obtain task-specific help by pressing <F1> at any point in the program. For example, if you are performing a scatterplot analysis, you can press <F1> to see the help for the SCATTERPLOT task.

If you prefer to browse through a list of the available help topics, select Help from the pull-down menu at the top of the screen and select the **Help Topics** option. At this point, you will be provided a list of topic areas. A closed-book icon represents each topic. To see what information is available in a given topic area, double-click on a book to "open" it. (For this version of the software, use only the "Student

ExplorIt" section of help; do not use the "Student MicroCase" section.) When you double-click on a book graphic, a list of help topics is shown. A help topic is represented by a graphic with a piece of paper with a question mark on it. Double-click on a help topic to view it.

If you have questions about Student ExplorIt, try the online help described above. If you are not familiar with software or computers, you may want to ask a classmate or your instructor for assistance.

EXITING FROM STUDENT EXPLORIT

If you are continuing to the next section of this workbook, it is not necessary to exit from Student ExplorIt quite yet. But when you are finished using the program, it is very important that you properly exit the software—do not just walk away from the computer. To exit Student ExplorIt, return to the main menu and select the [Exit Program] button that appears on the screen.

◆ EXERCISE 1 ◆
DEFINING "SOCIAL PROBLEMS"

Tasks: Univariate, Historical Trends
Data Files: ELECTION, TRENDS

Get any group of people together and start them talking about "what's wrong with the world today." Then observe carefully. What will you hear? Well, probably a lot of things. But if you pay close attention, you will notice that this kind of discussion tells you about a lot more than just the problems facing human beings, or even about our own society, today. Dialogue like this also reveals a great deal about the people who are talking about these troubles. It helps you to see what worries and matters most to them, and what their ideals and aspirations for themselves and society are. Some of the essential, and quite different, ways that people have of looking at the world become very evident when they talk about those problems that they believe are troubling contemporary society. And as you step back and look at the conversation as a whole, you might also find the realities that some people "know" to be "serious problems" are considered by others not to be problems at all, or may even be regarded as blessings by some.

If you used this exchange to learn about what may or may not be properly regarded as a true "social problem," you might conclude that the latter, like beauty, is something that only exists "in the eye of the beholder." And to an extent, you would be right. After all, as Malcolm Spector and John I. Kitsuse point out, "Social problems are what people think they are."[1] Thus, to understand, with regard to any group of people, why they view some realities and not others as social problems, we must know how they construct such definitions.[2] Understanding this process involves knowing what their values and norms are.[3] It is also important to look at the role that various, often powerful, groups play in promoting (or downplaying) the idea that people should be concerned, and "do something about," some particular state of affairs.[4]

However, while it is also true that definitions of social problems vary, and understanding those often very subjective processes by which some things rather than others come to be classified as social problems *is* important, many sociologists maintain that we can have a bit more guidance than this in determining what objective conditions do or do not constitute true social problems. These sociologists would commonly point to some or all of the following.

---

[1] 1987, *Constructing Social Problems*, Hawthorne: Aldine de Gruyter, page 73.

[2] Ibid., page 75.

[3] For our purposes here, let's simply say that *values* are people's ideas about what is right and wrong, good and evil, while *norms* are rules (formal or informal) that guide people's conduct (cf. Thomas J. Sullivan, 2000, *Introduction to Social Problems,* 5th ed., Boston: Allyn and Bacon, pages 5–6; and Linda A. Mooney, David Knox, and Caroline Schacht, *Understanding Social Problems,* 3rd ed., Belmont, Calif.: Wadsworth, page 6).

[4] Ibid., page 5; Spector and Kitsuse, op cit., pages 73–96.

First, they would argue that true social problems really harm people in measurable ways.[5] They would admit that whether or not a particular reality is "harmful" is often a matter of debate, but would still insist that real social problems have objective adverse effects. Generally, they also often either state or imply that these problems, and the harm accompanying them, must be relatively persistent, rather than very transitory.[6]

Next, they would highlight the idea that a social problem must in fact be "social." This includes the notion that, to be a *social* problem, a difficulty must be a public, rather than private, one. This latter insight was pursued in a famous essay by C. Wright Mills, who distinguished between "personal troubles" and "public issues."[7] Social problems certainly do lead to private struggles, but every personal tribulation is not a public concern.

Natural disasters, such as earthquakes, are not social problems either, even though such calamities certainly can create or worsen social problems, and their impacts may be lessened or increased by social factors.[8] As many sociologists point out, all true social problems are caused wholly or to a great extent by social conditions and can at least theoretically be addressed through collective, public action.[9] Thus, for example, racial discrimination may be a social problem, but hurricanes are not.

Next, (though no one can say for sure how "large" is large enough), most sociologists are hesitant to identify something as a social problem unless it affects a sizable number of people.[10] The abuse of alcohol is more likely to be seen as a social problem than, say, "getting high" by sniffing paint thinner. This is *not* because alcohol abuse is more dangerous to individuals who are involved in doing it, but because it directly or indirectly harms millions more people.

In addition, some sociologists would add that a significant number of people must view something as a threat before it can be properly regarded as a social problem.[11] However, it must be noted that many

---

[5] A good example of this concern for "objective" harm can be found in Jerome G. Manis, 1974, "Assessing the Seriousness of Social Problems," in pages 1–15 of *Social Problems*, vol. 22; see also Vincent N. Parillo, 2002, *Contemporary Social Problems,* 5th ed., Boston: Allyn and Bacon, page 5; and Daniel J. Curran and Claire M. Renzetti, 2000, *Social Problems: Society in Crisis,* 5th ed., Boston: Allyn and Bacon, page 3. This idea is discussed and critiqued by Joel Best. 1989, "Introduction: Typification and Social Problems Construction," pages xv–xvii in Joel Best (Ed.), *Images of Issues: Typifying Contemporary Social Problems*, New York: Aldine de Gruyter, page xv. It is also discussed and critiqued (but not wholly rejected) by D. Stanley Eitzen and Maxine Baca Zinn, 2000, *Social Problems,* 8th ed., Boston: Allyn and Bacon, pages 4–5 and 8–10.

[6] Cf. Parillo, op cit., pages 6–8.

[7] 1959, *The Sociological Imagination*, New York: Oxford University Press, pages 8–9.

[8] Sullivan, op cit., pages 5–6; Michael P. Soroka and George J. Bryjak, 1999, *Social Problems: A World At Risk,* Boston: Allyn and Bacon, pages 6–9. See also the discussion and critique of this view in Spector and Kitsuse, op cit., pages 46–48.

[9] Sullivan, op cit., pages 5–6; this view is also identified briefly in Best, op cit., page xv.

[10] Sullivan, op cit., page 5; this view is also briefly identified by Best, op cit., page xv. See also Robert H. Lauer, 1998, *Social Problems and the Quality of Life*, Boston: McGraw-Hill, page 5; Diana Kendall, 2001, *Social Problems in a Diverse Society,* 2nd ed., Boston: Allyn and Bacon, page 4; and Curran and Renzetti, op cit., pages 2–3.

[11] For a recent example of such an insistence in social problems texts, see J. John Palen, 2001, *Social Problems for the Twenty-First Century*, Boston: McGraw-Hill, page 10; also William Kornblum and Joseph Julian, 1998, *Social Problems,* 9th ed., Upper Saddle River, N.J.: Prentice-Hall, page 5.

sociologists would sharply disagree with this idea[12] and, again, saying just how many persons represent a "significant number" is basically impossible.[13]

Regardless of what criterion we employ to determine just what is or is not a social problem, we sociologists certainly do agree that it is important to know what people in general think are social problems, whether or not we agree with them. If sociologists like myself are to understand society and social problems, and devise means to correct the latter, it is vital that we know what various publics are concerned about and what they think needs to be done to address these concerns, as well as how and why opinions about all of these things vary.

The 1998 and 2000 American National Election Studies (NES), which are the 25th and 26th installments in a series of studies of political attitudes and behavior conducted by the Center for Political Studies and the Survey Research Center,[14] are excellent sources of such information. Your ELECTION data set combines both of these and includes a selection of items from them.

In 1998 and 2000, NES researchers asked respondents to identify the "most important problems facing this country." Respondents mentioned up to four. Of course, answers ranged widely, but they can be grouped into logical categories. Just about all of the answers given by the NES respondents potentially fit most of the criteria that sociologists would use to define "social problems." Let's take a look at some of what these answers reveal.

As we do this, I encourage you to follow along on your computer. Use the ExplorIt Guide, which lists the steps necessary to replicate what we are presenting here. If you are unsure how to use the ExplorIt Guide, review the *Getting Started* section at the beginning of this book. Throughout this book, performing the indicated steps in order to follow along with your own computer whenever you see these guides will help you to master the ExplorIt program. It will also get you ready to complete the worksheets associated with each exercise.

First, after starting up your ExplorIt software, open your ELECTION data set. Then, choose the UNIVARIATE task. We will start by looking at **variable** 25 (DOMPROB). What is a "variable"? It is simply something that varies![15] (By contrast, something that does not vary, such as the speed of light, would be called a "**constant**.") Let's take a look.

---

[12] This disagreement can arise from diverse theoretical perspectives. Cf. Manis, op cit., page 1; Spector and Kitsuse, op cit., pages 31–36, 74; Soroka and Bryjak, op cit., page 9; Curran and Renzetti, op cit., pages 3–4; Eitzen and Baca Zinn, op cit., pages 6–7.

[13] Kitsuse and Spector, op cit., page 32; Soroka and Bryjak, op cit., page 9.

[14] The American National Election Studies in 1998 and 2000 were conducted by the Center for Political Studies of the Institute for Social Research, under the general direction of Principal Investigators Virginia Sapiro and Steven Rosenstone (1998), then Nancy Burns and Donald R. Kinder (2000).

[15] Cf. Mooney et al., op cit., page 18.

> *Data File:* **ELECTION**
> *Task:* **Univariate**
> *Primary Variable:* **25) DOMPROB**
> *View:* **Pie**

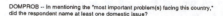

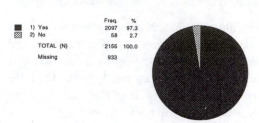

DOMPROB -- In mentioning the "most important problem(s) facing this country," did the respondent name at least one domestic issue?

		Freq.	%
■	1) Yes	2097	97.3
▨	2) No	58	2.7
	TOTAL (N)	2155	100.0
	Missing	933	

To reproduce this graphic on the computer screen using ExplorIt, it may be helpful to review the instructions in the "Getting Started" section. For this example, first select OPEN FILE, then open the ELECTION data file, if you have not done so already. (Remember, the ➤ symbol indicates which steps you need to perform if you are doing all examples as you follow along in the text. So, in the next example, you will not need to open a new data file, because the ELECTION file will already be open.)

Now, select the UNIVARIATE task. Next, select Variable 25) DOMPROB. Use the cursor keys and scroll bar to move through the Variables list, if necessary. After highlighting DOMPROB, click on the arrow next to "Primary Variable" to choose this variable for the UNIVARIATE task. Click [OK]. The "Pie" view should already be selected so that the pie graph appears automatically; if not, select that option (under "Graphs").

Notice that, both when you select the variable and when you produce the graph, you can see the exact survey question or a description of the item. What "varies" here is simply whether or not at least one of the problems mentioned by the respondent dealt with a domestic issue. This included a wide range of possible answers, such as unemployment, Social Security, crime, or race relations. As the graphic above shows, most (about 97%) of the 1998 and 2000 NES respondents who answered this question mentioned at least one domestic problem.

What about problems related to foreign/international issues, such as world hunger, communism, or the Middle East conflicts? Let's see.

> *Data File:* **ELECTION**
> *Task:* **Univariate**
> *Primary Variable:* **26) FORPROB**
> *View:* **Pie**

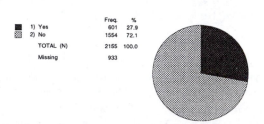

FORPROB -- In mentioning the "most important problem(s) facing this country," did the respondent name at least one foreign/international issue?

		Freq.	%
■	1) Yes	601	27.9
▨	2) No	1554	72.1
	TOTAL (N)	2155	100.0
	Missing	933	

If you are continuing from the previous example, just use the [⟲] button to return to the variable selection screen. Click "Clear All." Next, select 26) FORPROB as your Primary Variable, then click [OK].

Most of the respondents did *not* identify a foreign/international issue as at least one of the problems they were most concerned about. In fact, only about 28% did so.[16] How about those problems that researchers said were related to "government functioning," such as a Congress or Supreme Court that was perceived as overly powerful, government waste or inefficiency, or the view that government officials are dishonest and unethical?

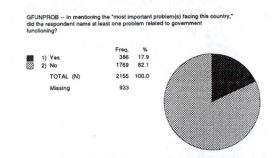

Data File: **ELECTION**

Task: **Univariate**

➤ Primary Variable: **27) GFUNPROB**

➤ View: **Pie**

GFUNPROB -- In mentioning the "most important problem(s) facing this country," did the respondent name at least one problem related to government functioning?

		Freq.	%
■	1) Yes	386	17.9
▨	2) No	1769	82.1
	TOTAL (N)	2155	100.0
	Missing	933	

Respondents were *least* likely to identify a government functioning issue as one of the problems they were most concerned about. The percentage here was only roughly 18%, which is less than one out of five.

What types of problems did NES respondents name as either the *only*, or the *single most important*, problem they believed was facing their country? Let's take a look.

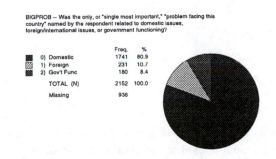

Data File: **ELECTION**

Task: **Univariate**

➤ Primary Variable: **22) BIGPROB**

➤ View: **Pie**

BIGPROB -- Was the only, or "single most important," "problem facing this country" named by the respondent related to domestic issues, foreign/international issues, or government functioning?

		Freq.	%
■	0) Domestic	1741	80.9
▨	1) Foreign	231	10.7
▨	2) Gov't Func	180	8.4
	TOTAL (N)	2152	100.0
	Missing	936	

Once again, domestic issues dominated respondents' attention. About 81% chose a problem of the latter type as the only or biggest problem that concerned them. Roughly 11% selected a foreign/international problem, and 8% focused on an issue of government functioning.

What about specific types of social problems? Let's look at the degree of respondents' concern with a few of the areas we will address in this book. First, we'll find out how many respondents expressed a concern with racial and ethnic issues. This includes a range of responses, reflecting a broad spectrum

---

[16] Perhaps more respondents would have named such foreign/international problems after the September 11, 2001, terrorist attacks. Since the NES did not ask these "problem" questions in their 2002 survey (not included here), we don't know.

of political orientations, dealing with areas such as racial discrimination, affirmative action, general race relations, and even white respondents wishing to retain racial segregation! We will be looking at whether or not respondents identified at least one racial or ethnic problem.

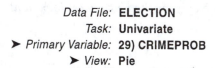

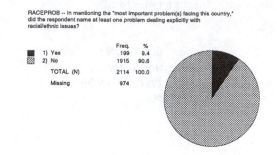

Perhaps surprisingly, only about 9% of the respondents clearly identified a racial or ethnic problem. We'll look at two more issues. First, we will see how often respondents listed something having to do with crime as a major problem (including such concerns as street crime, police brutality or incompetence, and wanting more or less gun control).

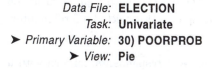

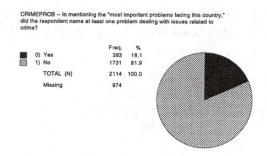

Approximately 18% of the respondents mentioned at least one crime-related issue. Now look at the respondent's level of concern with domestic poverty and unemployment (including worries about things such as support or opposition to welfare programs, homelessness, and hunger).

Data File: **ELECTION**
Task: **Univariate**
➤ *Primary Variable:* **30) POORPROB**
➤ *View:* **Pie**

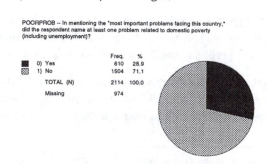

About 29% brought up at least one problem related to poverty and/or unemployment.

Investigating Social Problems

In thinking about these pie charts we've been looking at, keep a couple of things in mind. First, just because a particular issue didn't come to a respondent's mind as one of "the *most important* problems facing this country" does not mean that she or he did not regard it as a social problem. Someone can believe, for example, that the threat of domestic terrorism is a real social problem without labeling it one of "the most important" ones.

Second, notice that this information we have been looking at in these election surveys is supposed to accurately represent ("look like") the American public. Can we be sure that it does? Or, to be more specific, can we determine the extent to which these survey results accurately represent the ***population*** of (here, "adult") Americans generally? This is often a very important issue in social problems discussions and research. We do not wish to accept "findings" about any group of people that does not accurately represent them, as this leads to biased, distorted impressions of reality that make good analysis and decision-making impossible.

Many things can be "populations." Besides "adult Americans," we could talk about populations such as "residents of Paduga County" or "citizens of Malta." We might be interested in studying populations such as "major league baseball teams," "college students," or "members of the Beth Israel Synagogue on Howard Avenue." And one way to make sure that our study adequately represents the population we are researching would be to conduct a ***census***. That is, we could collect information from every member of the population.

But often it is not practical or desirable to conduct a census, especially when the population we are interested in is very large. So instead, when social scientists conduct surveys like the NES, they generally collect information from and/or about a ***sample*** (that is, a subset) of their target population. In doing so, if they want this sample to be representative of the latter, they make every effort to ensure that each member of the target population has an equal and known chance of being selected for their sample. For example, if a college had 5,000 students, drawing a "representative sample" of 500 of them would require making sure that each of the 5,000 students had a one-in-ten chance of being selected.

There are many methods for drawing representative samples, some of which are very complex. We will not go into these here![17] Generally, most are some type of ***probability sample***. However, one general rule of thumb is that, all other things being equal, the larger a sample, the better it will represent a population.

A key way in which a social scientist will find out how accurately a particular sample represents the population she is interested in is to estimate the degree of ***sampling error***. That is, she approximates the difference between the results she obtained with her sample and the "true" value in the population. For example, if a sample of Americans in the year 2000 is 10% African American, the sampling error for this last percentage is about 2%, since roughly 12% of all Americans are African American.[18]

---

[17] For extended discussion and training on this and other research methods issues, see my book *Experiencing Social Research: An Introduction Using MicroCase*, 2002, Belmont, Calif.: Wadsworth.

[18] This percentage is roughly correct, according to the 2000 U.S. Census. The specific figure is 12.3% for Americans who labeled themselves simply as "black," and 12.9% if those who named another race, in addition to "black," are included. I am relying here more on the former figure. *Census 2000, Profile of General Population Characteristics*, 2001, U.S. Census Bureau, U.S. Department of Commerce. Obtained from www.census.gov. Ibid, page 5; Spector and Kitsuse, op cit., pages 73–96.

Social scientists use estimates of sampling errors[19] to calculate the amount of "confidence" they can reasonably have in the accuracy of their findings. This is normally expressed in terms of **confidence levels** and **confidence intervals**. You will often see expressions like this in newspapers: "58% of Pennsylvanians surveyed indicated that they intended to vote for Candidate Smith. Results are accurate within plus or minus 2%." This means that pollsters are 95% confident that the "true" support for Smith among Pennsylvanians is between 56% and 60%.[20] The *confidence level* being used here is 95% (which is the most common one used by social scientists), and the *confidence interval* at this level is 56% to 60%.

In the 2000 American National Election Survey, if 30% of their sample agreed with a particular statement, you could be 95% certain that the "true" percentage of Americans who would have agreed with that same statement would be (roughly) between 27.6% and 32.4% (that is, plus or minus about 2.4%). If the percentage agreeing was 10%, you could be 95% certain that the "true" percentages among Americans would be (roughly) between 11.6% and 8.4% (plus or minus about 1.6%).[21] While confidence intervals in the NES vary according to the results and the proportion of respondents who are asked and/or answer items, overall, the NES represents the American population well. Generally, its results are accurate within about plus or minus 2%.

Still, no matter how accurate the percentages are as they apply to Americans as a whole, we want to know more about how, and to what degree, different *types* of Americans vary in their assessment of what the major problems facing their society are. As a general rule, sociologists are primarily interested in social regularities and patterns. In fact, when we collect information from and about **individuals**, as the NES does, we do so mainly so that we can combine this data in various ways in order to better describe and explain broader social patterns and variations by studying various **aggregates** (that is, collections, or groups, of people). Part of this involves categorizing people within the populations we are studying, and then analyzing variations that we discover among them. For example, when I look at American views about different social problems, I want to know if people of different races, genders, marital statuses, social classes, religions, and so on vary in these views and, if so, how and why they differ.

We can work with this a little bit using the ELECTION data set and something known as "Subsets." We'll start by seeing if there are differences in the degree to which African Americans, as opposed to whites, named a race or ethnic issue as one of the "major problems facing this country."

---

[19] These are called *standard errors*.

[20] Perhaps an even better way to put this is to say that, in repeat probability samples of Pennsylvanians, researchers can expect that 95% of the time, the percentage who say they intend to vote for Candidate Smith will be between 56% and 60%. See the brief, lucid explanation in Rodney Stark, 2001, *Sociology,* 8th ed., Belmont, Calif.: Wadsworth, pages 101–102.

[21] Nancy Burns, Donald R. Kinder, Steven J. Rosenstone, Virginia Sapiro, and the National Election Studies, 2001, *American National Election Studies: 2000 Pre- and Post-Election Study Codebook,* Ann Arbor: University of Michigan, Center for Political Studies, Institute for Social Research.

Data File: **ELECTION**

Task: **Univariate**

➤ Primary Variable: **28) RACEPROB**

➤ Subset Variable: **8) RACE**

➤ Subset Category: **Include: Black**

➤ View: **Pie**

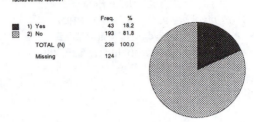

RACEPROB -- In mentioning the "most important problem(s) facing this country," did the respondent name at least one problem dealing explicitly with racial/ethnic issues?

		Freq.	%
■	1) Yes	43	18.2
▨	2) No	193	81.8
	TOTAL (N)	236	100.0
	Missing	124	

[Subset]

If you are continuing from the previous example, just use the [[↩]] button to return to the variable selection screen. Click "Clear All." Next, select 28) RACEPROB as your Primary Variable. Then, select 8) RACE as your Subset Variable. When you do this, a "Subset By Categories" box will come up. You will see the various categories of this variable. Select "Black" as your subset category, and choose the [Include] option. Then click [OK] and continue as usual.

Approximately 18% of African Americans named a race or ethnic issue as a major problem. Now let's look at the results for whites.

Data File: **ELECTION**

Task: **Univariate**

Primary Variable: **28) RACEPROB**

Subset Variable: **8) RACE**

➤ Subset Category: **Include: White**

➤ View: **Pie**

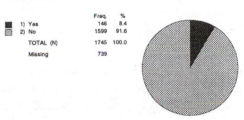

RACEPROB -- In mentioning the "most important problem(s) facing this country," did the respondent name at least one problem dealing explicitly with racial/ethnic issues?

		Freq.	%
▨	1) Yes	146	8.4
▨	2) No	1599	91.6
	TOTAL (N)	1745	100.0
	Missing	739	

[Subset]

Now, just use the [↩] button to return to the variable selection screen again, click "Clear All," and then select 28) RACEPROB as your Primary Variable. Next, select 8) RACE as your Subset Variable, as you did before. This time, when the "Subset By Categories" box comes up, select "White" as your subset category, and then choose the [Include] option. Then click [OK] and continue as usual.

Only 8.4% of whites named a race or ethnic issue as a major problem—nearly 10 percentage points less than African Americans. Given the historical experience of African Americans in this country as a minority suffering discrimination, it should not surprise us that this group was more than twice as likely as whites to identify such an issue as a major problem. Perhaps, in similar ways, we ought to expect poorer people to be more likely than wealthier people to identify at least one issue related to poverty or unemployment as a major problem. Let's find out.

Data File: **ELECTION**

Task: **Univariate**

➤ Primary Variable: **30) POORPROB**

➤ Subset Variable: **5) FAMINCOME**

➤ Subset Category: **Include: <$25,000**

➤ View: **Pie**

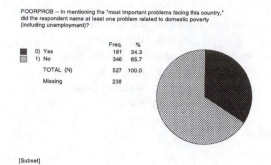

POORPROB -- In mentioning the "most important problems facing this country," did the respondent name at least one problem related to domestic poverty (including unemployment)?

		Freq.	%
■	0) Yes	181	34.3
▨	1) No	346	65.7
	TOTAL (N)	527	100.0
	Missing	238	

[Subset]

When we look at responses from those respondents earning $25,000 or less per year, just more than 34% named a problem related to domestic poverty. What about those respondents earning more than $65,000 a year?

Data File: **ELECTION**

Task: **Univariate**

Primary Variable: **30) POORPROB**

Subset Variable: **5) FAMINCOME**

➤ Subset Category: **Include: $65,000+**

➤ View: **Pie**

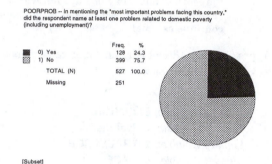

POORPROB -- In mentioning the "most important problems facing this country," did the respondent name at least one problem related to domestic poverty (including unemployment)?

		Freq.	%
■	0) Yes	128	24.3
▨	1) No	399	75.7
	TOTAL (N)	527	100.0
	Missing	251	

[Subset]

Among wealthier people approximately 24% named a problem related to poverty—again, nearly a 10-percentage-point difference. Could it be true that those who are most directly threatened by a problem are also most likely to be concerned about it?

Looking at these "subsets" has helped us to see that there is much to learn by looking at the differences between diverse groups of people within a society, including variations in their views about social problems. But we sociologists are interested in other types of variation within societies as well. One of these is variation across *time*. For example, how have people's concerns about social problems in the United States changed over the past few decades?

So far, the survey data we have looked at is ***cross-sectional***. That is, it looks at a fixed point in time, like a snapshot. To answer the latter type of question, we will often want to turn to some kind of *longitudinal study*. This is a study in which the data are collected over an extended period of time.[22]

The General Social Survey (GSS) is a major national survey conducted by the National Opinion Research Corporation (NORC).[23] You will be looking at lots of cross-sectional data from that survey in

---

[22] Some social scientists reserve the term "longitudinal study" for cases in which the same people are observed over time, rather than in the general sense I am using the term here. However, the general way that the term is being used here is widely accepted and, in fact, probably more common.

[23] James A. Davis is the Principal Investigator and Tom W. Smith is the Director and Co-Principal Investigator. The National Science Foundation sponsors the project.

Investigating Social Problems

this workbook, since that is what your GSS data set consists of. However, the GSS has been conducted most years since 1972,[24] and many of its items have been repeated over time (or replaced with questions that collect basically the same information). And like the NES, though the specific respondents change from year to year, the samples are always designed to mirror the U.S. population as a whole and yield results that are generally accurate within plus or minus 2 percentage points. Thus, GSS data are very good for tracking changes among Americans over time.

A little longitudinal GSS information is summarized in your TRENDS data set. This includes some data that shed a little light on changes in American concerns with various social problems over time. For example, one series of questions consistently asked in the GSS over the years has to do with whether or not respondents think that the government is "spending too little" to address various areas of social concern. Of course, there are other ways to address problems than through more government spending. However, these items at least give us a rough idea of the kinds of things that people think we ought to collectively "do more about." Let's take a look, starting with the area of poverty and welfare.

➤ *Data File:* **TRENDS**
  ➤ *Task:* **Historical Trends**
➤ *Variable:* **4) WELF $**

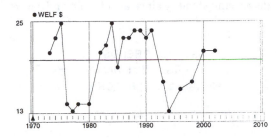

Percent who say that government is spending too little on welfare

To reproduce this map, you need to open the TRENDS data file and then select the HISTORICAL TRENDS task. After this, the process for selecting the variable is the same as you have been using.

Notice that the percentage of GSS respondents between 1973 and 2002 who indicated that they thought the government was spending "too little" on welfare never exceeded 25%, but varied between that and a low of 13%. Generally, it appears that Americans were more likely to be concerned about levels of welfare spending being too low in the 1980s than they have been since then.

Let's see similar trends in the other two areas we have looked at already, crime and race. We'll look at how Americans have changed over time in believing that the government is spending "too little" to deal with crime and problems confronting African Americans.

---

[24] It used to be done every year, but especially in recent times, it has been done every other year.

Data File: **TRENDS**
     Task: **Historical Trends**
➤ Variable: **8) CRIME $**

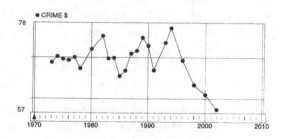

Percent who say the government is spending too little on
"halting the rising crime rate"

If you are continuing from the previous example, just use the [↺] button to return to the variable selection screen. Click "Clear All." Next, select 8) CRIME $ as your variable, then click [OK].

The percentage of respondents who think that the government needs to spend more on "halting the rising crime rate" is usually fairly high (from a low of about 57% to a high of about 77%), but has been decreasing steadily since about 1994 and was much lower in 2002 than it was in 1973.

Data File: **TRENDS**
     Task: **Historical Trends**
➤ Variable: **6) BLACK $**

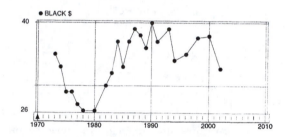

Percent who say the government is spending too little on improving
the conditions of blacks

The range of percentages of respondents who believed that the government was "spending too little on improving the conditions of blacks" has ranged from 26% to 40%. This percentage has generally risen since 1980, though it fell to about 33% in 2002, from 38% in 2000. Note that this trend has moved in a slightly opposite direction than the trend for crime prevention spending.

I want you to keep learning more about what kinds of problems most concern Americans, how various categories of Americans differ with regard to what things that society is facing today trouble them the most, and how views among Americans have changed over time. But it's time for you to do more of this investigation on your own. And you'll get a chance to do so, as you turn now to the worksheets that follow.

Investigating Social Problems

Workbook exercises and software are copyrighted. Copying is prohibited by law.

REVIEW QUESTIONS

Based on the first part of this exercise, answer True or False to the following items:

Knowing what people value and/or are threatened by helps us to understand what they are more likely to define as "social problems."	T F
Most sociologists would agree that there are no objective means for determining whether something is or is not a "social problem."	T F
Most sociologists are unlikely to call something a "social problem" unless it affects a large number of people.	T F
NES respondents were more likely to name issues related to crime, than issues related to poverty or unemployment, as "major problems facing this nation."	T F
Sociologists often sample populations by conducting censuses.	T F
In order to adequately represent a population in a sample, each member of that population should have had an equal chance of being selected for that sample.	T F
The typical confidence level used by sociologists is 99%.	T F
When sociologists say that they are 95% certain that a "true" percentage in a population is between 56% and 60%, they are expressing a *confidence interval*.	T F
Most African-American NES respondents named issues related to race or ethnicity as "major problems facing this country."	T F
Longitudinal data are used to see variation over time.	T F
Since 1973, Americans have been more likely to think that their government spends too little on crime than they have been to think that their government spends too little on improving conditions for African Americans.	T F

EXPLORIT QUESTIONS

You will need to use the ExplorIt software for the remainder of the questions. Make sure you have already gone through the "Getting Started" section that appears before the first exercise.

1. One area commonly addressed by social problems scholars and texts is that of health-related social problems. Let's look at public opinions about this in detail here, starting with more information from our ELECTION data set regarding proportions of Americans who named some health or health care issue as a "major problem facing this country."

a. Open the ELECTION data set.

b. Write in the description for 31) HEALTHPROB, exactly as it appears:

_____

_____

c. Look at the percentage in ELECTION that named a health-related issue as a major problem. Then, fill in that percentage (Yes) below.

> *Data File:* **ELECTION**
> *Task:* **Univariate**
> *Primary Variable:* **31) HEALTHPROB**
> *View:* **Pie**

    To select this pie using ExplorIt, open the ELECTION data file, select the UNIVARIATE task, and then select 31) HEALTHPROB as the primary variable.

Yes: _____%

2. Perhaps older people are more likely than younger people to be concerned with such health-related issues. Let's find out.

a. Look at the percentage of older people in ELECTION that named a health-related issue as a major problem. Then, fill in that percentage below.

> *Data File:* **ELECTION**
> *Task:* **Univariate**
> *Primary Variable:* **31) HEALTHPROB**
> *Subset Variable:* **3) AGE**
> *Subset Category:* **Include: 65+**
> *View:* **Pie**

    If you are continuing from the previous item, just use the [⟲] button to return to the variable selection screen. Next, select 3) AGE as your Subset Variable. When you do this, a "Subset By Categories" box will come up. You will see the various categories of this variable. Select "65+" as your subset category, and then choose the [Include] option. Then click [OK] and continue as usual.

Yes: _____%

b. Now, look at the percentage of younger people in ELECTION that named a health-related issue as a major problem. Then, fill in that percentage below.

> Data File: **ELECTION**
> Task: **Univariate**
> Primary Variable: **31) HEALTHPROB**
> Subset Variable: **3) AGE**
> ➤ Subset Category: **Include: <30**
> ➤ View: **Pie**

Use the [[↺]] button to return to the variable selection screen. Leave 31) HEALTHPROB as your Primary Variable. Click on AGE under Subset Variables to highlight it, then delete AGE (press "Delete" on your keyboard). Select 3) AGE as your Subset Variable again. When the "Subset By Categories" comes up, select "< 30" as your subset category, and choose the [Include] option. Then click [OK] and continue as usual.

Yes: _____%

c. Is there much difference between elderly and younger people with regard to whether or not they selected a health-related issue as a "major problem"? If so, why do you think this difference exists? If not, why do you think that both older and younger people are about equally likely to be concerned about such issues?

3. Perhaps people with less income differ from people with more income in whether or not they are concerned with health-related issues. Let's find out.

a. Look at the percentage of people with less income in ELECTION that named a health-related issue as a major problem. Then, fill in that percentage below.

> Data File: **ELECTION**
> Task: **Univariate**
> Primary Variable: **31) HEALTHPROB**
> ➤ Subset Variable: **5) FAMINCOME**
> ➤ Subset Category: **Include: <$25,000**
> ➤ View: **Pie**

Yes: _____%

b. Now, look at the percentage of people with more income in ELECTION that named a health-related issue as a major problem. Then, fill in that percentage below.

> Data File: **ELECTION**
> Task: **Univariate**
> Primary Variable: **31) HEALTHPROB**
> Subset Variable: **5) FAMINCOME**
> ➤ Subset Category: **Include: $65,000+**
> ➤ View: **Pie**

Yes: _____%

c. Is there much difference between people with less and more income with regard to whether or not they selected a health-related issue as a "major problem"? Which group is more likely to name such an issue as a concern?

d. Did these results surprise you? Why or why not? (Be specific.)

4. Now, let's look at related data in the TRENDS data set. We'll see how the percentage of GSS respondents saying that the government is not spending enough on improving the nation's health has changed between 1973 and 2002.

a. Open the TRENDS data set.

b. Write in the description for 5) HEALTH $, exactly as it appears:

    _____

    _____

c. Look at the Historical Trends chart for 5) HEALTH $. Then answer the following questions about what you see there.

> ➤ *Data File:* **TRENDS**
> ➤ *Task:* **Historical Trends**
> ➤ *Select Variable:* **5) HEALTH $**

d. The *lowest* percentage during this time period was _____%.
    (Tip: Look at the number at the bottom, left side of the graph.)   _____%

e. The *highest* percentage during this time period was _____%.
    (Tip: Look at the number at the top, left side of the graph.)   _____%

f. Overall, do you think that the percentage of GSS respondents who believed that the government was spending too little on improving the nation's health increased, decreased, or stayed about the same during the period 1973 to 2002? (Circle one.)

Increased

Decreased

Stayed About the Same

5. Another area commonly addressed by social problems scholars and texts is that of drug and alcohol abuse. Let's again start by looking at information from our ELECTION data set regarding proportions of Americans who named some issue related to drug and/or alcohol abuse as a "major problem facing this country."

a. Open the ELECTION data set.

b. Write in the description for 33) DRUGPROB, exactly as it appears:

_____

_____

_____

c. Look at the percentage in ELECTION that named an issue related to drug and/or alcohol abuse as a major problem. Then, fill in that percentage below.

> ➤ *Data File:* **ELECTION**
> ➤ *Task:* **Univariate**
> *Primary Variable:* **33) DRUGPROB**
> ➤ *View:* **Pie**

Yes: _____%

6.   Perhaps African Americans and whites differ in the degree to which they named drug and/or alcohol abuse as a major social problem. Let's find out.

    a. Look at the percentage of whites in ELECTION that named drug and/or alcohol abuse as a major problem. Then, fill in that percentage below.

> Data File: **ELECTION**
> Task: **Univariate**
> Primary Variable: **33) DRUGPROB**
> ➤ Subset Variable: **8) RACE**
> ➤ Subset Category: **Include: White**
> ➤ View: **Pie**

Yes: _____%

    b. Now, look at the percentage of African Americans in ELECTION that named drug and/or alcohol abuse as a major problem. Then, fill in that percentage below.

> Data File: **ELECTION**
> Task: **Univariate**
> Primary Variable: **33) DRUGPROB**
> Subset Variable: **8) RACE**
> ➤ Subset Category: **Include: Black**
> ➤ View: **Pie**

Yes: _____%

    c. Were whites or African Americans more likely to name drug and/or alcohol abuse as a major problem? (Circle one.)

                                                          Whites

                                        African Americans

                                  No meaningful difference
between them

    d. If you believe that these pie charts revealed a meaningful difference between whites and African Americans with regard to whether or not they selected an issue related to drug and/or alcohol abuse as a "major problem"—why do you think this difference exists?

7. Since we're in the "general area" of race and ethnicity, let's look at how often Hispanics mentioned a drug and/or alcohol related issue as a major problem.

    a. Look at the percentage of Hispanics who named a drug- and/or alcohol-related issue as a major problem. Then, fill in that percentage below.

    >   Data File: **ELECTION**
                     Task: **Univariate**
         Primary Variable: **33) DRUGPROB**
      ➤ Subset Variable: **9) HISPANIC**
      ➤ Subset Category: **Include: Yes**
      ➤   View: **Pie**

    Yes: _____%

    b. Looking back at the pie charts for white and African American respondents (question 6), which chart was the Hispanic percentage most like? (Circle one.)

                                                                              Whites

                                                                     African Americans

8. How about gender? Could males and females differ in how likely they were to name a drug- and/or alcohol-related issue as a major problem?

    a. Look at the percentage of males who named a drug- and/or alcohol-related issue as a major problem. Then, fill in that percentage below.

                    Data File: **ELECTION**
                         Task: **Univariate**
             Primary Variable: **33) DRUGPROB**
      ➤   Subset Variable: **2) GENDER**
      ➤   Subset Category: **Include: MALE**
      ➤   View: **Pie**

    Yes: _____%

    b. Look at the percentage of females who named a drug- and/or alcohol-related issue as a major problem. Then, fill in that percentage below.

                    Data File: **ELECTION**
                         Task: **Univariate**
             Primary Variable: **33) DRUGPROB**
             Subset Variable: **2) GENDER**
      ➤   Subset Category: **Include: FEMALE**
      ➤   View: **Pie**

    Yes: _____%

c. Were males or females more likely to name drug and/or alcohol
    abuse as a major problem? (Circle one.)

Males

Females

No meaningful difference
between them

9. Finally, let's once again look at related data in the TRENDS data set. We'll see how the percentage of
    GSS respondents saying that the government is not spending enough to deal with drug addiction has
    changed between 1973 and 2002.

    a. Open the TRENDS data set.

    b. Write in the description for 7) DRUG $, exactly as it appears:

    _____

    _____

    c. Look at the HISTORICAL TRENDS chart for 7) DRUG $. Then answer the following questions
        about what you see there.

        ➤ Data File: **TRENDS**
            ➤ Task: **Historical Trends**
        ➤ Select Variable: **7) DRUG $**

    d. The *lowest* percentage during this time period was: _____%

    e. The *highest* percentage during this time period was: _____%

    f. Overall, do you think that the percentage of GSS respondents who believed that
        the government was spending too little to deal with drug addiction increased,
        decreased, or stayed about the same during the period 1973 to 2002?
        (Circle one.)   Increased

Decreased

Stayed About the Same

    g. Why do you think that the percentages of GSS respondents indicating that they thought the gov-
        ernment needed to do more to deal with drug addiction was so different from the percentages of
        NES respondents who named drug and/or alcohol addiction as a major problem?

◆ **EXERCISE 2** ◆

RACE & ETHNICITY, GENDER, AND SOCIAL CLASS: INDIVIDUAL LIFE EXPERIENCES AND PERSPECTIVES

Tasks: Univariate, Cross-tabulation
Data Files: ELECTION, GSS

Opinions about and experiences with social problems vary, often enormously, among people occupying different positions in society. These facts are obvious to any careful observer of society. Certainly, they were already evident in some of the analyses in our first exercise. Understanding such variations in individual life experiences and perspectives is important to comprehending the nature, extent, causes, and solutions of social problems.

In this exercise, we will explore some of these social differences. Specifically, we will look first at how people's experiences with those realities that are associated with social class vary by race, ethnicity, and gender. Then later on, you will have the opportunity to sample some ways in which people's general policy perspectives vary across these different social groups in ways that are likely to impact their approaches to solving social problems.

Judith Lorber has argued that race, ethnicity, social class, and gender are "the most commonly used categories in sociology."[1] So, what are they? **Social classes** are complex and there is a great deal of controversy in sociology as to how to define them. We will treat them here simply as groups marked by different levels of wealth, social prestige (or "honor"), and power.[2] By **races** we are referring to categories people are placed in as a result of biological differences, especially "skin color, hair texture, and facial features."[3] Sociologists studying race have typically been most concerned with the "social consequences" of such categorizations.[4] **Ethnic groups**, which are closely related to racial groups, are characterized by the perception of a shared common ancestry or homeland, and history; as well as cultural realities such as language, ceremonies and rituals, and fashion. People within an ethnic group view themselves as a distinct people, and are seen as such by others.[5] Finally, by **gender** we mean "the division of people into...'men' and 'women';"[6] more specifically, the social roles and identities that people are given by their cultures because of their biological sex.[7]

---

[1] 2000, "Gender," pages 1057–1066 in *Encyclopedia of Sociology*, Vol. 2, 2nd ed., Edgar F. Borgatta (Ed.), New York: Macmillan, page 1057.

[2] Cf. David B. Grusky, 2000, "Social Stratification," pages 2807–2821 in ibid. Vol. 4, page 2807; also Andrew J. Cherlin, 2002, *Public and Private Families,* 3rd ed., Boston: McGraw-Hill, pages 113–114.

[3] Susan R. Pitchford, 2000, "Race," pages 2329–2335 in Edgar F. Borgatta (Ed.), op cit., Vol. 4, page 2329. See also Richard D. Alba, 2000, "Ethnicity," pages 840–852 in ibid., Vol. 2, page 841; and Mooney et al., op cit., page 186.

[4] Pitchford, op cit.

[5] Ibid., Alba, op cit.

[6] Lorber, op cit., pages 1057–1058. Note that Lorber points out that a few societies allow for more than two gender possibilities; here of course we will focus only on male and female identities.

[7] Ibid.; see also Cherlin, op cit., page 31.

By looking at social class differences across people of various races, ethnicities, and genders, you will be examining social realities that are practically and theoretically important in many social problems areas. Let's start with race, by comparing whites and African Americans. We will look at the relationship between race and both income and occupational prestige (that is, the amount of status, or esteem, or "high regard," that people associate with particular jobs).[8] This time, we will use data from the General Social Survey (GSS). The data set supplied with this workbook combines the GSS for the years 2000 and 2002.

➤ *Data File:* **GSS**
➤ *Task:* **Univariate**
➤ *Primary Variable:* **16) $FAMRANK**
➤ *Subset Variable:* **3) RACE**
➤ *Subset Category:* **Include: White**
➤ *View:* **Pie**

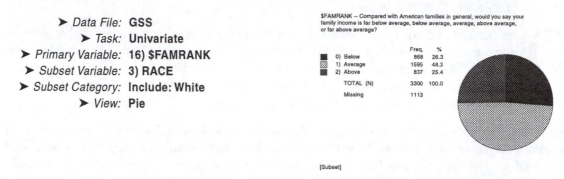

$FAMRANK -- Compared with American families in general, would you say your family income is far below average, below average, average, above average, or far above average?

		Freq.	%
■	0) Below	868	26.3
▨	1) Average	1595	48.3
▨	2) Above	837	25.4
	TOTAL (N)	3300	100.0
	Missing	1113	

[Subset]

Select "Open File," then open the GSS data file. Recall the procedure for using Subset Variables. Select 16) $FAMRANK as your Primary Variable. Then, select 3) RACE as your Subset Variable. When the "Subset By Categories" box comes up, select "White" as your subset category, and then choose the [Include] option. Then click [OK] and continue.

Looking just at the results for white respondents, we see that just over 26% believe their family income is "below average," while 25% consider their income "above average." Let's see how this compares with results for African American respondents.

Data File: **GSS**
Task: **Univariate**
Primary Variable: **16) $FAMRANK**
Subset Variable: **3) RACE**
➤ *Subset Category:* **Include: Black**
➤ *View:* **Pie**

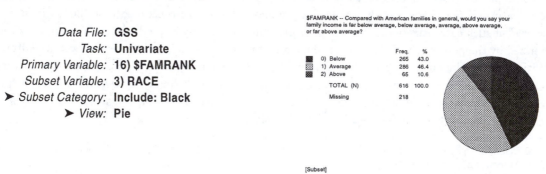

$FAMRANK -- Compared with American families in general, would you say your family income is far below average, below average, average, above average, or far above average?

		Freq.	%
■	0) Below	265	43.0
▨	1) Average	286	46.4
▨	2) Above	65	10.6
	TOTAL (N)	616	100.0
	Missing	218	

[Subset]

Remember to use the [⟲] button to return to the variable selection screen. Keep 16) $FAMRANK as your Primary Variable. Highlight RACE under Subset Variables and delete it, then select 3) RACE again as your Subset Variable. When the "Subset By Categories" box comes up, select "Black" as your subset category, and choose the [Include] option. Then click [OK] and continue.

---

[8] Here, we will be using data created by scoring the prestige of respondents' occupations using a standard and highly regarded scoring system, with possible scores from 0 to 100, which reflect the public's perception of the prestige associated with occupations. For example, news carriers score 15, waiters rank 20, and sales clerks 29; while physicians score 82, judges rank 76, and most college professors are at about 78.

Compared to whites, African Americans are much more likely to rate themselves as "below average" (43%) and much less likely to consider themselves to be "above average" in family income (almost 11%).

Let's try an easier way to get the same information that we just looked at, called a ***cross-tabulation***.[9] This is a single table with two variables on it.

> *Data File:* **GSS**
> ➤ *Task:* **Cross-tabulation**
> ➤ *Row Variable:* **16) $FAMRANK**
> ➤ *Column Variable:* **3) RACE**
> ➤ *View:* **Tables**
> ➤ *Display:* **Column %**

$FAMRANK   by   RACE
Cramer's V: 0.160 **

		RACE			
		White	Black	Missing	TOTAL
$FAMRANK	Below	868	265	73	1133
		26.3%	43.0%		28.9%
	Average	1595	286	119	1881
		48.3%	46.4%		48.0%
	Above	837	65	38	902
		25.4%	10.6%		23.0%
	Missing	1113	218	105	1436
	TOTAL	3300	616	335	3916
		100.0%	100.0%		

> **Click [Menu] to return to the main menu and then select the CROSS-TABULATION task. Select 16) $FAMRANK as the row variable and 3) RACE as the column variable, and click [OK]. Once the table appears, select the [Column %] option.**

For this type of table, you will always read the results across the rows, not down the columns. Look closely at the percentages at the different family income levels for African Americans and whites. They are the same as in the previous two pie charts; for example, 26% of whites, versus 43% of African Americans, identify their family income as "below average."

Now, let's take a look at occupational prestige differences for these two racial groups. We'll continue using cross-tabulation.

> *Data File:* **GSS**
> *Task:* **Cross-tabulation**
> ➤ *Row Variable:* **20) PRESTIGE**
> ➤ *Column Variable:* **3) RACE**
> ➤ *View:* **Tables**
> ➤ *Display:* **Column %**

PRESTIGE   by   RACE
Cramer's V: 0.136 **

		RACE			
		White	Black	Missing	TOTAL
PRESTIGE	Lower Half	1998	517	180	2515
		47.5%	66.2%		50.4%
	Upper Half	2209	264	135	2473
		52.5%	33.8%		49.6%
	Missing	206	53	20	279
	TOTAL	4207	781	335	4988
		100.0%	100.0%		

The results are as we might expect from the differences in family income we have already seen. 47.5% of whites have an occupation with a prestige score among the lower half of GSS respondents, while roughly 66% of African Americans have such an occupational prestige score. While 52.5% of whites rank in the upper half of GSS respondents on this variable, only about 34% of African Americans possess such higher rankings.

---

[9] I am grateful to Steven E. Barkan (*Discovering Sociology: An Introduction Using ExplorIt*, Belmont, Calif.: Wadsworth, 1998, page 37) for this particular way of using univariate distributions and subsets to introduce cross-tabulation.

Now, let's examine some class differences by ethnicity, looking at Hispanics as compared to non-Hispanic whites. "Hispanics" are an ethnic group (or more exactly, a collection of related ethnic groups). This is clear in the definition used by the 2000 U.S. Census: people "who classify themselves" or "identify their origin" as "Spanish, Hispanic, or Latino."[10]

We will see how Hispanics differ from non-Hispanic whites in their family income and self-identified social class. To do so, we will return to the NES.[11]

➤ *Data File:* **ELECTION**
➤ *Task:* **Cross-tabulation**
➤ *Row Variable:* **5) FAMINCOME**
➤ *Column Variable:* **9) HISPANIC**
➤ *View:* **Tables**
➤ *Display:* **Column %**

FAMINCOME   by   HISPANIC

Cramer's V: 0.109 **

		HISPANIC			
		Yes	No	Missing	TOTAL
FAMINCOME	< $25,000	57	370	130	427
		40.4%	26.2%		27.5%
	$25K-64.9K	59	581	261	640
		41.8%	41.1%		41.2%
	$65,000 +	25	461	183	486
		17.7%	32.6%		31.3%
	Missing	33	214	110	357
	TOTAL	141	1412	684	1553
		100.0%	100.0%		

Rounding out percentages, we can see that Hispanics do not do as well on average as non-Hispanic whites. Notice in the first row that 40.4% of white Hispanics report family incomes of less than $25,000 as compared to 26.2% of non-Hispanic whites.

Data File: **ELECTION**
Task: **Cross-tabulation**
Row Variable: **7) CLASS**
Column Variable: **9) HISPANIC**
➤ *View:* **Tables**
➤ *Display:* **Column %**

CLASS   by   HISPANIC

Cramer's V: 0.123 **

		HISPANIC			
		Yes	No	Missing	TOTAL
CLASS	Working	13	172	170	185
		50.0%	25.4%		26.3%
	Middle	4	298	308	302
		15.4%	44.0%		43.0%
	Other	9	207	183	216
		34.6%	30.6%		30.7%
	Missing	148	949	23	1120
	TOTAL	26	677	684	703
		100.0%	100.0%		

Results in this last table are similar to those in the previous table. About 50% of Hispanics report being members of the working class, compared to just 25% of non-Hispanic whites. Meanwhile, 44% of the latter say they are middle class, compared to only about 15% of Hispanics.

So far, we have used cross-tabulations to point out differences in areas such as income, occupational prestige, and self-reported class between Whites and African Americans and/or between Hispanics and non-Hispanic Whites. But how do we know that the differences in percentages that we have been looking at are not just "flukes"? Do these racial and ethnic differences in the GSS and NES samples

---

[10] "Origin" refers to "heritage, nationality group, lineage, or country of birth of the person's parents or ancestors before their arrival in the United States." U.S. Census Bureau, 2000, *2000 Census of the United States and Housing,* Technical Documentation, U.S. Department of Commerce, Washington, D.C., page B-8.

[11] This variable does not include African American respondents, dropping nine black respondents who were also classified as "Hispanic." This allows us to easily compare Hispanics with non-Hispanic whites.

Investigating Social Problems

accurately represent what is going on in the general population, or are they simply accidents—meaningless coincidences?

Social scientists employ something called **tests of statistical significance** in order to figure out if such differences in samples accurately reflect the population that the sample is supposed to represent, or if they are instead just the product of random chance. The general idea used to calculate statistical significance is that differences which are too small, and/or which are found in samples that are too small, should be disregarded, because in such cases it is too likely that these differences simply occurred by accident.

The rule of thumb social scientists use is that they do not want to treat differences as "significant" unless the possibility that they are just "flukes" is no greater than 5%. That is, they want to be sure that the differences they are looking at would occur simply because of chance no more than 5 out of 100 times. This figure is sometimes referred to as the "probability of error"—and social scientists want this probability to be no more than .05. Sometimes, social scientists will apply even tighter rules, seeking a probability of error of no more than .01 (1%).

Look carefully just above the top left corner of the cross-tabulations we have done so far. You will see a figure called "Cramer's V." This number is a "measure of association" that reflects the degree to which the variables in a cross-tabulation are related to each other (or we could say, how powerful the observed differences in the table are). Notice that there are asterisks to the right of each of the V's. One asterisk means that the differences are statistically significant at the .05 (5%) level, while two asterisks indicate that the probability of error is less than .01 (1%). No asterisk means that the differences in the cross-tabulation are _not_ significant and thus _should be treated as if there were not any differences_. Since the V's in each of our cross-tabulations have two asterisks, we conclude that each of these differences is very statistically significant. This means that by combining information about the size of the samples and the size of the differences (or, power of the measure of association, which in this case is Cramer's V), we can conclude that it is not very likely that these results occurred by chance.

There is one caveat in all of this. Because of the way that statistical significance is calculated, it is possible that even tiny differences (for example, groups differing by only 2 or 3 percentage points) will appear as "significant" if the samples being used are very large. When this happens, you should conclude that, while the difference in the sample probably does accurately reflect the population, it is not very powerful or meaningful. Looking at the size of the Cramer's V number helps here. As a general rule, V's greater than .30 show strong relationships, those between .10 and .30 ought to be regarded as moderate, and V's under .10 are weak.[12] The Cramer's V's for the last two tables were .109 and .123, respectively. This suggests that Hispanic status is moderately related to self-perceived class and family income among whites.

Now, let's go back to looking at the relationships among race, ethnicity, gender, and social class by briefly examining the latter two. Here, we will return to the GSS to compare the occupational prestige and personal incomes of men and women who are working full-time.

---

[12] I am using guidelines laid out by Barkan, op cit., page 38.

➤ *Data File:* **GSS**
➤ *Task:* **Cross-tabulation**
➤ *Row Variable:* **21) HIPRESTIGE**
➤ *Column Variable:* **2) GENDER**
➤ *Subset Variable:* **18) FULL TIME?**
➤ *Subset Category:* **Include: Yes**
➤ *View:* **Tables**
➤ *Display:* **Column %**

HIPRESTIGE by GENDER

Cramer's V: 0.047 *

HIPRESTIGE		Male	Female	TOTAL
		GENDER		
	Yes	324	344	668
		20.9%	24.9%	22.8%
	No	1224	1038	2262
		79.1%	75.1%	77.2%
	Missing	12	14	26
	TOTAL	1548	1382	2930
		100.0%	100.0%	

Here we see that women who are working full-time are a <u>little</u> *more* likely than men to hold high prestige positions (about 25% versus 21%). These differences are significant but weak (V = 0.047*).

Data File: **GSS**
Task: **Cross-tabulation**
➤ *Row Variable:* **17) OWN INCOME**
➤ *Column Variable:* **2) GENDER**
➤ *Subset Variable:* **18) FULL TIME?**
➤ *Subset Category:* **Include: Yes**
➤ *View:* **Tables**
➤ *Display:* **Column %**

OWN INCOME by GENDER

Cramer's V: 0.217 **

OWN INCOME		Male	Female	TOTAL
		GENDER		
	0-14.9	140	251	391
		10.1%	20.6%	15.0%
	15-24.9	221	319	540
		16.0%	26.2%	20.7%
	25+	1023	649	1672
		73.9%	53.2%	64.2%
	Missing	176	177	353
	TOTAL	1384	1219	2603
		100.0%	100.0%	

Gender disparities in the personal *incomes* of men and women who work full-time are not only significant, but moderately large (V = 0.217**). Women are more likely to have lower incomes (about 21% for incomes less than $14,999 and 26% at $15,000 to $24,999 levels, versus roughly 10% and 16% respectively for men). And they are much less likely to be in the higher income category (about 53% versus 74%). The paradox is that women are more likely to have high prestige jobs, yet get paid less on average, than men.

It is almost time to consider how people of diverse races, ethnicities, genders, and social classes may differ with regard to their general policy perspectives in ways that are likely to impact the types of solutions to social problems that they favor. But first, we will look briefly at one other variation in perspectives. Let's look at different *sociological* viewpoints on social problems; in other words, competing sociological *theories*.

Sociological theories are fairly abstract, general explanations of observed social regularities. That is, they attempt to identify the causes for, and processes behind, the latter. Formulating theories involves attempting to identify the relationships of different social facts to each other, and the reasons for these associations.

In addition to theories, there are even broader perspectives that inform and distinguish sociologists studying social problems. Different theories often tend to be associated with these basic orientations toward doing sociology. Let's look at two key ways in which the essential approaches of sociologists often differ.

First, they can prefer **micro** or **macro** levels of analysis. *Micro* sociologists are most interested in small-scale social realities, such as personal interaction and small groups, which are directly observable. *Macro* sociologists look at large-scale phenomena, such as changes in entire societies over time, or variations among nations, states and provinces, counties, cities, and the like.[13] This includes considering how large-scale social structures impact "individual thought and action."[14] For example, consider the way each type of sociologist might try to understand why murders are sometimes committed during armed robberies. A micro sociologist might look closely at individual incidents in order to determine what types of victim actions, interruptions, bystander behavior, and so on may commonly precipitate such killings. A macro sociologist might want to know whether or not the rates of such murders are influenced by things like the general availability of guns, poverty and unemployment rates, community disorganization, and so on.

George Ritzer uses the term "Social Factists" for all theoretical schools that prefer a macro-approach.[15] He has identified two key groups of related sociological theories that have a strong micro-orientation. One group, which he calls the "Social Definitionists," focuses on "the way [people] define their social situations and the effect of these definitions on ensuing action and interaction."[16] Consider our earlier discussion about defining "social problems." Social Definitionists would be very interested in people's diverse definitions of the latter, how and why these were arrived at, and what all of this means for the ways people react to such problems.

Another group, which Ritzer labels the "Social Behaviorists," focuses on individual behavior, especially "the rewards that elicit desirable behaviors and the punishments that inhibit undesirable behavior."[17] These theories are used in a number of social problems areas such as, where it is necessary, to consider why individuals perform destructive actions, including domestic assaults, drug and alcohol abuse, rape, murder, and so on.

In addition to this basic micro-macro distinction, there is a second major way in which sociological approaches may differ, which is important in social problems study and this book. Sociologists may adopt either a **conflict** or **consensus** frame of reference.[18]

Consensus sociologists believe that most basic social structures and processes support social harmony and benefit most members of society. They believe that it is natural for different elements of societies to be integrated with each other, and they are inclined to see people within healthy societies as being in general agreement ("consensus") about the more important aspects of social life. Disruptions do occur, and these may be caused by pervasive social inequalities, but they are not "natural." They must be dealt with through social reforms that are designed to restore integration, reduce inequality, broaden opportunities, or help individuals who are not in harmony with the social order to comply with social expectations and rules.

---

[13] Cf. Mooney et al., op cit., page 13.

[14] George Ritzer, 2000, *Modern Sociological Theory,* 5th ed., Boston: McGraw-Hill, pages 497–498.

[15] Ibid.

[16] Ibid., page 498.

[17] Ibid.

[18] In the way that I characterize the conflict and consensus approaches (below), I am very grateful for the excellent summary of these competing perspectives in Ralf Dahrendorf, 1959, *Class and Class Conflict in Industrial Society,* Stanford, Calif.: Stanford University Press; especially pages xi and 157–165. My presentation here is modified from my earlier (2002) book, op cit., pages 33–34.

Conflict sociologists look at how basic social arrangements are often contested and changing. To these sociologists, people with different ideals, perspectives, and material interests often disagree about major aspects of society in very fundamental, profound ways. Social structures and processes that are good for some people may be bad for others. And since those with greater resources are in a better position to "win" social contests, there is a tendency for existing social arrangements to favor people at the "top of the heap."[19] For example, feminist sociologists emphasize the ways that social orders may advantage men relative to women. Marxists focus on how those with greater property are advantaged relative to those with less property. Other conflict sociologists might concentrate on the nature and effects of inequalities rooted in racial and ethnic competition. As remedies for social problems, conflict sociologists tend to support far-reaching, fairly radical, social changes, which they believe will fundamentally address and even eliminate various inequalities.

Sociologists favoring either a conflict or a consensus approach might prefer doing analysis at either a micro or a macro level. Likewise, a sociologist can be a "factist," "behaviorist," or "definitionist" (using Ritzer's terms) and adopt either a conflict or consensus perspective (or even both). We should also recognize that there is value in all of these ways of analyzing and looking at social problems. I like to think of each as a set of "optical lenses" that helps us to see some things that we might miss if we were wearing a different set of "glasses."[20]

Hypotheses are valuable tools that we use, among other things, to apply and test these general theories and approaches. We will often use them in this workbook. A hypothesis is simply a precise prediction regarding the relationship between two or more variables.[21]

Now, armed with the various distinctions and concepts we've laid out so far, let's move on to considering how race, ethnicity, gender, and social class may be associated with support for some different basic policy approaches for dealing with social problems. We will do this by formulating and testing specific hypotheses that are consistent with a very general, simple proposition: *within a given society, those who are disadvantaged are more likely than those who are advantaged to support policies which they believe could significantly and directly alleviate these disadvantages, while the advantaged will be more likely to resist such changes to the status quo.* This proposition is consistent with the definitionist idea that people's life experience will effect how they view reality, which will in turn shape their actions. It is also compatible with the insights of some behaviorists that those in advantaged positions will be motivated to protect and exploit their privileges while the disadvantaged will often find their most "rewarding" option is to challenge and/or undermine the relative value of such advantages.[22] And though this proposition is obviously consistent with conflict theory, it would find agreement among many if not most in the consensus camp as well.[23]

---

[19] Ibid.

[20] Apparently, Parillo (op cit., page 14) also likes this metaphor!

[21] Cf. Mooney et al., op cit., page 18.

[22] See Jonathan H. Turner's excellent discussion of the compatibility of most aspects of exchange theory with conflict theory (1998, *The Structure of Sociological Theory*, 6th ed., Belmont, Calif.: Wadsworth, pages 258–259).

[23] For example, this idea is compatible with much of Robert K. Merton's "structural strain" theory of deviance, as seen in instances such as his discussion of the nature and genesis of "rebellion" and "innovation" (1968, "Social Structure and Anomie" and "Continuities in the Theory of Social Structure and Anomie," in *Social Theory and Social Structure: 1968 Enlarged Edition*, Robert K. Merton ([Ed.], New York: The Free Press, pages 185–248). His theory is, however, of the consensus type.

We will start by looking at people's basic political orientation, focusing on whether or not they consider themselves to be politically "liberal," "moderate," or "conservative." Our specific predictions will reflect the idea that those who are relatively advantaged will be more likely to call themselves "conservative" than those who are relatively disadvantaged. Let's consider this hypothesis first: *Whites will be more likely to call themselves "conservative" than African Americans*. Let's use the ELECTION data set.

➤ *Data File:* **ELECTION**
➤ *Task:* **Cross-tabulation**
➤ *Row Variable:* **21) POLVIEW**
➤ *Column Variable:* **8) RACE**
➤ *View:* **Tables**
➤ *Display:* **Column %**

POLVIEW by RACE
Cramer's V: 0.075 *

		RACE			
		White	Black	Missing	TOTAL
POLVIEW	Liberal	351	42	34	393
		24.4%	29.2%		24.8%
	Moderate	494	61	31	555
		34.4%	42.4%		35.1%
	Conservatv	593	41	44	634
		41.2%	28.5%		40.1%
	Missing	1046	216	135	1397
	TOTAL	1438	144	244	1582
		100.0%	100.0%		

Notice that the hypothesis is confirmed. For example, approximately 41% of whites called themselves "conservative," as opposed to 28.5% of African Americans. The race difference in political views is weak, but statistically significant (V = 0.075*).

How about another hypothesis? *The wealthier people are, the more likely they will be to call themselves "conservative."*

Data File: **ELECTION**
Task: **Cross-tabulation**
Row Variable: **21) POLVIEW**
➤ *Column Variable:* **5) FAMINCOME**
➤ *View:* **Tables**
➤ *Display:* **Column %**

POLVIEW by FAMINCOME
Cramer's V: 0.058 *

		FAMINCOME				
		< $25,000	$25K-64.9K	$65,000 +	Missing	TOTAL
POLVIEW	Liberal	87	158	120	62	365
		22.8%	25.9%	25.4%		24.9%
	Moderate	155	208	145	78	508
		40.7%	34.0%	30.7%		34.7%
	Conservatv	139	245	207	87	591
		36.5%	40.1%	43.9%		40.4%
	Missing	384	473	306	234	1397
	TOTAL	381	611	472	461	1464
		100.0%	100.0%	100.0%		

Again, the hypothesis is supported. Among those with family incomes of less than $25,000 per year, 36.5% considered themselves to be conservative, while that percentage was about 44% among those making $65,000 or more per year. These differences are statistically significant (V = 0.058*), although again not terribly large.

I'd like you to continue exploring hypotheses related to our general proposition (above) by looking at differences in basic policy perspectives among people of diverse races, ethnicities, classes, and genders. This will include a little more examination of differences in the degree of self-identified conservatism. But now it's time for you to do this a bit more on your own. In other words, your turn!

REVIEW QUESTIONS

Based on the first part of this exercise, answer True or False to the following items:

"Ethnic groups" are primarily biological, rather than cultural, realities.	T	F
The concept of "gender" has to do with social roles and identities that we associate with biological sex.	T	F
Whites are more likely than African Americans to have jobs that place them in the upper half of the population in terms of occupational prestige rankings.	T	F
The term "Hispanic" has more to do with race than with ethnicity.	T	F
Social scientists are usually willing to accept findings as "statistically significant" if the probability of error is less than 10%.	T	F
Statistical significance takes into account the strength of differences as well as the sizes of samples.	T	F
On average, women who work full-time make less money than men who work full-time.	T	F
Social definitionists and social behaviorists are both micro sociologists.	T	F
All social factist theories are consensus theories.	T	F
Only conflict theorists believe that social inequalities may have negative consequences for people.	T	F
African Americans are less likely to call themselves "conservative" than whites.	T	F

EXPLORIT QUESTIONS

1. Let's continue where we just left off. We will test this hypothesis: *Non-Hispanic whites will be more likely than Hispanics to call themselves "conservative."*

    a. Open the ELECTION data set (if it is not open already).

    b. Cross-tabulate 21) POLVIEW with 9) HISPANIC. Then, fill in the percentage claiming to be conservative.

> *Data File:* **ELECTION**
> *Task:* **Cross-tabulation**
> *Row Variable:* **21) POLVIEW**
> *Column Variable:* **9) HISPANIC**
> *View:* **Tables**
> *Display:* **Column %**

	YES	NO
CONSERVATIVE	_____%	_____%

Now, get the Cramer's V and the significance level for these two variables.

c. Record the value of Cramer's V for this table. (Include asterisks, if any.)   V = _____

d. Is the relationship between HISPANICS and POLVIEW statistically significant? (Circle one.)   Yes   No

e. Was the hypothesis supported? (Circle one.)   Yes   No

f. Do these results surprise you? Why or why not?

2. Now, we will test this hypothesis: *Among people who work full-time, men will be more likely than women to call themselves "conservative."*

a. Cross-tabulate 21) POLVIEW with 2) GENDER, focusing only on those who work full-time. Then, fill in the percentage claiming to be conservative.

> *Data File:* **ELECTION**
> *Task:* **Cross-tabulation**
> *Row Variable:* **21) POLVIEW**
> *Column Variable:* **2) GENDER**
> *Subset Variable:* **12) WORK FT**
> *Subset Category:* **Include: Yes**
> *View:* **Tables**
> *Display:* **Column %**

	MALE	**FEMALE**
CONSERVATIVE	_____%	_____%

Now, get the Cramer's V and the significance level for these two variables.

b. Record the value of Cramer's V for this table. (Include asterisks, if any.)   V = _____

c. Is the relationship between GENDER and POLVIEW statistically significant? (Circle one.)   Yes   No

d. Is the relationship between GENDER and POLVIEW weak, moderate, strong, or not significant? (Circle one.)

Weak

Moderate

Strong

Not Significant

e. Was the hypothesis supported? (Circle one.)   Yes   No

3. There are lots of battles in the United States over inequalities of wealth. One major controversy has to do with whether or not the government should play much of a role in reducing such inequalities. Regardless of whether or not one tends to see such involvement as a good or a bad thing, it seems that generally, most of those who strongly want to see such inequalities significantly reduced or eliminated favor giving the government a major role in doing so. Thus, if our general proposition is true (that the relatively disadvantaged will be more likely than the relatively advantaged to want policies which they think could significantly and directly alleviate these disadvantages), we ought to be able to predict which groups will be more or less likely to support such government involvement. Let's start with this hypothesis: *Lower income people will be more likely than upper income people to believe that government should play an active role in reducing income inequalities.* We will switch to the GSS to test this hypothesis.

a. Open the GSS data set.

b. Write in the description for 49) EQUALIZE$, exactly as it appears:

_____

_____

_____

c. Cross-tabulate 49) EQUALIZE$ with 16) $FAMRANK. Then, fill in the percentages of those who strongly feel that government should do something to correct income inequalities.

➤ *Data File:* **GSS**
➤ *Task:* **Cross-tabulation**
➤ *Row Variable:* **49) EQUALIZE$**
➤ *Column Variable:* **16) $FAMRANK**
➤ *View:* **Tables**
➤ *Display:* **Column %**

	BELOW	AVERAGE	ABOVE
STR SHOULD	_____%	_____%	_____%

Now, get the Cramer's V and the significance level for these two variables.

d. Record the value of Cramer's V for this table. (Include asterisks, if any.)   V = _____

e. Is the relationship between $FAMRANK and EQUALIZE$ statistically significant? (Circle one.)   Yes   No

f. Is the relationship between GENDER and POLVIEW weak, moderate, strong, or not significant? (Circle one.)

Weak

Moderate

Strong

Not Significant

g. Was the hypothesis supported? (Circle one.)   Yes   No

4. Now we'll check out this hypothesis: *African Americans will be more likely than Whites to believe that government should play an active role in reducing income inequalities.* We'll stick with the GSS.

a. Cross-tabulate 49) EQUALIZE$ with 3) RACE. Then, fill in the percentages of those who strongly feel that government should do something to correct income inequalities.

Data File: **GSS**
Task: **Cross-tabulation**
Row Variable: **49) EQUALIZE$**
➤ *Column Variable:* **3) RACE**
➤ *View:* **Tables**
➤ *Display:* **Column %**

	WHITE	BLACK
STR SHOULD	_____%	_____%

Now, get the Cramer's V and the significance level for these two variables.

b. Record the value of Cramer's V for this table. (Include asterisks, if any.)   V = _____

c. Is the relationship between RACE and EQUALIZE$ statistically
    significant? (Circle one.)   Yes   No

d. Is the relationship between RACE and EQUALIZE$ weak, moderate,
    strong, or not significant? (Circle one.)   Weak

                                                                              Moderate

                                                                                Strong

                                                                           Not Significant

e. Was the hypothesis supported? (Circle one.)   Yes   No

5. Last, let's try this hypothesis: *Women will be more likely than men to believe that government should
    play an active role in reducing income inequalities.* We'll stick with the GSS.

    a. Cross-tabulate 49) EQUALIZE$ with 2) GENDER. Then, fill in the percentages of those who
        strongly feel that government should do something to correct income inequalities.

                Data File: **GSS**
                    Task: **Cross-tabulation**
            Row Variable: **49) EQUALIZE$**
        ➤ Column Variable: **2) GENDER**
                ➤ View: **Tables**
             ➤ Display: **Column %**

                                MALE   **FEMALE**

        STR SHOULD   _____%   _____%

    Now, get the Cramer's V and the significance level for these two variables.

    b. Record the value of Cramer's V for this table. (Include asterisks, if any.)   V = _____

    c. Is the relationship between GENDER and EQUALIZE$ statistically
        significant? (Circle one.)   Yes   No

d. Is the relationship between GENDER and EQUALIZE$ weak, moderate, strong, or not significant? (Circle one.)

Weak

Moderate

Strong

Not Significant

e. Was the hypothesis supported? (Circle one.)   Yes   No

6. This is a good time to look at another item that measures the degree to which respondents seem to be sympathetic to government involvement in solving social problems. This will be our hypothesis: *Lower income people will be* <u>less</u> *likely than upper income people to see big government as meddling in things it should leave alone, and* <u>more</u> *likely than upper income people to see big government as a reasonable response to today's problems.* We will switch to the ELECTION data set to test it.

a. Open the ELECTION data set.

b. Write in the description for 38) GOV MEDDLE, exactly as it appears:

_____

_____

_____

c. Cross-tabulate 38) GOV MEDDLE with 5) FAMINCOME. Then, fill in the appropriate column percentages.

> ➤ Data File: **ELECTION**
> ➤ Task: **Cross-tabulation**
> ➤ Row Variable: **38) GOV MEDDLE**
> ➤ Column Variable: **5) FAMINCOME**
> ➤ View: **Tables**
> ➤ Display: **Column %**

	< $25,000	$25K–$64.9K	$65,000 +
GOVT MEDL	_____ %	_____ %	_____ %
BGR PROBS	_____ %	_____ %	_____ %

Now, get the Cramer's V and the significance level for these two variables.

d. Record the value of Cramer's V for this table. (Include asterisks, if any.)   V = _____

   e.   Is the relationship between FAMINCOME and GOV MEDDLE statistically significant? (Circle one.)   Yes   No

   f.   Is the relationship between FAMINCOME and GOV MEDDLE weak, moderate, strong, or not significant? (Circle one.)   Weak

                                                                     Moderate

                                                                      Strong

                                                   Not Significant

   g.   Was the hypothesis supported? (Circle one.)   Yes   No

7.   Our next hypothesis: *African Americans will be less likely than whites to see big government as meddling in things it should leave alone, and will be more likely to see big government as a reasonable response to today's problems.*

   a.   Cross-tabulate 38) GOV MEDDLE with 8) RACE. Then, fill in the appropriate column percentages.

                   Data File: **GSS**
                       Task: **Cross-tabulation**
            Row Variable: **38) GOV MEDDLE**
     ➤ *Column Variable:* **8) RACE**
             ➤ *View:* **Tables**
          ➤ *Display:* **Column %**

	WHITE	**BLACK**
GOVT MEDL	_____%	_____%
BGR PROBS	_____%	_____%

Now, get the Cramer's V and the significance level for these two variables.

   b.   Record the value of Cramer's V for this table. (Include asterisks, if any.)   V = _____

   c.   Is the relationship between RACE and GOV MEDDLE statistically significant? (Circle one.)   Yes   No

   d.   Is the relationship between RACE and GOV MEDDLE weak, moderate, strong, or not significant? (Circle one.)   Weak

                                                                   Moderate

                                                                      Strong

                                                   Not Significant

e. Was the hypothesis supported? (Circle one.)   Yes   No

8. Our next hypothesis: *Hispanics will be less likely than non-Hispanic whites to see big government as meddling in things it should leave alone, and will be more likely to see big government as a reasonable response to today's problems.*

    a. Cross-tabulate 38) GOV MEDDLE with 9) HISPANIC. Then, fill in the appropriate column percentages.

               Data File: **GSS**
                  Task: **Cross-tabulation**
         Row Variable: **38) GOV MEDDLE**
   ➤ *Column Variable:*   **9) HISPANIC**
            ➤ *View:*   **Tables**
        ➤ *Display:*   **Column %**

	YES	NO
GOVT MEDL	_____%	_____%
BGR PROBS	_____%	_____%

Now, get the Cramer's V and the significance level for these two variables.

    b. Record the value of Cramer's V for this table. (Include asterisks, if any.)   V = _____

    c. Is the relationship between HISPANIC and GOV MEDDLE statistically significant? (Circle one.)   Yes   No

    d. Is the relationship between HISPANIC and GOV MEDDLE weak, moderate, strong, or not significant? (Circle one.)

                                                   Weak

                                             Moderate

                                              Strong

                                     Not Significant

    e. Was the hypothesis supported? (Circle one.)   Yes   No

    f. Do these results surprise you? Why or why not?

9. Our last hypothesis: *Women will be less likely than men to see big government as meddling in things it should leave alone, and will be more likely to see big government as a reasonable response to today's problems.*

    a. Cross-tabulate 38) GOV MEDDLE with 2) GENDER. Then, fill in the appropriate column percentages.

    Data File: **GSS**
    Task: **Cross-tabulation**
    Row Variable: **38) GOV MEDDLE**
    ➤ Column Variable: **2) GENDER**
    ➤ View: **Tables**
    ➤ Display: **Column %**

	MALE	**FEMALE**
GOVT MEDL	_____%	_____%
BGR PROBS	_____%	_____%

    Now, get the Cramer's V and the significance level for these two variables.

    b. Record the value of Cramer's V for this table. (Include asterisks, if any.)   V = _____

    c. Is the relationship between GENDER and GOV MEDDLE statistically significant? (Circle one.)   Yes   No

    d. Is the relationship between GENDER and GOV MEDDLE weak, moderate, strong, or not significant? (Circle one.)

    Weak

    Moderate

    Strong

    Not Significant

    e. Was the hypothesis supported? (Circle one.)   Yes   No

10. Look over the results from all previous nine items (questions 1–9) in these worksheets. In which cross-tabulations was the general proposition we are testing here (from page 28) not supported, if any? If there were any, in your opinion, why do you think that these exceptions occurred? That is, with regards to those "exception" tables, why did the groups being compared not differ significantly on the item being addressed?

♦ EXERCISE 3 ♦

RACE & ETHNICITY, GENDER, AND SOCIAL CLASS: COMPARATIVE PERSPECTIVES

Tasks: Mapping, Scatterplot
Data Files: STATES, COUNTRIES

As we learned in Exercise 1, sociologists want to understand social regularities. When they do this by directly examining individual people (as micro sociologists often do), their **units of analysis** (that is, the entities they are specifically studying) are individuals.

However, in trying to comprehend larger social processes, groups, and structures, sociologists, especially macro sociologists, frequently analyze "units made up of more than one person."[1] For example, they may wish to study organizations, towns, counties, states, or nations. Sociologists often do this by combining (or "aggregating") data from individual cases in order to derive single pieces of information that describe these larger entities. For example, rather than comparing the SAT scores of individuals, an educational sociologist could calculate and compare the "average SAT scores" of ethnic groups, schools, school districts, or even states. This type of data is called **aggregate data**, and such units of analysis are classified as **aggregate**.

When aggregate data applies to geographic units, it is called **ecological data**. Using the latter to compare units of analysis such as cities, counties, states, and countries is known as **comparative research**. In this exercise, we will continue looking at race, ethnicity, gender, and social class by doing some comparative, macro-level research of our own.

When looking at ecological data in this workbook, you will notice that most of the variables are special types of aggregate figures that allow us to make meaningful comparisons among units of different sizes, because raw numbers don't allow us to do this properly. Let's say that the number of African Americans in both State "X" and State "Y" is 500,000. Does this mean that each state is equally African American? Probably not. If the population of State X is 1,000,000 and the population of State Y is 5,000,000 then the **percentage** of African Americans in State X is 50% (divide 500,000 by 1,000,000, then multiply the result by 100), but in State Y it is 10% (divide 500,000 by 5,000,000, then multiply the result by 100). In State X, 50 out of every 100 people are African American, while in State Y, 10 out of every 100 people are.

Rates are similar to percentages. They are calculated by multiplying divisions such as those we just did by numbers such as 1,000, 10,000, or 100,000, instead of by 100. They are used when percentages would be too small (typically, less than 1%).[2] For example, assume that 5,000 people died in both State X and State Y (above). The death rate per 1,000 people in State X would be 5 (divide 5,000 by 1,000,000, then multiply the result by 1,000), but in State Y it would be 1 (divide 5,000 by 5,000,000, then multiply that figure by 1,000).

---

[1] Rodney Stark, 2001, *Sociology*, 8th ed., Belmont, Calif.: Wadsworth, page 8.

[2] Barkan, op cit., page 3.

There are other types of aggregate figures used in this workbook. ***Ratios*** compare the relative proportions of two things. For example, student/teacher ratios tell us how many students there are per teacher (the number of students divided by the number of teachers). ***Averages*** (or "means") describe what is mathematically "typical" in a population, while ***medians*** tell us what the "middle" point is. Consider the difference between the average and median incomes for 125 people. You would find the average by adding all of the incomes and then dividing that figure by 125. But you would determine the median by locating the middle person (number 63) on a list of these 125 individuals ranked (highest to lowest) by income.

Let's look at some aggregate figures related to social class, gender, race, and ethnicity, and see how they help us to compare large units of analysis. We will turn to your STATES data file to do so, starting with percentages of African American.

> ➤ *Data File:* **STATES**
> ➤ *Task:* **Mapping**
> ➤ *Variable 1:* **10) %BLACK00**
> ➤ *View:* **Map**
> ➤ *Display:* **Legend**

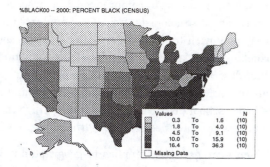

First select "Open File," then open the STATES data file, if you have not done so already. Now, select the MAPPING task. Next, select Variable 10) %BLACK00. Use the cursor keys and scroll bar to move through the Variables list, if necessary. After highlighting 10) %BLACK00, click on the arrow next to "Variable 1" to choose this variable for the MAPPING task. Then click [OK]. Finally, check the box for "Legend."

This map uses five colors to display the data. Looking at the legend, you can see that the highest percentages of African Americans are shown on the map with the darkest color. The lowest percentages of African Americans are shown on the map with the lightest color. Therefore, the percentages of African Americans are heaviest in the Southeast, which should not surprise us since these were slave states until the Civil War. You may want to try using your cursor arrow to "click" on various states. When you do so, you will notice that the state will turn green, and some additional information on that state will be provided at the bottom of your screen. For example, click on "Mississippi," and you will see that 36.3% of the people of this state are African American, giving Mississippi the highest ranking on this variable. Click on Montana, and you can see that less than 1% (0.3%) of its population is African American, placing it last among states on this variable. Now, let's look at the percentages of Hispanics for states.

Data File: **STATES**
Task: **Mapping**
➤ Variable 1: **13) %HISP.00**
➤ View: **Map**

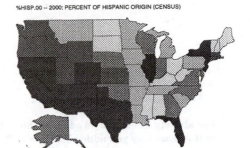

%HISP.00 -- 2000: PERCENT OF HISPANIC ORIGIN (CENSUS)

As you can see, Hispanics are most heavily concentrated in the South*west*. However, there are also high concentrations in Florida, Illinois, and parts of the Northeast, as well as some other Western states. Why don't we take a look at a ranking of states by percent Hispanic?

Data File: **STATES**
Task: **Mapping**
Variable 1: **13) %HISP.00**
➤ View: **List: Rank**

RANK	CASE NAME	VALUE
1	New Mexico	42.1
2	California	32.4
3	Texas	32.0
4	Arizona	25.3
5	Nevada	19.7
6	Colorado	17.1
7	Florida	16.8
8	New York	15.1
9	New Jersey	13.3
10	Illinois	12.3

With the map for 13) %HISP.00 still open, select the [List: Rank] option. Use the cursor keys and scroll bar to move through the list, if necessary.

We see that the highest ranked state is New Mexico, where 42.1% of the population identifies itself as a member of a Hispanic group (here, mostly Mexican-American). Maine and West Virginia, where less than 1% (0.7%) of the population are Hispanic, have the lowest rank. Why don't you take a moment now to find your own state on the list?

To compare rates, we'll examine some rather sad data. We'll look at infant mortality rates (per 1,000 live births) for whites and then for African Americans. Let's go right to ranks here, which reveal something that is rather disturbing.

Data File: **STATES**
Task: **Mapping**
➤ Variable 1: **24) WINFMRT99**
➤ Variable 2: **25) BINFMRT99**
➤ View: **List: Rank**

RANK	CASE NAME	VALUE
1	Oklahoma	8.0
2	South Dakota	7.7
3	West Virginia	7.3
4	Kentucky	7.1
5	Indiana	7.0

RANK	CASE NAME	VALUE
1	Iowa	20.6
2	Arizona	19.1
3	Missouri	18.9
3	Nebraska	18.9
5	Illinois	18.4

You already know how to add Variable 1. Here, just add Variable 2, in the appropriate slot, in the same way you added Variable 1. That is, highlight 25) BINFMRT99, and click on the arrow next to Variable 2 to choose this as the second variable for the MAPPING task. Then click [OK]. Finally, check the box next to [List: Rank] for both variables on the left side of the screen.

If you look carefully, you will see that in every state, infant mortality is much higher for African Americans than for whites. Moreover, you may notice that the *highest* rate for whites (8.0, in Oklahoma) is smaller than the *lowest* rate for blacks (9.8, in Massachusetts).

Let's take a look at a ratio, namely the ratio of males to females (specifically, the number of males per 100 females). This is a variable that, as we shall see soon, is important to a major sociological theory dealing with areas such as sex roles, gender equity, and discrimination.

Data File: **STATES**
Task: **Mapping**
➤ Variable 1: **6) SEX RAT.00**
➤ View: **Map**

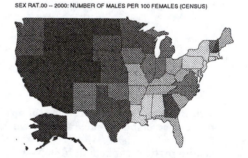

SEX RAT.00 -- 2000: NUMBER OF MALES PER 100 FEMALES (CENSUS)

Notice that, generally, the relative proportion of males to females is higher in the West than in the East. If you take a moment to look at the ranks here [List: Rank], you can see this very clearly. Alaska has the highest ratio of males to females—107 males for every 100 females. Close behind is Nevada with about 104 males for every 100 females. Meanwhile, at the other end of the spectrum, Massachusetts and Rhode Island each have about 93 males per 100 females.

Let's consider *median* family income and then *average* income per person (or, "per capita income"). This information is involved in many discussions of social class and is commonly used to make comparisons of wealth.

Data File: **STATES**
Task: **Mapping**
➤ Variable 1: **28) MED.FAM$00**
➤ Variable 2: **29) PER CAP$00**
➤ View: **Maps**

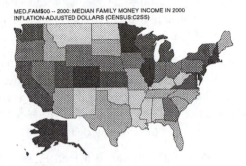

MED.FAM$00 -- 2000: MEDIAN FAMILY MONEY INCOME IN 2000
INFLATION-ADJUSTED DOLLARS (CENSUS:C2SS)

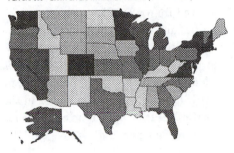

PER CAP$00 -- 2000: PER CAPITA MONEY INCOME (CENSUS:C2SS)

Notice that both maps look similar, indicating that, with various exceptions, incomes are higher in the Northeast and upper Midwest, and generally lower in areas west of the Mississippi and east of the Rocky Mountains, and in the Southeast. Looking at the ranks [List: Rank] provides even more detail. The highest median family and per capita money incomes are in New Jersey and Connecticut respectively ($65,182 and $29,145). The lowest median family and per capita money incomes are in West Virginia ($34,465 and $15,714).

You may recall that in Exercise 2, I pointed out that theories are very important in sociology and that they are ways of *explaining* social regularities. This involves trying to determine what *causes* the latter. For example, in trying to understand and solve various social problems, we realize that it is critical to formulate and test theories about what causes them.

When social scientists try to find out what causes something, they are seeking to discover factors that make this thing *more* or *less* likely to occur or exist. They are *not* generally looking for factors that *always* lead to this thing. This is to say that social scientists deal in *probabilities*. So, for example, when a sociologist says that "getting married at a young age is a cause of divorce," she is *not* saying "every person who gets married young will get divorced!" She is saying "people who get married at a young age are *more likely* to get divorced than people who do not get married at a young age."

Likewise, sociologists generally do not believe that a "cause" for something is its *only* cause. Most, if not all, social facts that sociologists try to explain have multiple, and often very complex, causes. To continue with our previous example, our sociologist would *not* be saying "early marriage is the *only* reason that people get divorced," but rather "early marriage is *one of many* factors that increases the risk of getting divorced."

When sociologists talk about causes and effects, they carefully distinguish the variables they are studying. An **independent variable** is the one they are treating as a possible cause, and the **dependent variable** is the effect they are trying to explain.[3]

Sociologists understand that if their independent variable is a cause of their dependent variable, then these variables must be associated with each other. Changes in the independent variable must be accompanied by changes in the dependent variable. They must "vary together." For example, if racial discrimination leads to lower relative wages for African Americans, then as racial discrimination decreases, relative African American wages ought to increase.

In 1983, Marcia Guttentag and Paul F. Secord set forth a fascinating theory about sex ratios and gender roles.[4] For reasons too involved to set forth here, they asserted that the more males there are relative to females, the more bound women will be to traditional gender roles. (This is an insight mostly derived from a conflict perspective.) If this is true, then, since having lots of children is part of these traditional roles, it is very likely that the following hypothesis will be supported: *the fertility rate* (that is, estimated births per 1,000 women of childbearing age) *will be higher in places where the ratio of men to women is higher than in places where this ratio is lower*. You may recall that the ratio of males to females is higher in the West than in the East. Guttentag and Secord's theory would suggest that the fertility rate ought to be higher in the West than in the East. Let's find out. Here, we will use the ExplorIt MAPPING function to compare maps of these two variables next to each other. Notice that "sex ratio" is our independent variable, and "fertility rate" is our dependent variable.

Data File:	**STATES**
Task:	**Mapping**
➤ *Variable 1:*	**6) SEX RAT.00**
➤ *Variable 2:*	**27) FERTIL00**
➤ *View:*	**Maps**

SEX RAT.00 – 2000: NUMBER OF MALES PER 100 FEMALES (CENSUS)

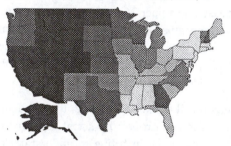

FERTIL00 – 2000: FERTILITY RATE--BIRTHS PER 1,000 WOMEN AGED 15-44 YEARS ESTIMATED (NCHS)

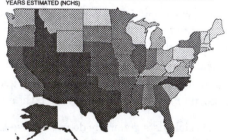

---

[3] Cf. Mooney et al., op cit., page 18.

[4] *Too Many Women? The Sex Ratio Question*, Beverly Hills, Calif.: Sage.

Just by looking at the two maps, you get the sense that our hypothesis may be supported. In both maps, the West is generally darker and the East is generally lighter, indicating that states that are higher in the ratio of males per females also tend to be higher in fertility. But how can we be *sure* that the association between sex ratios and fertility rates is real and meaningful?

Well, you may recall that in Exercise 2, we settled these kinds of questions in cross-tabulations by looking at a "measure of association" called Cramer's V. Before we accepted an association as "real," V had to be statistically significant. If V was followed by one asterisk, this meant that the chance of error was less than 5% (.05), while two asterisks meant that the chance of error was less than 1% (.01). If asterisks did not follow V, you were directed to treat any associations between the two variables in the cross-tabulation as non-existent.

If you look closely at the upper right-hand side of the lower map, you will see something called an *r*. Like Cramer's V, *r* is a measure of association, generally called a **correlation coefficient**. An *r* is always a decimal number between "0" (no correlation) and "1" or "–1" (either number indicating a perfect correlation). Because it was invented by someone named Karl Pearson, this figure is referred to as a "Pearson's '*r*.' " The asterisks here mean the same thing as they do when they are next to a "V." In this case, r = .496**. It appears that the association between sex ratio and fertility here is significant, with a chance of error less than 1%.

Pearson's *r* is also like Cramer's V in that even if the correlation coefficient is significant, it may show only a weak association between two variables. A good rule of thumb is to consider any *r* that is less than .30 to indicate a weak relationship and an *r* between .30 and .60 to suggest a moderate one, with an *r* greater than .60 showing a strong association.[5] Thus, the above analysis reveals a moderate correlation between sex ratios and fertility rates.

By drawing a **scatterplot**, you can look at this kind of information visually, and also get a Pearson's *r*. Let's take a look at a scatterplot of the above two variables, and then I'll explain to you what you are seeing.

Data File:	**STATES**
➤ *Task:*	**Scatterplot**
➤ *Dependent Variable:*	**27) FERTIL00**
➤ *Independent Variable:*	**6) SEX RAT.00**

r = 0.496**   Prob. = 0.000   N = 50   Missing = 0

As you can see, the *r* is shown at the bottom, along with the exact probability of error (well under 1%), the number of cases (50), and the number of cases with missing data (none). Focusing on the scatterplot itself now, notice that the independent variable is laid out along the horizontal line at the bottom (called the **X axis**), while the dependent variable is represented along the vertical line to the left (called the **Y axis**). Each "dot" represents a particular case (here, a state). For each particular case a

---

[5] Again, I am indebted to Barkan (op cit., page 21) for these rules of thumb.

point is placed where its value on the independent variable (along the X axis) intersects with its value on the dependent variable (along the Y axis).

In ExplorIt, you can get information on any point on a scatterplot by simply clicking on it with your mouse. Click on the point that is farthest to the right of this scatterplot, and what I just told you (above) about what the "dots" represent ought to become very clear.

Data File: **STATES**
Task: **Scatterplot**
Dependent Variable: **27) FERTIL00**
Independent Variable: **6) SEX RAT.00**
➤ View: **Find Case**
➤ Display: **Alaska**

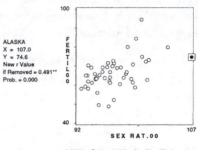

As you can see, a red box is drawn around that point, and information about it is shown on the left. You can see that the point is Alaska. Its sex ratio in 2000 was about 107 males for every 100 females (which is why it is placed along the far right of the X axis). Its fertility rate was about 75 births per 1,000 women between 14 and 44 years old. So Alaska's "point" was placed 75 "notches" straight above the 107th "notch" of the horizontal (X) axis.

Now, click anywhere on the white part of the screen (not the menu areas) that is outside of the scatterplot box itself and this special Alaska information will disappear. With the scatterplot open, I want you to look at one other feature of the scatterplot that helps you to grasp what is going on in the relationship of the two variables on it: the regression line. A *regression line* is the best straight line one can use to represent the distribution of all the points.

Data File: **STATES**
Task: **Scatterplot**
Dependent Variable: **27) FERTIL00**
Independent Variable: **6) SEX RAT.00**
➤ View: **Reg. Line**

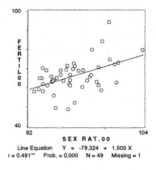

To view the regression line, select the [Reg. Line] option from the menu in the gray area on the left side of the screen.

Notice that the regression line makes it clear that as states' values on the X axis (independent variable) increase, their values on the Y axis (dependent variable) also increase. This type of relationship is called a *positive* correlation. That is, both variables "move" in the same direction. If X rises, Y increases too. If X falls, so does Y. In positive correlations, the regression line on a scatterplot slopes *up* from left to right.

Investigating Social Problems

Correlations can also be **negative** (or, "inverse"). That is, they can be associated but "move" in opposite directions. In negative correlations, if X rises, Y *falls*; and if X falls, Y *rises*. An easy way to picture negative correlations is to think of a "seesaw" on a playground. As one child goes up, the other goes down, and vice versa. In negative correlations, the regression line on a scatterplot slopes *down* from left to right.

Notice that in this last example, if the correlation had been negative, the hypothesis would not have been supported, even if the correlation had been significant. That is because the hypothesis predicted a positive correlation—as the ratio of males to females increased, fertility was supposed to increase, and vice versa. Let's use Guttentag and Secord's theory to derive a hypothesis that predicts a *negative* correlation: *as the ratio of males to females <u>increases</u>, the percentage of females in the labor force will <u>decrease</u>*. To test this, we'll go back to a time when female labor force involvement challenged social norms more so than it does today, 1940.

Data File:	**STATES**
Task:	**Scatterplot**
➤ *Dependent Variable:*	**53) %FEM LAB40**
➤ *Independent Variable:*	**8) SEX RAT.40**
➤ *View:*	**Reg. Line**

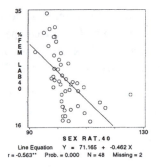

Line Equation   Y = 71.165 + -0.462 X
r = -0.563**   Prob. = 0.000   N = 48   Missing = 2

Notice that the line now slopes *down* from left to right. This is opposite of the last scatterplot. Take a look at *r* and you will see that it is not only very significant, but it is also now a negative number ($r = -0.563**$). Our hypothesis predicted a significant negative correlation between sex ratio and female labor force participation, and it appears to be supported.

Well, so far we have seen that in order to determine if an independent variable "causes" (has an effect on) a dependent variable, these two variables must be significantly correlated. In testing Guttentag and Secord's ideas so far, we have seen that sex ratio appears to be related to gender role variables as their theory predicts. Does this mean that changes in sex ratios cause these gender role changes? No. *Correlation, in and of itself, does not establish cause.* Two other things must be true before we can have greater confidence in the idea that sex ratios actually cause changes in fertility or female employment.

First, changes in sex ratios must have preceded changes in these dependent variables in time. A cause must occur *before* its effect! But in social science it is often hard to be certain which variable—the independent or dependent— "came first." In this case, logic suggests that changes in the dependent variables probably did not occur first. For example, it is unlikely that changes in fertility or female employment rates would alter sex ratios. However, the question of which variable came first is still a sticky one here, as it often is.[6] To complicate matters further, it is frequently true that the independent and dependent variables *both* affect each other!

---

[6] However, to be fair, the time-order issue does appear to be addressed well by Guttentag and Secord (op cit.).

Second, in order for sex ratios to affect dependent variables such as fertility and female employment, the correlation between them must not be *spurious*. A correlation is spurious when it exists only because each of the variables is correlated with some other variable(s).

Suppose someone told you that kids who come from homes where operas are regularly played do better in school than kids who don't come from such homes. You might point out (correctly) that this is probably just because people who enjoy listening to opera are, on average, better-educated and wealthier than people who don't. So it is not surprising that their kids do better in school! In this case, the relationship between "exposure to opera" and "academic performance" is spurious. This correlation exists only because both of these variables are related to parents' wealth and education. Consider another example. Believe it or not, it is true that people who have been arrested are significantly more likely to be employed full-time than people who have never been arrested. Does this mean that getting arrested improves people's job prospects? Of course not! Males are more likely than females to be arrested, and they are also more likely than women to have full-time jobs.

You've covered a lot of ground so far in this exercise. Congratulations! Now, it's time for you to work on your own doing some further comparative research and hypothesis-testing focusing on race, ethnicity, gender, and social class. You'll not only look at some more STATES data, but get into some international comparisons as well (COUNTRIES). Have fun!

NAME:

COURSE:

DATE:

Workbook exercises and software are copyrighted. Copying is prohibited by law.

REVIEW QUESTIONS

Based on the first part of this exercise, answer True or False to the following items:

When aggregate data represents geographic units, it is called "ecological data."	T	F
Rates are always figures expressed in terms of either "per 1,000" or "per 10,000."	T	F
Among states, the highest infant mortality rate for whites is less than the lowest infant mortality rate for African Americans.	T	F
Dependent variables are causes, and independent variables are effects.	T	F
The Guttentag and Secord theory predicts that traditional sex roles will be more associated with places where men outnumber women than with places where women outnumber men.	T	F
An r must be a number between 0 and either +1 or −1.	T	F
We would treat this number—$r = 0.324^*$— as if there were no correlation between the two variables.	T	F
In a scatterplot, the dependent variable is represented along the X axis.	T	F
In a scatterplot, if the regression line slopes downward from left to right, the correlation is negative.	T	F
Among states in 1940, as the ratio of males to females increased, the percentage of employed women increased.	T	F
If two variables are significantly correlated, we can be certain that one causes the other.	T	F
If x does not precede y, the relationship between x and y is "spurious."	T	F

EXPLORIT QUESTIONS

1. We will start by continuing to look at the STATES file, exploring in a general way the relationship of race, ethnicity, and poverty. In Exercise 2, we saw that African American survey respondents were more likely than whites to be in lower income categories. Let's find out if this association between race and income shows up in our STATES ecological data as well.

   a. Open the STATES data set (if it is not open already).

b. Create maps showing state differences in the percent that are poor. Look carefully at the variable descriptions that appear above the maps.

> Data File: **STATES**
> Task: **Mapping**
> Variable 1: **48) %POOR00**
> Variable 2: **10) %BLACK00**
> View: **Maps**

c. Compare the two maps. Would you say that they are "very similar," "somewhat similar," "not at all similar," "somewhat opposite," or "very opposite?" Circle what you think is the best answer.

Very Similar

Somewhat Similar

Not At All Similar

Somewhat Opposite

Very Opposite

d. Now look at the rank for each variable.

Data File: **STATES**
Task: **Mapping**
Variable 1: **48) %POOR00**
Variable 2: **10) %BLACK00**
> View: **List:Rank**

e. Provide the state name and value (%) for the 10 _highest_ ranked states on each of the above two variables.

	48) %POOR00			**10) %BLACK00**	
	STATE	VALUE		STATE	VALUE
1.	_____	_____	1.	_____	_____
2.	_____	_____	2.	_____	_____
3.	_____	_____	3.	_____	_____
4.	_____	_____	4.	_____	_____
5.	_____	_____	5.	_____	_____

	48) %POOR00			10) %BLACK00	
	STATE	VALUE		STATE	VALUE
6.	_____	_____	6.	_____	_____
7.	_____	_____	7.	_____	_____
8.	_____	_____	8.	_____	_____
9.	_____	_____	9.	_____	_____
10.	_____	_____	10.	_____	_____

f. How many states appear in the top 10 rank lists for *both* of the above variables, rather than appearing in the top 10 for only *one* of these variables? Fill in the correct answer below.   _____

g. Now, remove the ranks and go back to the map view for both of these variables. When you have done so, look at Pearson's *r*.

> Data File: **STATES**
> Task: **Mapping**
> Variable 1: **48) %POOR00**
> Variable 2: **10) %BLACK00**
> ➤ View: **Maps**

> **With the previous screen still open, just select [Map] for both Variable 1 and Variable 2. The ranks will disappear and be replaced by maps, with Pearson's *r* displayed to the upper right of the lower (%BLACK00) map.**

h. Provide Pearson's *r* (including asterisks, if any, and the direction sign, if any). $r =$ _____

i. Is this correlation significant *and* negative, significant *and* positive, or not significant? (Circle one.)

Significant *and* Negative

Significant *and* Positive

Not Significant

j. Are increases in the percent African American associated with increases in the percent poor? (Circle one.)   Yes   No

2. Let's look at the associations between poverty and Hispanics.

    a. Draw two maps, one showing state variations in the percent poor, and the other showing state variations in the percent Hispanic. Look at the rank for 13) %HISP.00.

> Data File: **STATES**
> Task: **Mapping**
> Variable 1: **48) %POOR00**
> ➤ Variable 2: **13) %HISP.00**
>   ➤ View: **List:Rank**

    b. Provide the state name and value (%) for the 10 _highest_ ranked states on 13) %HISP.00.

13) %HISP.00

	STATE	VALUE
1.	_____	_____
2.	_____	_____
3.	_____	_____
4.	_____	_____
5.	_____	_____
6.	_____	_____
7.	_____	_____
8.	_____	_____
9.	_____	_____
10.	_____	_____

    c. How many states that appeared in the top 10 rank list for %HISP.00 also appeared in the top 10 rank list for %POOR00? Fill in the correct answer.   _____

    d. Now, remove the rank and go back to the map view for %HISP.00. When you have done so, look at Pearson's *r*.

> Data File: **STATES**
> Task: **Mapping**
> Variable 1: **48) %POOR00**
> Variable 2: **13) %HISP.00**
> ➤ View: **Map**

    e. Provide Pearson's *r* (including asterisks, if any, and the direction sign, if any).   *r* = _____

    f. Is this correlation significant *and* negative, significant *and* positive, or not significant? (Circle one.)

> Significant *and* Negative
>
> Significant *and* Positive
>
> Not Significant

    g. Are increases in the percent Hispanic associated with increases in the percent poor? (Circle one.)

> Yes   No

    h. Is the correlation between %POOR00 and %HISP.00 weak, moderate, strong, or not significant? (Circle one.)

> Weak
>
> Moderate
>
> Strong
>
> Not Significant

    i. Based on what you learned in questions 1 and 2, briefly describe the association between the percentage of Hispanics and African Americans in a state and its percentage of people who are poor.

3. Sociologists have noted that women who head families are disproportionately likely to be poor. This is part of a growing phenomenon called the **feminization of poverty**.[7] Let's explore this hypothesis: *as the percentages of households with children that are headed by single mothers increases, the percentage of poor people will increase.* We're still in the STATES file.

---

[7] See, for example, Eitzen and Baca Zinn, op cit., pages 180–181; and Sullivan, op cit., pages 162–163.

a. Does this hypothesis predict a negative or a positive correlation? (Circle one.)   Negative

Positive

Look carefully at the variable description for 45) F HEAD/C00.

b. Construct a scatterplot that represents the association between 45) F HEAD/C00 and 48) %POOR00. Don't forget to select [Reg. Line].

Data File:	**STATES**
➤ Task:	**Scatterplot**
➤ Dependent Variable:	**48) %POOR00**
➤ Independent Variable:	**45) F HEAD/C00**
➤ View:	**Reg. Line**

c. Select [Find: Case]. When the "Select One Case" box pops up, select the state you are in right now. Then, fill in the values for the state you are in, for each of these variables, below. Remember, the X axis ("X") is the independent variable, and the Y axis ("Y") is the dependent variable. When you are done filling in the percentages for your state (below), just click anywhere in the white area outside the scatterplot itself to make this special information disappear.

48) F HEAD/C00: _____%

45) %POOR00: _____%

d. Provide Pearson's *r*. (Include asterisks, if any.)   *r* = _____

e. Is this correlation significant *and* negative, significant *and* positive, or not significant? (Circle one.)

Significant *and* Negative

Significant *and* Positive

Not Significant

f. Is the relationship between %POOR00 and F HEAD/C00 weak, moderate, strong, or not significant? (Circle one.)

Weak

Moderate

Strong

Not Significant

g. Is the hypothesis supported? (Circle one.)   Yes   No

h. Does this scatterplot show that increases in percentages of female-headed households with children *lead to* (cause) increases in percentages of people who are poor? Why or why not?

i. Do you <u>think</u> that increases in percentages of female-headed households with children *lead to* (cause) increases in percentages of people who are poor? Why or why not? (Be specific.)

4. Let's finish these worksheets by testing some more hypotheses derived from Guttentag and Secord's theory about sex ratios and gender roles. To do so, we will now switch to international ecological data, using your COUNTRIES data set.

   Previously, we looked at the association between sex ratios and female labor force involvement among American states in 1940. Now, let's look at the same issue internationally in the 1990s. Here is our hypothesis: *as the ratio of males to females increases, the percentage of the labor force that is female will decrease.*

   a. Does this hypothesis predict a negative or a positive correlation? (Circle one.)

      Negative

      Positive

   b. Open the COUNTRIES data set. Look carefully at the variable descriptions for both 17) SEX RATIO and 40) %WKR WOMEN.

   c. Draw two maps. One should show national sex ratios, and the other should show national percentages of the work force that is female.

      ➤ Data File: **COUNTRIES**
      ➤ Task: **Mapping**
      ➤ Variable 1: **17) SEX RATIO**
      ➤ Variable 2: **40) %WKR WOMEN**
      ➤ View: **Maps**

   d. Use your mouse to "click" on Mexico (on either of the two maps). Then, fill in the values (note: not the ranks) for Mexico for each of these variables, below. When you are done filling in the information, just click anywhere in the white area on your screen that is outside of the maps to make this special information disappear.

      17) SEX RATIO: _____%

      40) %WKR WOMEN: _____%

   e. Provide Pearson's *r* (including asterisks, if any, and the direction sign, if any).   *r* = _____

f.   Is this correlation significant *and* negative, significant *and* positive, or not significant? (Circle one.)

Significant *and* Negative

Significant *and* Positive

Not Significant

g.   Is the correlation weak, moderate, strong, or not significant? (Circle one.)

Weak

Moderate

Strong

Not Significant

h.   Is the hypothesis supported? (Circle one.)

Yes   No

5.   Now, let's test another hypothesis we have already looked at, dealing with the relationship of sex ratios to fertility rates: *as the ratio of males to females increases, the fertility rate will increase.*

a.   Does this hypothesis predict a negative or a positive correlation? (Circle one.)

Negative

Positive

b.   Look carefully at the description for 8) FERTILITY.

c.   Construct a scatterplot that represents the association between 17) SEX RATIO and 8) FERTILITY.

> Data File: **COUNTRIES**
> ➤ Task: **Scatterplot**
> ➤ Dependent Variable: **8) FERTILITY**
> ➤ Independent Variable: **17) SEX RATIO**
> ➤ View: **Reg. Line**

d.   Provide Pearson's *r* (including asterisks, if any, and the direction sign, if any).   *r* = _____

e.   Is this correlation significant *and* negative, significant *and* positive, or not significant? (Circle one.)

Significant *and* Negative

Significant *and* Positive

Not Significant

f.   Is the correlation weak, moderate, strong, or not significant? (Circle one.)

Weak

Moderate

Strong

Not Significant

g.   Is the hypothesis supported? (Circle one.)

Yes   No

h. Does this scatterplot show that increases in the ratio of females to males *lead to* (cause) decreases in fertility? Why or why not?

6. Finally, let's test one more hypothesis that appears consistent with the idea that the more females there are relative to males, the less bound women will be to traditional gender roles: *as the ratio of males to females increases, the percentage of women using contraceptives will decrease.*

    a. Does this hypothesis predict a negative, or a positive, correlation? (Circle one.)   Negative

                                                                                Positive

    b. Look carefully at the description for 12) CONTRACEPT.

    c. Construct a scatterplot that represents the association between 17) SEX RATIO and 12) CONTRA-CEPT.

> Data File: **COUNTRIES**
> Task: **Scatterplot**
> ➤ Dependent Variable: **12) CONTRACEPT**
> ➤ Independent Variable: **17) SEX RATIO**
> ➤ View: **Reg. Line**

    d. Provide Pearson's *r* (including asterisks, if any, and the direction sign, if any).   *r* = _____

    e. Is this correlation significant *and* negative, significant *and* positive, or not significant? (Circle one.)

                                                       Significant *and* Negative

                                                         Significant *and* Positive

                                                         Not Significant

    f. Is the correlation weak, moderate, strong, or not significant? (Circle one.)   Weak

                                                         Moderate

                                                         Strong

                                                        Not Significant

    g. Is the hypothesis supported? (Circle one.)   Yes   No

7. In this exercise overall—in questions 4–6 (above) and in the text preceding these worksheets—how well have hypotheses derived from Guttentag and Secord's theory been supported? Detail your answer, citing facts you have uncovered.

SEXUAL ACTIVITY AND ORIENTATION AND THE "CULTURE WARS"

Tasks: Univariate, Historical Trends, Cross-tabulation
Data Files: ELECTION, TRENDS, GSS

In modern American life, few things appear to stir up passionate debate as readily as issues of sexual activity and orientation. There are numerous points of controversy, for example, related to sex between unmarried heterosexuals. To what extent and under what conditions does such sexual activity constitute a "problem" at all? Are the solutions to fallout related to nonmarital sex such as unmarried teen pregnancy and sexually transmitted diseases (STDs) to be found mainly or solely in promoting premarital abstinence and postmarital sexual faithfulness? Or should social responses to sex outside marriage focus on, or at least include, such things as increased access to contraception and abortion, education of youth and others that promotes responsible sex, and heightened public support for single mothers?

Discussion becomes even more heated when the debate turns to homosexuality. Is sex between people of the same gender inherently dysfunctional and morally wrong? Are those who practice it misguided or sinful? Or do such views lead to, or even constitute, *homophobia* (that is, "an unreasonable fear of or hostility toward homosexuals")?[1] To many who affirm this last point, it is not homosexuality, but "homophobia," that is a true "social problem." Important related questions abound. The most significant in contemporary America have to do with the extent to which government should protect and/or extend the civil rights of homosexuals. Should gay and lesbian couples be allowed to legally marry or adopt children? Is the traditional presumption against homosexuals in child-custody disputes fair? To what extent should gay and lesbian employees enjoy civil rights protections similar to those granted women and minorities?

Many social scientists believe that debates such as these are part of broader conflicts over core values, lifestyles, and policies that divide America today. They say, in fact, that America is in the midst of a "culture war." James Davison Hunter, a leading proponent of this idea, describes competing "moral visions [which] take expression as *polarizing impulses* or *tendencies* in American culture . . . toward *orthodoxy* and . . . *progressivism.*"[2]

Cultural war theorists tend to think that the most fundamental difference between the latter two camps is a disagreement over the nature and source of morality.[3] The "orthodox" hold that moral truths are ultimately rooted in authority that is unchanging, absolute, knowable, and above human beings.[4] "Progressives" see moral values as changing and relative, determined by and subject to reason,

---

[1] Curran and Renzetti, op cit., page 204.

[2] 1990, *Culture Wars*, New York: Basic Books, page 43. Emphasis is in the original. See also Gertrude Himmelfarb, 2001, *One Nation, Two Cultures*, New York: Vintage Books, pages 117–141. Those who support the idea of a culture war generally recognize numerous subfactions within these two larger, competing "cultures," as well as different levels of commitment to core beliefs, and stridency, among both traditionalists and progressives.

[3] Cf. Himmelfarb, ibid., pages 117–141; and Hunter, op cit., pages 44–46.

[4] Ibid., page 44. Hunter states that this "authority" may emanate from a divine source, nature, natural law, or some other source external to people. Most of the orthodox are religious, he states, though some are secularists.

human experience and needs.[5] Differences in views about sexual practices and orientation are thought to figure prominently in these divergent ethical views.[6]

In an excellent study of female "pro-life" versus "pro-choice" abortion activists, Kristin Luker discussed some of the differences in moral, including sexual, views that culture war theorists are talking about.[7] According to Luker, the pro-life activists believed that morality is rooted in clear, unchanging rules that "originate in a Divine Plan." These activists also regarded all forms of sex outside the traditional, heterosexual marital bond as immoral. Thus, they stressed abstinence education for teenagers, and they rejected programs that provided confidential contraception and abortion services to teens. The pro-choice activists held almost opposite views. They used subjective reasoning in arriving at moral judgments. They did "not see certain activities as intrinsically right or wrong," but instead tried to determine, in any situation, what the most "loving thing to do" was. Sex outside of marriage, including by teenagers, was acceptable to them so long as it was protected and responsible.[8]

Not all social scientists accept the culture wars thesis. For example, in recent years Alan Wolfe has eloquently opposed it. After doing in-depth interviews with 200 American suburbanites, Wolfe said "that there is little truth to the charge that middle-class Americans, divided by a culture war, have split into two hostile camps."[9] Generally, his interviewees embraced tolerance. They tended to allow beliefs and behaviors that diverged from their own provided that those who held them were personally responsible. They believed in intrinsic values but did not wish to impose them on others. To deal with moral challenges, they looked at their own experiences and the situations present in particular cases, balancing compassion and principle. These respondents often embraced contradictory ideals and opinions.[10]

In this exercise, we will explore sexual attitudes and behaviors among the American public. We will also test the culture war theory by looking at differences between Christian conservatives, liberals, and others in these areas. Our foci will be on heterosexual sex among teens and unmarried adults, and on homosexuality. Let's begin with teen sex.

Recent reports have indicated that teen pregnancy has been dropping nationally since about 1990.[11] ("Pregnancy" includes births, abortions, and miscarriages.) This has been attributed to both decreased sexual activity and increased use of contraception among teens. Let's look at some data in your TRENDS data set to see if and how much this is true. We'll start with the pregnancy rate per 1,000 for women aged 15 to 19.

---

[5] Ibid., pages 44–45. Hunter says that these include both religious people and secularists.

[6] Cf. ibid., pages 50, 93–96, 188–194; Himmelfarb, op cit.

[7] 1984, *Abortion & the Politics of Motherhood*, Berkeley: University of California Press.

[8] Ibid, pages 174, 159–161, 172–173, 185, 176, and 182–183 (pages in the order presented).

[9] 1999, *One Nation After All*, New York: Penguin Books, pages 320–321.

[10] Ibid., pages 278–283.

[11] Cf. NCHS Press Office, "Pregnancy Rate Reaches a Record Low in 1997," U.S. Department of Health and Human Services, National Center for Health Statistics, Bethesda, MD.

> *Data File:* **TRENDS**
> > *Task:* **Historical Trends**
> *Variable:* **27) TEENPREG**

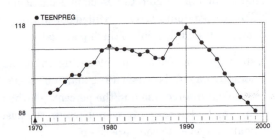

Pregnancy rate for women aged 15 to 19 (per 1,000 women)

You may recall that to reproduce this chart, you need to open the TRENDS data file, and then select the HISTORICAL TRENDS task.

This chart certainly seems to support these reports! From a high of about 117 per 1,000 in 1990, pregnancy among teens had dropped to about 88 per 1,000 in 1999. What about the rate for even younger women, say, 14 and under?

Data File: **TRENDS**
Task: **Historical Trends**
> *Variable:* **24) PREGRATE14**

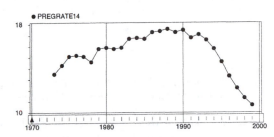

Pregnancy rate for women aged 14 or less (per 1,000 women)

We see the same pattern. From a high of almost 18 per 1,000 in 1990, the pregnancy rate for these younger women had dropped to about 11 per 1,000 in 1999.

Now we ought to look at the extent to which these declines in pregnancy represent teens having less sex![12] To do so, we will examine data from the Youth Risk Behavior Survey (YRBS)[13] that is summarized in your TRENDS data set. The YRBS is conducted every other year by the Centers for Disease Control and Prevention (CDC) with a random sample of a large number[14] of high school students from across the United States.

You may wonder how surveys like the YRBS get honest answers to questions about sensitive topics such as sexual practices. Although not all respondents tell the complete truth on such surveys, the researchers use methods to make sure that respondents are aware that their answers are anonymous.

---

[12] We will look at recent trends in teen contraceptive use in the worksheets in this exercise.

[13] You also have many variables from the senior portion of this survey, given in 2001, in your data set titled "YRBS." We will be making use of your YRBS data set in subsequent exercises, but not this one.

[14] For example, in 2001, 13,601 surveys were completed. *2001 National School-based Youth Risk Behavior Survey: Public Use Documentation*, U.S. Department of Health and Human Services, Centers for Disease Control and Prevention, Atlanta, GA, page ii.

That is, no one is able to associate a particular respondent with any answers he or she gave. In the YRBS, respondents privately filled out written questionnaires and there was no way to trace the questionnaire they filled out to them personally.[15]

Well, on we go. We'll start by seeing what changes, if any, occurred in levels of sexual intercourse among teenagers between 1991 and 2001. Let's look at two measures—the percentage who have ever had sexual intercourse and the percentage who are "currently sexually active" (measured by the YRBS as having had sexual intercourse within the past 3 months). We'll put both variables on the same chart to make it easier to compare them.

Data File: **TRENDS**
Task: **Historical Trends**
➤ Variable: **10) TEENSEX**
      15) TNSEXACTV

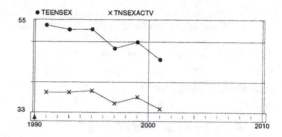

• Percent of high school students who have ever had sexual intercourse

x Percent of high school students who are currently sexually active (that is, who have had sexual intercourse within 3 months of being surveyed)

When using the HISTORICAL TRENDS task, you can select many variables to be displayed together. Just select the second variable the same way that you selected the first.

Notice that both of these measures clearly declined between 1991 and 2001. The percentage of high school students who had ever had sexual intercourse went from about 54% in 1991 to about 46% in 2001, while the "currently sexually active" declined from 37.5% in 1991 to a little over 33% in 2001. Though these rates rose a little bit between 1997 and 1999, they both went down again, to the lowest point in all 10 years, in 2001.

These figures combine older and younger students, since they include all grades from 9th to 12th. Since younger students are less sexually active, this decreases the percentages. Why don't we find out to what extent American young people have had sexual intercourse by the 12th grade, and how this changed between 1993 and 2001?

Data File: **TRENDS**
Task: **Historical Trends**
➤ Variable: **12) SEXGRD12**

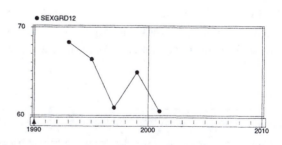

Percent of 12th grade students who have ever had sexual intercourse

---

[15] Ibid.

The pattern of change in this measure between 1993 and 2001 was the same for 12th graders as for high school students as a whole, namely a general decline, with some increase only between 1997 and 1999. As expected the percentages of those who had ever had sex were much higher for 12th graders. They ranged from about 68% in 1993 to a 2001 low of 60.5%.

How do Americans feel about teens having sex and what should be done about it? Let's find out by looking at the General Social Survey (GSS) and an item that asks respondents how they feel about sex between "early teens" (14 to 16 years old).

> *Data File:* **GSS**
> *Task:* **Univariate**
> *Primary Variable:* **28) TEEN SEX?**
> *View:* **Pie**

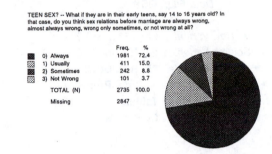

TEEN SEX? -- What if they are in their early teens, say 14 to 16 years old? In that case, do you think sex relations before marriage are always wrong, almost always wrong, wrong only sometimes, or not wrong at all?

		Freq.	%
■	0) Always	1981	72.4
▦	1) Usually	411	15.0
■	2) Sometimes	242	8.8
▦	3) Not Wrong	101	3.7
	TOTAL (N)	2735	100.0
	Missing	2847	

As we can see, such activity is generally frowned upon! About 72% of respondents said that sex between young teens is "always wrong." So, what do Americans think ought to be done about teen sex? Let's first take a look at what Americans think about sex education in the schools.

> *Data File:* **GSS**
> *Task:* **Univariate**
> *Primary Variable:* **29) SEX ED**
> *View:* **Pie**

SEX ED -- Would you be for or against sex education in the public schools?

		Freq.	%
■	0) For	2379	87.7
▦	1) Against	335	12.3
	TOTAL (N)	2714	100.0
	Missing	2868	

An overwhelming majority, nearly 88% of respondents, approved of sex education in the schools. Do most Americans also approve of providing birth control to younger teens even if their parents do not approve?

> *Data File:* **GSS**
> *Task:* **Univariate**
> *Primary Variable:* **30) TEEN BC OK**
> *View:* **Pie**

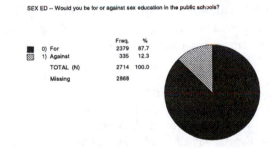

TEEN BC OK -- Do you strongly agree, agree, disagree, or strongly disagree that methods of birth control should be available to teenagers between the ages of 14 and 16 if their parents do not approve?

		Freq.	%
■	0) Agree	1597	58.8
▦	1) Disagree	1117	41.2
	TOTAL (N)	2714	100.0
	Missing	2868	

Nearly 59% of respondents do think younger teens should have access to birth control, even if their parents do not approve. Both of these measures appear to have a great deal of public support.

So, how about the "culture war"? Let's find out if religious fundamentalists are significantly more conservative than religious moderates or liberals in their views in these areas. We will focus only on those identifying themselves as Protestant.

Data File:	**GSS**
➤ *Task:*	**Cross-tabulation**
➤ *Row Variable:*	**28) TEEN SEX?**
➤ *Column Variable:*	**23) R.FUND/LIB**
➤ *Subset Variable:*	**25) RELIGION**
➤ *Subset Category:*	**Include: Protestant**
➤ *View:*	**Tables**
➤ *Display:*	**Column %**

TEEN SEX?   by   R.FUND/LIB

Cramer's V: 0.099 **

		R.FUND/LIB				
		Fundam.	Moderate	Liberal	Missing	TOTAL
TEEN SEX?	Always	645	252	241	27	1138
		83.0%	81.3%	70.3%		79.6%
	Usually	77	39	68	4	184
		9.9%	12.6%	19.8%		12.9%
	Sometimes	36	14	26	4	76
		4.6%	4.5%	7.6%		5.3%
	Not Wrong	19	5	8	1	32
		2.4%	1.6%	2.3%		2.2%
	Missing	784	346	355	30	1515
	TOTAL	777	310	343	66	1430
		100.0%	100.0%	100.0%		

Recall the procedure for using Subset Variables. Select your Row and Column Variables. Then select 25) RELIGION as your Subset Variable. When the "Subset By Categories" box comes up, select "Protestant" as your subset category and choose the [Include] option. Then click [OK] and continue.

On the issue of teen sex, fundamentalist Protestants (83%) differ little from the moderates (81.3%), though both are more likely than liberals (70.3%) to feel it is always wrong (V = 0.099**). However, there is still far more agreement than disagreement on this issue, with overwhelming majorities in all three groups categorically opposing sex between young teens.

Data File:	**GSS**
Task:	**Cross-tabulation**
➤ *Row Variable:*	**29) SEX ED**
➤ *Column Variable:*	**23) R.FUND/LIB**
➤ *Subset Variable:*	**25) RELIGION**
➤ *Subset Category:*	**Include: Protestant**
➤ *View:*	**Tables**
➤ *Display:*	**Column %**

SEX ED   by   R.FUND/LIB

Cramer's V: 0.118 **

		R.FUND/LIB				
		Fundam.	Moderate	Liberal	Missing	TOTAL
SEX ED	For	621	264	307	32	1192
		80.6%	85.4%	91.1%		84.2%
	Against	149	45	30	4	224
		19.4%	14.6%	8.9%		15.8%
	Missing	791	347	361	30	1529
	TOTAL	770	309	337	66	1416
		100.0%	100.0%	100.0%		

Fundamentalists (80.6%) are less likely than moderates (85.4%) or liberals (91.1%) to support sex education, but there is still substantial agreement among all three groups in favor of it (V = 0.118**).

Data File:	**GSS**	
Task:	**Cross-tabulation**	
➤ *Row Variable:*	**30) TEEN BC OK**	
➤ *Column Variable:*	**23) R.FUND/LIB**	
➤ *Subset Variable:*	**25) RELIGION**	
➤ *Subset Category:*	**Include: Protestant**	
➤ *View:*	**Tables**	
➤ *Display:*	**Column %**	

TEEN BC OK   by   R.FUND/LIB

Cramer's V: 0.121 **

		R.FUND/LIB				
		Fundam.	Moderate	Liberal	Missing	TOTAL
TEEN BC OK	Agree	360	171	209	18	740
		46.8%	54.6%	61.1%		51.9%
	Disagree	410	142	133	18	685
		53.2%	45.4%	38.9%		48.1%
	Missing	791	343	356	30	1520
	TOTAL	770	313	342	66	1425
		100.0%	100.0%	100.0%		

On the issue of birth control for young teens without parental consent, fundamentalists (46.8%) are significantly less likely than moderates (54.6%) or liberals (61.1%) to support it (V = 0.121**). But even here the differences between these groups are not overwhelming. So far, we have not seen much of a cultural divide between conservative and liberal Protestants.

Now, let's turn to consenting sex between unmarried adults. What proportion of unmarried adults have had sex (defined by the GSS as "vaginal, oral, or anal")?[16]

Data File:	**GSS**	
➤ *Task:*	**Univariate**	
➤ *Primary Variable:*	**34) SEXSINCE18**	
➤ *Subset Variable:*	**8) MARITAL**	
➤ *Subset Category:*	**Include: Nev Mar**	
➤ *View:*	**Pie**	

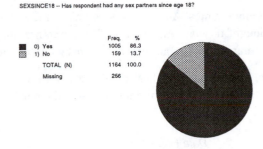

SEXSINCE18 -- Has respondent had any sex partners since age 18?

		Freq.	%
■	0) Yes	1005	86.3
▨	1) No	159	13.7
	TOTAL (N)	1164	100.0
	Missing	256	

[Subset]

Here we see that a large majority (about 86%) of unmarried adults have had sex at least once since age 18. What about the numbers of sex partners during the past year?

Data File:	**GSS**	
Task:	**Univariate**	
➤ *Primary Variable:*	**32) SX.PRTNERS**	
➤ *Subset Variable:*	**8) MARITAL**	
➤ *Subset Category:*	**Include: Nev Mar**	
➤ *View:*	**Pie**	

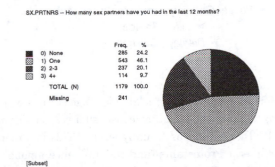

SX.PRTNRS -- How many sex partners have you had in the last 12 months?

		Freq.	%
■	0) None	285	24.2
▨	1) One	543	46.1
▦	2) 2-3	237	20.1
▨	3) 4+	114	9.7
	TOTAL (N)	1179	100.0
	Missing	241	

[Subset]

---

[16] When asking respondents for sensitive information about their own sexual activities and orientations, the GSS has respondents give anonymous answers through something called a "secret ballot." Even the interviewer does not know what answers the respondent gave. See Ayers, op cit., page 154.

While only about 24% had not had sex within a year of being surveyed, about 30% had two or more different sex partners during that year. Generally, to what extent do Americans approve or disapprove of consensual sexual activity by unmarried adults?

Data File: **GSS**
Task: **Univariate**
➤ Primary Variable: **27) PREM.SEX**
➤ View: **Pie**

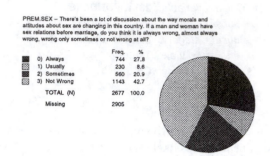

PREM.SEX -- There's been a lot of discussion about the way morals and attitudes about sex are changing in this country. If a man and woman have sex relations before marriage, do you think it is always wrong, almost always wrong, wrong only sometimes or not wrong at all?

		Freq.	%
■	0) Always	744	27.8
▨	1) Usually	230	8.6
▨	2) Sometimes	560	20.9
▨	3) Not Wrong	1143	42.7
	TOTAL (N)	2677	100.0
	Missing	2905	

> **Remember, after using the [⟲] button to return to the variable selection screen, click "Clear All" in order to clear the previous Subset Variable before selecting 27) PREM.SEX as your Primary Variable. Then click [OK] and continue as usual.**

Obviously, most Americans do not have difficulty accepting this type of sexual activity. Only about 28% thought it was "always wrong," with another almost 9% thinking it was usually wrong. The rest were willing to accept consensual sex among adults under most or all circumstances.

So, how about a cultural divide between the "orthodox" and the "progressives" here? Let's repeat our analysis comparing fundamentalist and other Protestants for the premarital sex variable.

Data File: **GSS**
➤ Task: **Cross-tabulation**
➤ Row Variable: **27) PREM.SEX**
➤ Column Variable: **23) R.FUND/LIB**
➤ Subset Variable: **25) RELIGION**
➤ Subset Category: **Include: Protestant**
➤ View: **Tables**
➤ Display: **Column %**

PREM.SEX by R.FUND/LIB

Cramer's V: 0.159 **

		R.FUND/LIB				
		Fundam.	Moderate	Liberal	Missing	TOTAL
PREM.SEX	Always	358	93	81	14	532
		46.9%	30.4%	24.5%		38.0%
	Usually	82	34	28	0	144
		10.7%	11.1%	8.5%		10.3%
	Sometimes	115	65	93	8	273
		15.1%	21.2%	28.2%		19.5%
	Not Wrong	209	114	128	13	451
		27.4%	37.3%	38.8%		32.2%
	Missing	797	350	368	31	1546
	TOTAL	764	306	330	66	1400
		100.0%	100.0%	100.0%		

Here, we find more of a "divide" that culture war theorists talk about. About 47% of fundamentalist Protestants thought that consensual sex outside marriage for adults was "always wrong," and about 11% thought it was "usually wrong." This is a more conservative position than that held by moderate or liberal Protestants (and the difference among these groups is moderately strong and statistically significant; V = 0.159**), but it is well to the "right" of the American public as a whole (where only about 27.8% thought that such sex was always wrong). However, contrary to formal fundamentalist Bible interpretation, most fundamentalists did not condemn *all* premarital sex. And as you can see by adding the rows "sometimes" and "not wrong," quite a large percentage (over 42%) of fundamentalists accepted premarital sex between consenting adults under all or many circumstances.

Investigating Social Problems

Finally, we will turn to homosexuality, which is generally defined as being oriented sexually toward, and/or having sexual relations with, "people of the same sex."[17] In the GSS, questions were asked that allow us to look at the last issue (but not the first), namely what percentage of respondents have had sex with people of the same sex. We will be looking only at respondents who had sex at least once since they were 18 years old. What percentage of these respondents had sex with others of the same sex?

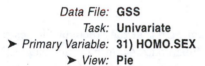

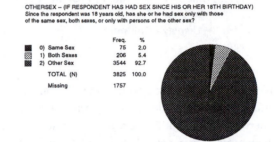

OTHERSEX -- (IF RESPONDENT HAS HAD SEX SINCE HIS OR HER 18TH BIRTHDAY)
Since the respondent was 18 years old, has she or he had sex only with those of the same sex, both sexes, or only with persons of the other sex?

		Freq.	%
0)	Same Sex	75	2.0
1)	Both Sexes	206	5.4
2)	Other Sex	3544	92.7
	TOTAL (N)	3825	100.0
	Missing	1757	

Data File: **GSS**
➤ Task: **Univariate**
➤ Primary Variable: **36) OTHERSEX**
➤ View: **Pie**

It appears that only 2% of these GSS respondents have had sex only with others of the same sex, but about another 5% have had sex with partners of both sexes, since age 18. This means that about 7% had at least one homosexual encounter since age 18.[18] None of these figures tell us what percentage of Americans is "truly homosexual," however. This is only a sample. And among those who had sex partners of both sexes, some probably regard themselves as homosexual and others regard themselves as heterosexual. Some of those with homosexual preferences have maintained abstinence. There are other problems too. However, determining what percentage of Americans is homosexual is a complicated, difficult undertaking, and we will not attempt to do so here! But what about the degree to which Americans approve or disapprove of homosexuality?

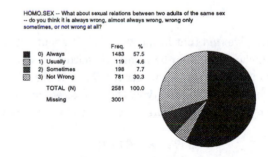

HOMO.SEX -- What about sexual relations between two adults of the same sex -- do you think it is always wrong, almost always wrong, wrong only sometimes, or not wrong at all?

		Freq.	%
0)	Always	1483	57.5
1)	Usually	119	4.6
2)	Sometimes	198	7.7
3)	Not Wrong	781	30.3
	TOTAL (N)	2581	100.0
	Missing	3001	

Data File: **GSS**
Task: **Univariate**
➤ Primary Variable: **31) HOMO.SEX**
➤ View: **Pie**

It appears that most Americans regard homosexuality as "always wrong" (about 57.5% in the GSS). The majority continues to reject this sexual orientation and practice. Now, let's look again at the "culture war" divide by comparing religious fundamentalists to other Protestants.

---

[17] Cf. *The American Heritage Dictionary*, and Mooney et al., op cit., page 249.

[18] For an overview of the percentages of those engaging in same-sex behavior, and self-identifying as homo-, bi-, and heterosexual, found in various surveys, see ibid., pages 252–253.

Data File: **GSS**
➤ Task: **Cross-tabulation**
➤ Row Variable: **31) HOMO.SEX**
➤ Column Variable: **23) R.FUND/LIB**
➤ Subset Variable: **25) RELIGION**
➤ Subset Category: **Include: Protestant**
➤ View: **Tables**
➤ Display: **Column %**

HOMO.SEX   by   R.FUND/LIB

Cramer's V: 0.129 **

| | | R.FUND/LIB | | | | |
		Fundam.	Moderate	Liberal	Missing	TOTAL
HOMO.SEX	Always	564	206	185	17	955
		77.4%	67.3%	58.7%		70.7%
	Usually	29	12	16	4	57
		4.0%	3.9%	5.1%		4.2%
	Sometimes	31	15	31	1	77
		4.3%	4.9%	9.8%		5.7%
	Not Wrong	105	73	83	9	261
		14.4%	23.9%	26.3%		19.3%
	Missing	832	350	383	35	1600
	TOTAL	729	306	315	66	1350
		100.0%	100.0%	100.0%		

While it is interesting that about 23% of fundamentalists do not view homosexual sex as "always wrong," about 77% do. This is much greater than the 57.5% in the general public who feel this way. There is also a significant difference among these three groups of Protestants (V = 0.129**) with fundamentalists being clearly the most likely to condemn homosexuality.

Finally, let's turn to the National Election Study to look at a major issue involving gay and lesbian rights today—homosexual adoption. How do Americans feel about this?

➤ Data File: **ELECTION**
➤ Task: **Univariate**
➤ Primary Variable: **41) GAY ADOPT**
➤ View: **Pie**

GAY ADOPT -- Do you think gay or lesbian couples, in other words, homosexual couples, should be legally permitted to adopt children?

	Freq.	%
0) Yes	747	41.9
1) No	909	51.0
2) Don't Know	126	7.1
TOTAL (N)	1782	100.0
Missing	1306	

Here, we find that in the 2000[19] NES, about 42% of respondents indicated that they thought "homosexual couples should be legally permitted to adopt children." Let's finish once again by comparing religious conservatives to others. We will see whether or not, among those who consider themselves "Christians" of some type, those who regard themselves as "born again" are more likely to reject gay adoption, as the culture wars theorists would predict.

Data File: **ELECTION**
➤ Task: **Cross-tabulation**
➤ Row Variable: **41) GAY ADOPT**
➤ Column Variable: **19) BORN AGAIN**
➤ View: **Tables**
➤ Display: **Column %**

GAY ADOPT   by   BORN AGAIN
Cramer's V: 0.254 **

| | | BORN AGAIN | | | |
		Yes	No	Missing	TOTAL
GAY ADOPT	Yes	136	398	213	534
		23.1%	46.7%		37.1%
	No	415	387	107	802
		70.6%	45.4%		55.7%
	Don't Know	37	68	21	105
		6.3%	8.0%		7.3%
	Missing	362	682	262	1306
	TOTAL	588	853	603	1441
		100.0%	100.0%		

---

[19] This question was not asked in 1998.

Investigating Social Problems

Obviously, the "born again" are only about half as likely as non-born-again Christians to accept gay or lesbian adoption (about 23% versus about 47%; V = 0.254**). Those who are "born again" are also much less likely than the general population to accept homosexual adoption.

It's time to continue exploring these issues on your own. In the worksheets, you will have more opportunity to look at teen and nonmarital adult heterosexual sex, and homosexuality, in more detail. You'll also test the culture wars theory a bit more. Enjoy!

REVIEW QUESTIONS

Based on the first part of this exercise, answer True or False to the following items:

Culture war theorists generally believe that Americans are deeply divided over the source and nature of moral values and rules.　　T　F

Alan Wolfe thinks that, among middle-class Americans, there is a broad consensus in favor of conservative sexual values.　　T　F

Teen pregnancy has declined in the 1990s for older teens, but not for younger teens.　　T　F

According to the YRBS, the percentage of American high school students who had ever had sexual intercourse, and the percentage who were currently sexually active, generally declined between 1991 and 2001, but rose between 1997 and 1999.　　T　F

According to the GSS, most Americans support both sex education in public schools and making contraceptives available without parental consent to teens between the ages of 14 and 16; but most Protestant fundamentalists disapprove of both.　　T　F

According to the GSS, most never-married Americans have had sex at least once since age 18, but most Americans regard consensual sex between unmarried adults as "always" or "usually" wrong.　　T　F

According to the GSS, over half of fundamentalists do not think that consenting sex between unmarried adults is "always wrong."　　T　F

According to the GSS, almost 20% of Americans have had sex with a partner of the same sex at least once since they were 18 years old.　　T　F

According to the GSS, most Americans believe that homosexual sex is always wrong.　　T　F

According to the 2000 NES, most Americans approve of gay couples adopting children, but most "born-again" Christians do not.　　T　F

EXPLORIT QUESTIONS

1.　We have already looked at public support for making contraceptives available to teens. And we saw that reports of declines in teen pregnancy credit increased use of contraceptives as one reason for this decline. Now, let's look at recent trends in teen use of contraceptives, based on your TRENDS data set.

a. Open the TRENDS data set and look carefully at the variable description for 18) TNCONDOM.

b. Look at the Historical Trends chart for 18) TNCONDOM. Then, answer the following questions about what you see there.

> ➤ *Data File:* **TRENDS**
>   ➤ *Task:* **Historical Trends**
> ➤ *Variable:* **18) TNCONDOM**

c. According to the YRBS, among American high school students, did the use of a condom at last intercourse increase, decrease, or stay about the same between 1991 and 2001? (Circle one.)

                                                    Increased

                                                    Decreased

                                                Stayed About the Same

d. Now look at the variable description for 19) TNPILL.

e. Look at the Historical Trends chart for 19) TNPILL. Then, answer the following questions about what you see there.

> *Data File:* **TRENDS**
>   *Task:* **Historical Trends**
> ➤ *Variable:* **19) TNPILL**

f. According to the YRBS, among American high school students, *overall* did the use of birth control pills at last intercourse increase, decrease, or stay about the same between 1991 and 2001? (Circle one.)

                                                    Increased

                                                    Decreased

                                                Stayed About the Same

g. What about the use of birth control pills at last intercourse between 1999 and 2001? Did it increase, decrease, or stay about the same? (Circle one.)   Increased

                                                    Decreased

                                            Stayed About the Same

h. Briefly, summarize the changes in contraception use among American high school students between 1991 and 2001 revealed by the YRBS.

2. Previously, we saw that most unmarried Americans have had sex at least once since age 18. How about age differences in this? It seems that younger people are more accepting of premarital sex than older people and perhaps also are more likely to have engaged in it. Let's find out. We'll test this hypothesis first: *the younger people are, the more likely they will be to say that premarital sex between adults is "not wrong."*

a. Open the GSS data set.

b. Cross-tabulate 27) PREM.SEX with 1) AGE. Then, fill in the percentages that say that premarital sex is "not wrong."

> ➤ *Data File:* **GSS**
> ➤ *Task:* **Cross-tabulation**
> ➤ *Row Variable:* **27) PREM.SEX**
> ➤ *Column Variable:* **1) AGE**
> ➤ *View:* **Tables**
> ➤ *Display:* **Column %**

	<30	30–49	50–64	65 AND UP
NOT WRONG	_____%	_____%	_____%	_____%

Now, get the Cramer's V and the significance level for these two variables.

c. Record the value of Cramer's V for this table. (Include asterisks, if any.)   V = _____

d. Is the relationship between AGE and PREM.SEX statistically significant? (Circle one.)   Yes   No

e. Was the hypothesis supported? (Circle one.)   Yes   No

3. Now, let's test this hypothesis: *among never-married people, the younger people are, the more frequently they will have had sex within the past year.*

a. Look carefully at the variable description for 33) SEX FREQ.

b. Cross-tabulate 33) SEX FREQ. with 1) AGE. Then, fill in the designated column percentages

> *Data File:* **GSS**
> *Task:* **Cross-tabulation**
> ➤ *Row Variable:* **33) SEX FREQ.**
> ➤ *Column Variable:* **1) AGE**
> ➤ *Subset Variable:* **8) MARITAL**
> ➤ *Subset Category:* **Include: Nev Mar**
> ➤ *View:* **Tables**
> ➤ *Display:* **Column %**

	<30	30–49	50–64	65 AND UP
1–3 MONTH	_____%	_____%	_____%	_____%
WEEKLY	_____%	_____%	_____%	_____%
>WEEKLY	_____%	_____%	_____%	_____%

Now, carefully examine the Cramer's V and the significance level for these two variables.

c. Is this relationship between AGE and SEX FREQ. weak, moderate, strong, or not significant? (Circle one.)

Weak

Moderate

Strong

Not Significant

d. Was the hypothesis supported? (Circle one.)

Yes   No

4. If the culture war theory would predict that religious conservatives hold more traditional sexual values than others, then it would seem they would also be less likely to engage in premarital sex. Let's find out by testing this hypothesis: *Young, never-married adults who grew up in religiously fundamental homes will be more likely to have "never" had sex within the past year than such adults who did not grow up in fundamentalist homes.*

a. Look carefully at the variable description for 24) R.FUND@16.

b. Cross-tabulate 33) SEX FREQ. with 24) R.FUND@16. Then, fill in the designated column percentages.

Data File:	**GSS**
Task:	**Cross-tabulation**
Row Variable:	**33) SEX FREQ.**
➤ Column Variable:	**24) R.FUND@16**
➤ Subset Variable 1:	**8) MARITAL**
➤ Subset Category:	**Include: Nev Mar**
➤ Subset Variable 2:	**1) AGE**
➤ Subset Category:	**Include: <30**
➤ View:	**Tables**
➤ Display:	**Column %**

	FUNDAM.	**MODERATE**	**LIBERAL**
NEVER	_____%	_____%	_____%

Now, carefully examine the Cramer's V and the significance level for these two variables.

c. Was the hypothesis supported? (Circle one.)   Yes   No

d. Did these results surprise you? Why or why not?

5. We move on now to looking closely at what Americans think about one recent controversy involving gay and lesbian rights. To do so, let's switch to the NES.

   a. Open the ELECTION data set and look carefully at the variable description for 42) GAYMIL SUP.

   b. Look at the percentage of respondents in ELECTION who believe that homosexuals should be allowed to serve in the armed forces. Then, fill in that percentage below.

> ➤ *Data File:* **ELECTION**
> ➤ *Task:* **Univariate**
> ➤ *Primary Variable:* **42) GAYMIL SUP**
> ➤ *View:* **Pie**

   ALLOWED: _____%

6. How about Americans' *personal feelings* toward homosexual people? We will remain in the ELECTION data set.

   a. Look carefully at the variable description for 43) GAY THERM.

   b. Look at the percentage of respondents in ELECTION who were cold, neutral, or warm toward homosexuals. Then, fill in the percentages in the pie for each of the categories below.

> *Data File:* **ELECTION**
> *Task:* **Univariate**
> ➤ *Primary Variable:* **43) GAY THERM**
> ➤ *View:* **Pie**

COLD: _____%

NEUTRAL: _____%

WARM: _____%

7. If the culture war theory would predict that religious conservatives hold more traditional sexual values than others, then it would seem they would also be less likely to agree with allowing homosexuals to serve in the armed forces. We'll find out by testing this hypothesis: *born-again Christians will be less likely than others to support allowing homosexuals to serve in the armed forces.* Again, we will remain in the ELECTION data set.

a. Cross-tabulate 42) GAYMIL SUP and 19) BORN AGAIN. Then, fill in the percentages of those who believe that homosexuals should be allowed to serve in the armed forces.

Data File:	**ELECTION**
➤ Task:	**Cross-tabulation**
➤ Row Variable:	**42) GAYMIL SUP**
➤ Column Variable:	**19) BORN AGAIN**
➤ View:	**Tables**
➤ Display:	**Column %**

	YES	NO
ALLOWED	_____%	_____%

    Now, carefully examine the Cramer's V and the significance level for these two variables.

b. Is this relationship between GAYMIL SUP and BORN AGAIN weak, moderate, strong, or not significant? (Circle one.)

    Weak

    Moderate

    Strong

    Not Significant

c. Was the hypothesis supported? (Circle one.)   Yes   No

d. Did a *majority* of born-again Christians support allowing homosexuals to serve in the armed forces? (Circle one.)   Yes   No

e. Did these percentages surprise you? Why or why not?

8. We'll test one more "culture war" hypothesis using ELECTION: *born-again Christians will be more likely than others to be "cool" toward homosexuals.*

    a. Cross-tabulate 43) GAY THERM with 19) BORN AGAIN. Then, fill in the percentages of those who felt "cold" toward homosexuals.

Data File:	**ELECTION**
Task:	**Cross-tabulation**
➤ Row Variable:	**43) GAY THERM**
➤ Column Variable:	**19) BORN AGAIN**
➤ View:	**Tables**
➤ Display:	**Column %**

	YES	NO
COLD	_____%	_____%

    Now, carefully examine the Cramer's V and the significance level for these two variables.

    b. Is this relationship between BORN AGAIN and GAY THERM statistically significant? (Circle one.)   Yes   No

    c. Was the hypothesis supported? (Circle one.)   Yes   No

◆ EXERCISE 5 ◆

ALCOHOL AND DRUG ABUSE

Tasks: Historical Trends, Scatterplot, Mapping, Cross-tabulation
Data Files: TRENDS, STATES, YRBS

In a famous song from the 1960s, the Beatles vocalized the following lyrics: "I get by with a little help from my friends; I get high with a little help from my friends; Going to try with a little help from my friends." And all but those who were woefully ignorant of the drug culture understood what these "friends" were!

Every year, millions of Americans "get high." Many do so regularly. Sometimes this involves illegal drug use such as the Beatles seemed to intone about. More often, we get "elevated" by abusing that highly popular legal drug known as alcohol (or depending on its form, by more interesting names such as booze, hooch, brew, and tipple). Regardless, Americans spend a great deal of time and money to get stoned, bombed, buzzed, zonked, spaced-out, tripped-out, doped-up, liquored-up, lit-up, coked-up, soaked, and tanked!

In this exercise, we will look at the use of *psychoactive drugs* (chemicals that alter "the perceptions and/or moods of people who take" them[1]). Our focus will be on the abuse of alcohol and "illicit" (illegal[2]) drugs *in order to get high*. We will not be concerned with the use of psychoactive substances (such as tobacco[3] and caffeine) or practices (such as moderate alcohol use or narcotics as postsurgical pain-killers) that are *not* designed to produce that intense alteration of consciousness that we normally identify with being "high."

Let's begin by examining some trends in the abuse of alcohol and illicit drugs, and attitudes toward it. Then, we'll look at geographic variations in it. Finally, we will investigate correlations between various social factors and substance abuse. This will allow us to "test" a couple of major theories that purport to explain variations in the latter.

Our exploration of this issue starts with 12th-grade students. This gives us some idea of what proportion of teens has abused alcohol or illicit drugs by the time they have completed high school. We will start by looking at data in your TRENDS file derived from the annual Monitoring the Future Study (MFS) that has been conducted by the University of Michigan since 1975. This survey is administered to a large[4] cross-section of American high school students through the use of an anonymous questionnaire that students fill out privately at school.[5]

---

[1] Eitzen and Baca Zinn, op cit., page 504.

[2] Note that many drugs known as "illicit" have legal uses (usually as prescription drugs) as well. These drugs become illicit when they are used and/or distributed in an illegal manner.

[3] Clearly, however, tobacco use is often abusive and destructive. Though it is not normally used to "get high," its use seems to me to be a "social problem." We will deal with tobacco consumption as a health issue in Exercise 14.

[4] Roughly 16,000 12th graders take the MFS survey each year. See information about the purpose and design of the study at http://monitoringthefuture.org/purpose.html.

[5] Ibid. This increases the honesty of responses. The MFS *slightly* underestimates substance abuse because it cannot include students who are absent or not enrolled when the surveys are administered, and these students are more likely to misuse drugs and alcohol than those who attend school regularly. However, the MFS does allow us to accurately chart substance abuse trends, and it is more accurate than many other studies of teen drug and alcohol abuse. See *Health United States*, 2001, National Center for Health Statistics, U.S. Department of Health and Human Services, Hyattsville, MD, page 249.

> *Data File:* **TRENDS**
> > *Task:* **Historical Trends**
> *Variable:* **30) EVPOT12GR**

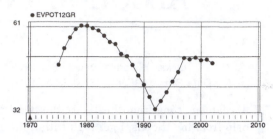

Percentage of 12th grade students who have ever smoked marijuana

Here, we see that the percentage of 12th graders who had ever tried marijuana increased sharply in the last half of the 1970s to about 60%, then rapidly declined to about 33% in 1992. But overall it has been slowly increasing since then. The 2002 percentage was about 48%.

Let's look at trends for "harder" drugs. We'll view the percentages of 12th-grade students who have ever used any illicit drug other than marijuana (not including alcohol or tobacco).

Data File: **TRENDS**
> *Task:* **Historical Trends**
> *Variable:* **39) EVILL12GR**

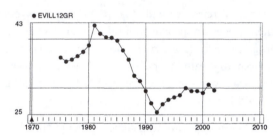

Percentage of 12th grade students who had ever used any illicit drug other than marijuana (not including alcohol or tobacco)

This is interesting. Notice that while the percentages are much lower than for marijuana, the *pattern of change* over time is quite similar. That is, use increased from the mid-1970s, declined from 1981 to 1992 (from about 43% to about 25%), then increased (more modestly) since then. Percentages have been holding fairly steady since 1997, however, and were 29.5% in 2002. Let's look at both of these last variables on the same chart in order to better see the similarity in trends for marijuana and use of harder drugs.

Data File: **TRENDS**
> *Task:* **Historical Trends**
> *Variables:* **30) EVPOT12GR**
> **39) EVILL12GR**

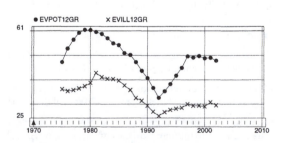

Percentage of 12th grade students who have ever smoked marijuana and used other illicit drugs

Investigating Social Problems

What about heavy drinking? First, what are the trends in "binge" drinking (defined as five or more drinks at one sitting and in a short period of time) among 12th-graders? Second, are trends in binge drinking similar to trends in marijuana or other illicit drug use?

Data File: **TRENDS**
Task: **Historical Trends**
➤ Variables: **30) EVPOT12GR**
39) EVILL12GR
41) BINGE12GR

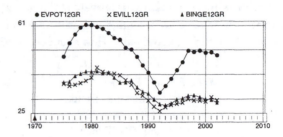

Percentage of 12th grade students who have ever smoked marijuana, used other illicit drugs, or binge drunk within the past two weeks

You can simply add 41) BINGE12GR to the last chart you did. Just click the [⟲] button to return to the variable selection screen, and use "Select Variables" to add BINGE12GR to the list of variables to be displayed. Don't "clear" the others.

Wow! This chart shows some interesting things. First of all, the trend in the percentage of 12th-graders who have engaged in binge drinking (in red) rose and fell at roughly the same times that the percentages that had ever smoked pot or used other illicit drugs did. Second, binge drinking is quite common. At the high point of 1981, about 41% of high school seniors had done so within two weeks prior to being surveyed. In 2002, that percentage was about 29%.

Now, let's move on to trends in *adult* substance abuse. Here, we will look at data summarized from the National Household Survey on Drug Abuse (NHSDA). This is another large, national study conducted annually, this time through interviews in households.[6] On each chart, we will graph three age groups: 18 to 25, 26 to 34, and 35 and older. First, let's check the percentage of adults who had smoked marijuana within the month prior to being surveyed.

Data File: **TRENDS**
Task: **Historical Trends**
➤ Variables: **43) POT1825**
44) POT2634
45) POT35+

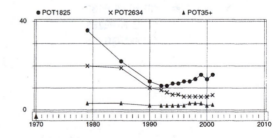

Percentage who had smoked marijuana and the past month among 18–25, 26–34, and 35+ age groups

---

[6] In the NHSDA, 68,929 persons were interviewed in 2001. Respondents completed sensitive items, such as those about drug abuse, privately in order to enhance honesty. See http://www.samhsa.gov/oas/nhsda/2k1nhsda/vol1/chapter1.htm#1.1, Substance Abuse & Mental Health Services Administration, U.S. Dept. of HHS.

As we can see, the older respondents were, the less likely they were to have recently smoked marijuana. Like the 12th graders, use for all three groups fell from the period around the late 1970s through 1992. Again like the high school seniors, percentages for 18- to 25- year-olds rose slightly after that. But between 1992 and 2001, usage for those aged 26 to 34 continued to decline (but much more slowly), while it remained relatively stable (*very* slight increase) among those 35 and older. In 2001, 16% of those aged 18 to 25 had recently smoked pot, compared to 7% of those 26 to 34 years old, and a mere 2% of those 35 and older. How about cocaine?

Data File: **TRENDS**
Task: **Historical Trends**
➤ Variables: **49) COKE1825**
          50) COKE2634
          51) COKE35+

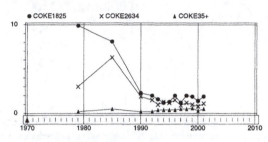

*Percentage who had used cocaine in the past month among
18–25, 26–34, and 35+ age groups*

Well, generally we can see that, like other measures of substance abuse we've looked at so far, usage declined going into the early 1990s, though for those 26 and older this was preceded by an increase from 1979 through the mid-1980s. Since 1992, with minor fluctuations, percentages have remained stable for all of these adult age groups. Notice too that while those 18 to 25 years old appear to use cocaine more than those in the older age groups, this gap between the three adult age groups became pretty small from 1992 forward. Finally, we can see that in 2001, 1.9% of those 18 to 25 years old had recently used cocaine, compared to 1.1% of those 26 to 34, and only 0.5% for those 35 and older. Now, what about binge drinking (5+ alcoholic drinks within a couple of hours) among adults?

Data File: **TRENDS**
Task: **Historical Trends**
➤ Variables: **46) BINGE1825**
          47) BINGE2634
          48) BINGE35+

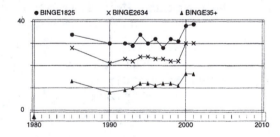

*Percentage who had drunk 5 or more alcoholic drinks within a couple of hours,
within the past month, among 18–25, 26–34, and 35+ age groups*

Once again, we see a general decline going into the early 1990s. Percentages were fairly steady from this point until 1999, but there was quite a rise in binge drinking from 1999 through 2001. Further, as before, as age increases, binge drinking decreases. In 2001, within a month prior to being surveyed, 39% of those aged 18 to 25 had engaged in binge drinking, compared to 30% of those 26 to 34, and 16% of those 35 and older.

How have American *attitudes* toward substance abuse changed over time? Let's start by looking at General Social Survey data summarized in your TRENDS file that measures what percentage of Americans favor the legalization of marijuana.

Data File: **TRENDS**
Task: **Historical Trends**
➤ Variable: **52) GRASS**

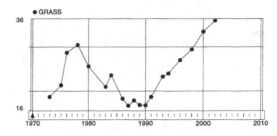

Percentage of Americans favoring the legalization of marijuana

Obviously, support for marijuana legalization declined from the late 1970s to the late 1980s, remaining in a range between about 17% and 19% in the years 1986 to 1991. Then it began rising again. Notice that this trend of support for marijuana legalization roughly follows the patterns for drug use overall that we have seen so far (that is, drop in the 1980s and rise in the 1990s)! Support for pot legalization in the year 2002 was the highest ever, at 36%. Now, let's look at support among 12th-grade students for the occasional use of marijuana, and experimentation with cocaine, by adults.

Data File: **TRENDS**
Task: **Historical Trends**
➤ Variables: **53) GRASS12?**
54) COKE12?

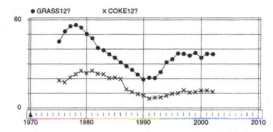

Percentage of 12th grade students who support occasional marijuana use, and cocaine experimentation, among adults

Wow! The same pattern again—drop in the late 1970s through the 1980s, and rise from the early 1990s on. *It appears that approval for illicit drug use or legalization may rise and fall with the use of these drugs itself.* However, for 12th graders, approval in recent years has not returned to or exceeded mid-1970s levels. In 2002, about 37% of high school seniors approved of occasional marijuana use, and about 11% approved of cocaine experimentation, by adults.

We have looked at variation in alcohol and illicit drug use in America over time. Now, let's examine *geographic* variation in the United States by mapping some comparative, ecological data dealing with substance abuse. Switch to the STATES data file. We will be looking at state-level data derived from the 1999 and 2000 NHSDA surveys.

➤ *Data File:* **STATES**
   ➤ *Task:* **Mapping**
➤ *Variable 1:* **42) POT00**
   ➤ *View:* **Map**

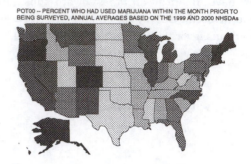

The percentage that had used marijuana within a month of being surveyed was highest in the West and Northeast. Let's look at the use of illicit drugs other than marijuana, and find out if it tends to be higher in the same states where marijuana use is greater.

Data File: **STATES**
Task: **Mapping**
Variable 1: **42) POT00**
➤ *Variable 2:* **41) ILCTDRG00**
   ➤ *View:* **Maps**

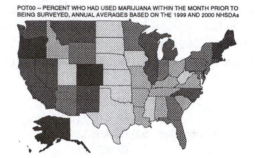

$r = 0.615**$

Remember, just click the [⟲] button to return to the variable selection screen, and then add 41) ILCTDRG00 as Variable 2. Don't "clear" 42) POT00.

States where marijuana use is greater tend to be states where other illicit drugs (other than marijuana) are also used more and, again, are primarily located in the West and Northeast. These two variables are strongly associated ($r = 0.615**$). Now, let's look at the distribution of binge drinking and find out if states with more of *it* also tend to have more pot smoking.

         Investigating Social Problems

Data File: **STATES**

Task: **Mapping**

Variable 1: **42) POT00**

➤ *Variable 2:* **38) BINGE00**

➤ *View:* **Maps**

POT00 -- PERCENT WHO HAD USED MARIJUANA WITHIN THE MONTH PRIOR TO BEING SURVEYED, ANNUAL AVERAGES BASED ON THE 1999 AND 2000 NHSDAs

BINGE00 -- PERCENTAGES WHO "BINGE DRANK" (THAT IS, 5+ ALCOHOLIC DRINKS AT THE SAME TIME/WITHIN A COUPLE OF HOURS) IN THE MONTH PRIOR TO BEING

Again, click the [[↺]] button to return to the variable selection screen, and then just add 38) BINGE00 as Variable 2. There is no need to "clear" Variable 1, 42) POT00.

Unlike pot smoking and other illicit drug use, binge drinking is most prevalent in the upper Mid-West, in places like the Dakotas, Wisconsin, and Minnesota! Notice that the correlation between these two measures is not significant ($r = 0.227$).

Social scientists have long noted that males are more likely than females to engage in behavior involving impulsivity, risk, and thrill. This includes many forms of non-drug-related criminality and also substance abuse. Some sociologists believe that these gender variations are due solely to differences in the ways males and females are *socialized* (that is, the processes by which they absorb, and are enabled to be involved in, their culture and society), and treated. Others think that biological—especially hormonal—differences between the sexes *also* play a role in causing these dissimilarities in impulsive, thrill-seeking, and/or high-risk behaviors.[7]

There are data on 12th graders in the Youth Risk Behavior Survey (YRBS)[8] that allow us to look at some of these gender differences. Let's look at the percentages of 12th graders who had driven a motor vehicle after drinking alcohol within a month prior to being surveyed. This is surely a high-risk behavior involving substance abuse! Go ahead and open your YRBS file now.

---

[7] A nice, short overview of these issues is provided in Stark, op cit., pages 188–190.

[8] You may recall we used YRBS data in the TRENDS file in Exercise 4. Now we will use the YRBS data file.

➤ *Data File:* **YRBS**
➤ *Task:* **Cross-tabulation**
➤ *Row Variable:* **7) DRVDRK**
➤ *Column Variable:* **1) GENDER**
➤ *View:* **Tables**
➤ *Display:* **Column %**

DRVDRK by GENDER
Weight Variable: WEIGHT
Cramer's V: 0.119 **

		GENDER			
		Female	Male	Missing	TOTAL
DRVDRK	Yes	250	376	0	626
		17.3%	27.2%		22.1%
	No	1195	1005	4	2200
		82.7%	72.8%		77.9%
	Missing	17	25	1	43
	TOTAL	1445	1381	5	2826
		100.0%	100.0%		

Males moderately exceeded females in this dangerous behavior (V = 0.119**). Look at the "Total" column and notice another sobering fact: in 2001, about 22% of 12th graders drove after drinking at least once (about 27% of the males and 17% of the females).

Some sociologists believe that pressures rooted in inequality lead to greater substance abuse among disadvantaged persons. This is particularly true for proponents of a macro-level, consensus[9] theory known as ***structural strain*** theory. In its classic form, this theory holds that social pressures cause some people to violate and/or reject approved social goals and/or the legitimate means for achieving them. Substance abuse involves "retreatism," in which *both* legitimate goals and means are rejected.[10] "The retreatist 'turns on and drops out.'"[11] The disadvantaged face many serious pressures such as poverty, unemployment, "dead-end" jobs, and the like. Thus, sociologists commonly interpret structural strain theory as predicting (among many other things) greater substance abuse among the poor and oppressed minorities.

Let's perform a "test" of this facet of structural strain theory. We'll use macro-level data to look at whether or not percentages of people who use illicit drugs other than marijuana are associated with percentages of people who are poor or African American.

➤ *Data File:* **STATES**
➤ *Task:* **Scatterplot**
➤ *Dependent Variable:* **41) ILCTDRG00**
➤ *Independent Variable:* **48) %POOR00**
➤ *View:* **Reg. Line**

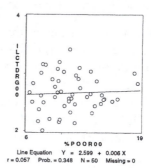

Line Equation   Y = 2.599 + 0.006 X
r = 0.057   Prob. = 0.348   N = 50   Missing = 0

Structural strain theory is not confirmed in this small test of it! There is no relationship between these two variables (*r* = 0.057).

---

[9] You may recall that these types of theories were overviewed in Exercise 2.

[10] Robert K. Merton, "Social Structure and Anomie," in *Social Theory and Social Structure*, New York: Free Press. Pages 185–214.

[11] John Palen, op cit., page 366.

Investigating Social Problems

Data File: **STATES**

Task: **Scatterplot**

Dependent Variable: **41) ILCTDRG00**

➤ Independent Variable: **10) %BLACK00**

➤ View: **Reg. Line**

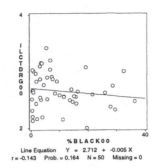

Line Equation Y = 2.712 + -0.005 X
r = -0.143 Prob. = 0.164 N = 50 Missing = 0

Not only is the correlation between the percentage of African Americans and the percentage of people who have abused illicit drugs other than marijuana *in*significant, it is also negative ($r = -0.143$). This fact defies both structural strain theory and popular racial stereotypes. We have obviously not "proved" here that structural strain theory or its predictions about substance abuse among the disadvantaged are incorrect. However, we can say that, in this instance, its predictions were not supported.

Since we're already challenging stereotypes, let's look at the connection between race/ethnicity and drugs once more, returning to the YRBS to "test" strain theory by looking at individual behavior. The issue will be use of cocaine (including freebase and crack).

➤ Data File: **YRBS**

➤ Task: **Cross-tabulation**

➤ Row Variable: **26) HWMNYCOC**

➤ Column Variable: **2) RACE**

➤ Subset Variable: **2) RACE**

➤ Subset Category: **Exclude: Other**

➤ View: **Tables**

➤ Display: **Column %**

HWMNYCOC   by   RACE

Weight Variable: WEIGHT
Cramer's V: 0.087 **

		RACE			
		Black	Hispanic	White NHis	TOTAL
HWMNYCOC	None	303	227	1772	2302
		97.8%	81.5%	87.2%	87.9%
	1-2	2	22	109	132
		0.6%	7.8%	5.4%	5.0%
	3+	5	30	151	186
		1.7%	10.7%	7.4%	7.1%
	Missing	8	4	6	19
	TOTAL	310	278	2032	2620
		100.0%	100.0%	100.0%	

Obviously, among high school seniors, African Americans were *less* likely to have used cocaine products than the others. Hispanic students were most likely to have done so but did not differ much from non-Hispanic whites. The overall differences are significant (V = 0.087**), but certainly do not support strain theory much if at all.

Now I would like you to continue analyzing the degree and distribution of, and explanations for, various types of substance abuse.

WORKSHEET

EXERCISE

5

NAME:

COURSE:

DATE:

Workbook exercises and software are copyrighted. Copying is prohibited by law.

REVIEW QUESTIONS

Based on the first part of this exercise, answer True or False to the following items:

All psychoactive drugs are used to get "high."   T   F

Among high school seniors since 1975, the pattern of changes in the percentages
using marijuana has not been similar to the pattern of changes in the percentages
using illicit drugs other than marijuana.   T   F

In the year 2002, close to a third of high school seniors had engaged in binge
drinking within two weeks prior to being surveyed.   T   F

The percentages using marijuana within a month of being surveyed increased
between 1992 and 2001 for adults of all age groups.   T   F

According to the GSS, support for the legalization of marijuana increased between
1990 and 2002.   T   F

States with higher percentages of recent marijuana smokers are not more likely
to have higher percentages of recent binge drinkers.   T   F

All social scientists agree that differences between levels of male and female
involvement in high-risk behaviors are caused only by differences in the
socialization of males and females.   T   F

In 2001, over one-third of male high school seniors drove a motor vehicle after drinking
alcohol within a month prior to being surveyed.   T   F

Many sociologists believe that classical social strain theory predicts that substance
abuse will be disproportionately high among the poor.   T   F

Among American states, the greater the percentages that are poor or African
American, the greater the percentages that have recently used illicit drugs other
than marijuana.   T   F

EXPLORIT QUESTIONS

1. We have looked at what percentages of 12th-grade students engaged in binge drinking within two
    weeks prior to being surveyed. But what percentages have *ever* gotten drunk?

    a. Open the TRENDS data set and look carefully at the variable description for 40) EVDRNK12GR.

    b. Look at the Historical Trends chart for 40) EVDRNK12GR. Then, answer the following questions
        about what you see there.

> *Data File:* **TRENDS**
> > *Task:* **Historical Trends**
> > *Variable:* **40) EVDRNK12GR**

c. The *lowest* percentage during this time period was _____% in the   _____%
   year _____. (Tip: To get the percentage, look at the number at the
   bottom left of the graph. To get the year, look at the dot that is lowest on   _____
   the graph, and then straight down to see what year marker that dot is over.
   The first marker on the left is 1991, the second 1992, and so on. These
   markers are on the horizontal bar at the bottom of the graph, and are light
   gray and vertical.)

d. The *highest* percentage during this time period was _____% in the   _____%
   year _____. (Tip: To get the percentage, look at the number at the
   top left of the graph. To get the year, follow the instructions provided in   _____
   part c above.)

e. Overall, do you think that the percentages of MFS 12th graders who have
   ever been drunk have increased, decreased, or stayed about the same
   during the period from 1996 to 2002? (Circle one.)   Increased

        Decreased

        Stayed About the Same

2. What about use of the *really* hard illicit drugs by high school seniors? Let's look at trends in the percentages of seniors who have ever used heroin or amphetamines.

   a. Carefully examine the variable descriptions for 33) EVHER12GR and for 36) EVAMP12GR.

   b. Look at the Historical Trends chart for 33) EVHER12GR and 36) EVAMP12GR. Then, answer the following questions about what you see there.

   > *Data File:* **TRENDS**
   > *Task:* **Historical Trends**
   > *Variables:* **33) EVHER12GR**
   >   **36) EVAMP12GR**

   c. The *highest* percentage during this time period was _____% in the   _____%
      year _____.

        _____

   d. The percentages of high school seniors who had ever used _____ were   _____
      higher than the percentages of seniors who had ever used _____.

        _____

e. Overall, do you think that the percentages of MFS 12th graders who have ever used amphetamines have increased, decreased, or stayed about the same during the period from 1981 to 2002? (Circle one.)

Increased

Decreased

Stayed About the Same

f. Overall, do you think that the percentages of MFS 12th graders who have ever used heroin have increased, decreased, or stayed about the same during the period from 1981 to 2002? (Circle one.)

Increased

Decreased

Stayed About the Same

3. Previously, we compared the *pattern* of change in the percentage of 12th graders who had ever used marijuana to the *pattern* of changes in the use of other drugs by these seniors. (That is, to what extent do percentages using these drugs rise, or fall, around the same times?) Let's do this again, comparing changes in the percentages that have ever used cocaine to changes in the percentages that have ever used pot.

a. Carefully examine the variable description for 34) EVCOKE12GR.

b. Look at the Historical Trends chart for 30) EVPOT12GR and 34) EVCOKE12GR. Then, answer the following questions about what you see there.

> Data File: **TRENDS**
> Task: **Historical Trends**
> ➤ Variables: **30) EVPOT12GR**
> **34) EVCOKE12GR**

c. The percentages of high school seniors who had ever used _____ were _____ *higher* than the percentages of seniors who had ever used _____.

_____

d. Overall, do you think that the pattern of change in the percentages of high school seniors who have ever used marijuana and the pattern of change in the percentages of seniors who have ever used cocaine (between the years 1975 and 2002) have been very similar, somewhat similar, or not at all similar? (Circle one.)

Very Similar

Somewhat Similar

Not At All Similar

e. Which of the following percentages appears to be closest to the percentage of high school seniors in the year 2002 that had ever used cocaine or crack? (Circle one.)

10%

20%

30%

Exercise 5: Alcohol and Drug Abuse

93

4. Now, let's compare the involvement of male and female high school seniors in high-risk behaviors and substance abuse, starting with riding with drivers who had been drinking alcohol. We'll use the YRBS.

a. Open the YRBS data set.

b. Carefully examine the variable description for 6) RDWDRK.

c. Cross-tabulate 6) RDWDRK with 1) GENDER. Then, fill in the percentages indicating that they had recently ridden in a car driven by someone who had been drinking.

> Data File: **YRBS**
> Task: **Cross-tabulation**
> Row Variable: **6) RDWDRK**
> Column Variable: **1) GENDER**
> View: **Tables**
> Display: **Column %**

	FEMALE	MALE
YES	_____%	_____%

Now, get the Cramer's V and the significance level for these two variables.

d. Record the value of Cramer's V for this table. (Include asterisks, if any.)   V = _____

e. Is the relationship between GENDER and RDWDRK statistically significant? (Circle one.)

Yes   No

f. Overall, were male or female high school seniors more likely to have recently ridden in a car driven by someone who had been drinking?(Circle one.)

Males More Likely

Females More Likely

Males and Females About the Same

5. Now, let's compare male and female involvements in binge drinking. We are still using the YRBS.

a. Carefully examine the variable description for 23) RECBINGE.

b. Cross-tabulate 23) RECBINGE with 1) GENDER. Then, fill in the percentages that indicated they had not recently engaged in binge drinking.

Data File: **YRBS**
Task: **Cross-tabulation**
➤ Row Variable: **23) RECBINGE**
➤ Column Variable: **1) GENDER**
➤ View: **Tables**
➤ Display: **Column %**

	FEMALE	MALE
NONE	_____%	_____%

Now, get the Cramer's V and the significance level for these two variables.

c. Record the value of Cramer's V for this table. (Include asterisks, if any.) V = _____

d. Is the relationship between GENDER and RECBINGE statistically significant? (Circle one.) Yes No

e. Overall, were male or female high school seniors more likely to have recently engaged in binge drinking?(Circle one.)

Males Much More Likely

Males a Little More Likely

Females Much More Likely

Females a Little More Likely

Males and Females About the Same

6. Now, let's compare male and female involvements in cocaine use in the YRBS.

a. Cross-tabulate 26) HWMNYCOC and 1) GENDER. Then, fill in the percentages that indicated they had *not* ever used any form of cocaine.

Data File: **YRBS**
Task: **Cross-tabulation**
➤ Row Variable: **26) HWMNYCOC**
➤ Column Variable: **1) GENDER**
➤ View: **Tables**
➤ Display: **Column %**

	FEMALE	MALE
NONE	_____%	_____%

Now, carefully examine the Cramer's V and the significance level for these two variables.

b. Is the relationship between GENDER and HWMNYCOC statistically significant? (Circle one.)   Yes   No

c. Overall, were male or female high school seniors more likely to have ever used any form of cocaine?(Circle one.)

Males Much More Likely

Males a Little More Likely

Females Much More Likely

Females a Little More Likely

Males and Females About the Same

7. (Answer this item only if one gender was more likely to have been involved in being in a motor vehicle with a driver who had been drinking and/or binge drinking and/or using cocaine.) In your opinion, why were males (or females) more likely to have been involved in these behaviors than females (or males)? That is, in your opinion, what is the reason (or reasons) for this gender difference?

8. Let's finish up by looking at more ecological, comparative, state-level data. We'll start by examining differences in the percentage of traffic fatalities involving drunk drivers and comparing these percentages with levels of binge drinking.

a. Open the STATES data set and look carefully at the variable description for 34) CAR HBA.

b. Draw two maps, one showing state variations in 34) CAR HBA 98 and the other showing state variations in 38) BINGE00.

> Data File: **STATES**
> Task: **Mapping**
> Variable 1: **34) CAR HBA 98**
> Variable 2: **38) BINGE00**
> View: **Maps**

c. Provide Pearson's r (including asterisks, if any, and the direction sign, if any).   r = _____

d. Is this correlation negative or positive? (Circle one.)

Negative

Positive

e. Is this correlation between CAR HBA 98 and BINGE00 weak, moderate, strong, or not significant? (Circle one.)

Weak

Moderate

Strong

Not Significant

f. Are increases in the percentage of traffic fatalities involving drunk drivers associated with increases in binge drinking? (Circle one.)

Yes   No

9. Finally, let's test a couple of hypotheses related to classical social strain theory. Both will be based on the notion that this theory would predict that greater percentages of poor or otherwise disadvantaged people should be associated with greater levels of substance abuse. Our first hypothesis will be: *As percentages of African Americans increase, marijuana use will also increase.*

a. Does this hypothesis predict a negative or a positive correlation? (Circle one.)

Negative

Positive

b. Construct a scatterplot that represents the association between 10) %BLACK00 and 42) POT00. Don't forget to select [Reg. Line].

> Data File: **STATES**
> ➤ Task: **Scatterplot**
> ➤ Dependent Variable: **42) POT00**
> ➤ Independent Variable: **10) %BLACK00**
> ➤ View: **Reg. Line**

Carefully examine Pearson's *r* (looking for asterisks and the direction sign, if any).

c. Is the correlation negative or positive? (Circle one.)

Negative

Positive

d. Is this correlation between POT00 and %BLACK00 weak, moderate, strong, or not significant? (Circle one.)

Weak

Moderate

Strong

Not Significant

e. Is the hypothesis supported? (Circle one.)

Yes   No

f.   Explain exactly why the hypothesis is or is not supported, drawing on the statistical evidence above.

10.   Our second, and last, hypothesis will be: *as percentages of poor people increase, binge drinking will also increase.*

     a.   Does this hypothesis predict a negative or a positive correlation? (Circle one.)   Negative

                                                                                                 Positive

     b.   Construct a scatterplot that represents the association between 48) %POOR00 and 38) BINGE00.

                      Data File: **STATES**
                             Task: **Scatterplot**
          ➤ *Dependent Variable:*   **38) BINGE00**
         ➤ *Independent Variable:*   **48) %POOR00**
                     ➤ *View:*   **Reg. Line**

Carefully examine Pearson's *r* (looking for asterisks and the direction sign, if any).

     c.   Is the correlation negative or positive? (Circle one.)   Negative

                                                                                                Positive

     d.   Is this correlation between BINGE00 and %POOR00 weak, moderate, strong, or not significant? (Circle one.)   Weak

                                                                         Moderate

                                                                                Strong

                                                                    Not Significant

     e.   Is the hypothesis supported? (Circle one.)   Yes   No

     f.   Explain exactly why the hypothesis is or is not supported, drawing on the statistical evidence above.

CRIME AND PUNISHMENT IN THE UNITED STATES

Tasks: Historical Trends, Cross-tabulation, Scatterplot, Univariate
Data Files: TRENDS, YRBS, GSS, ELECTION, STATES

C rime and punishment. This phrase is more than the title of Dostoyevsky's famous novel. Assuming that polls are fairly accurate gauges of public opinion, crime and punishment have been major concerns for Americans over the past several decades. And yet the perception that most Americans have of both of these things appears to often be flawed.

In this exercise we will take a brief "tour" of crime and punishment in America. What *are* some of the major types of crimes, and how are they most commonly measured? Can these measurements be trusted? How much do these crimes actually occur? Are they increasing or decreasing? Have levels of punishments such as imprisonment and execution changed much over time? What are Americans' beliefs about crime and punishment? Finally, how do all of these things vary across different places and types of people, and what implications do these variations have for some sociological theories about crime? That's a lot to do, so let's get started.

Perhaps the "granddaddy" of U.S. crime measurements is the Federal Bureau of Investigation's (FBI) *Uniform Crime Reports* (UCR), which has been published annually since 1930. Information in the UCR ultimately comes from police departments around the country, and it is provided in the form of raw numbers and rates per 100,000.

While the UCR contains information on close to 30 categories of crime, its centerpiece is the ***crime index***. This is a set of eight crimes regarded by the FBI as the most serious and as a rough indicator of overall crime. Four of these are defined as ***violent***, because they "involve force or threat of force." These are ***homicide*** (the deliberate and unjustified killing of a human being), ***forcible rape*** (having or attempting to have sexual intercourse with a "female forcibly and against her will"), ***robbery*** ("taking or attempting to take anything of value" from another "by force or threat of force or violence and/or . . . ear"), and ***aggravated assault*** (unjustified attack on another with a weapon and/or to inflict severe bodily injury). The four ***property*** index crimes are directed toward "money or property" and involve "no force or threat of force." They are ***burglary*** ("unlawful entry of a structure to commit a felony or theft"), ***larceny-theft*** (stealing another's property from him or her without the use of force, violence or fraud), ***motor vehicle theft*** (stealing or attempting to steal a motorized vehicle that "runs on the surface and not on rails"), and ***arson*** (willfully burning or attempting to burn many kinds of property). In this exercise, we will focus on all of these index crimes except arson.[1]

Let's take a look at trends in various UCR rates. We will look at violent and property crime rates, and then at homicide.

---

[1] Arson is hard to detect and has not been included in the crime index consistently. All quotes and definitions are from the *Uniform Crime Reports, 2000*, Federal Bureau of Investigation, U.S. Department of Justice, Washington D.C., 2001. See pages 11, 14, 25, 29, 34, 38, 41, 46, 52, and 56. Violent crime is sometimes called "personal crime."

> *Data File:* **TRENDS**
> > *Task:* **Historical Trends**
> *Variable:* **57) VIOLUCR**

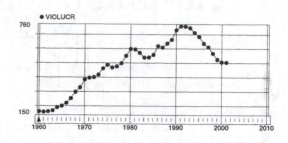

Violent crime rates per 100,000 (includes homicide, robbery, aggravated assault, and forcible rape)

Violent index crimes rose steadily from 1960 until 1991, reaching a high of 760 per 100,000. Since 1991, violent crimes have declined to about 500 per 100,000. Let's see if this pattern is similar to property crime rates.

> *Data File:* **TRENDS**
> > *Task:* **Historical Trends**
> *Variable:* **77) PROPUCR**

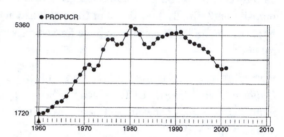

Property crimes per 100,000 (arson excluded). Includes burglary, larceny-theft, and motor vehicle theft.

Property crimes have a slightly different pattern. Again, we see a dramatic increase that peaks in 1980. However, property crimes then fell in the mid-1980s, began rising again, and then declined steadily from 1991.

> *Data File:* **TRENDS**
> > *Task:* **Historical Trends**
> *Variable:* **70) UCRMURDER**

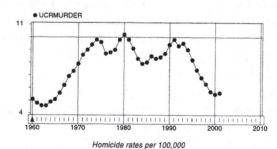

Homicide rates per 100,000

Interestingly, the pattern of change in homicide rates has been similar to that in property crimes rates. As with property crimes, there was a general increase in homicides through 1980, a small decline in the mid-1980s, followed by another peak in 1991, and a dramatic increase after that. Note also the dramatic drops in all three rates since 1991. In fact, each of the seven UCR index crimes we are looking at in this exercise has fallen a great deal since 1991 or 1992.

However, the UCR is based on *reported* crimes. This does not give a completely accurate picture of crime. Most crimes are not reported. While this is not a major problem with homicide since most homi-

Investigating Social Problems

cides are reported, it leads to significant undercounting of other offenses. Moreover, reports and police records are often inaccurate and/or incomplete in other ways. These and other problems mean that social scientists are not comfortable relying solely on the UCR as a measure of crime.

Another source of crime data, known as the *National Crime Victimization Survey* (NCVS), relies on surveys of crime *victims*. Done since 1973, NCVS researchers interview people 12 and older in about 49,000 households every 6 months about crimes in which they have been victims. Obviously, homicides are not included (one cannot interview corpses!). Neither are crimes against businesses. The NCVS provides information about offenses that the police don't know about. Thus, while NCVS figures commonly reveal *patterns of change* that are similar to UCR trends, the *amounts* of crime detected by the NCVS are much higher. To see the difference, let's compare totals of violent index offenses from the UCR versus the NCVS.[2]

Data File: **TRENDS**
    Task: **Historical Trends**
➤ Variables: **55) #VIOLNCVS**
            56) #VIOLUCR

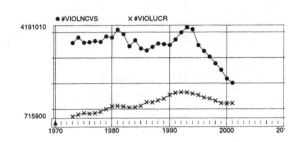

Number of serious violent crimes reported by NCVS and number of serious violent crimes reported to police

As you can see, NCVS totals are much higher than those from the UCR. However, the pattern is roughly similar, with both declining since the early 1990s. According to the NCVS, victimizations from serious violent crimes rose to 1981, then dropped to 1986, then rose again to an "all-time" peak in 1993 (4,191,000). The decrease since 1993 has been great—the 2001 total of 2,014,400 is less than half the 1993 amount and is the lowest since the NCVS began. The 2001 totals also represented much less than 1% of the total U.S. population.

NCVS property crime rates have also dropped since the early 1990s. However, the pattern before this time period is quite different from the corresponding UCR rate.[3] Let's look.

Data File: **TRENDS**
    Task: **Historical Trends**
➤ Variable: **78) PROPNCVS**

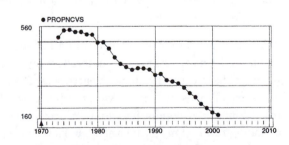

Property crimes per 1,000 (includes burglary, larceny-theft, and motor vehicle theft

---

[2] The homicide component of the NCVS violent crimes totals comes from the UCR.

[3] This is probably because the NCVS does not include offenses against businesses.

Now, let's examine age and gender differences in victimization.

Data File: **TRENDS**
Task: **Historical Trends**
➤ Variables: **67) VIOLML**
68) VIOLFM

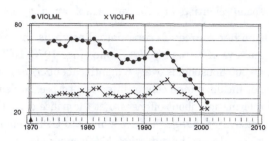

Violent victimization rates per 1,000 for males and females.

Though the "gender gap" in victimization has narrowed considerably in recent years, males are more likely than females to be victims of violence. What about age differences? Let's find out if younger adults are more likely to be victims of violence than females or older adults.

Data File: **TRENDS**
Task: **Historical Trends**
➤ Variables: **60) VIOL2024**
63) VIOL5064
64) VIOL65+

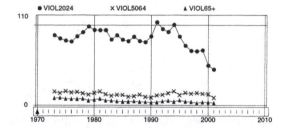

Violent victimization rates per 1,000 for ages 20–24, 50–64, and 65 and older.

Yes again! Younger adults are far more likely to suffer from such crime than older adults. In fact, those most likely to be victims of violent crime are in their late teens to mid-twenties.

The NCVS is an important addition to our crime data. However, it is not perfect. For example, inaccurate, under- and over-reporting do occur in victim surveys for various reasons.

Another major means of measuring crime is to ask people to report on their own violations of the law. This is called *self-report*. Of course, we have already seen self-report data. In Exercise 5, we saw respondents admitting to their use of illegal drugs.

Ask yourself whether or not you would be willing, even under conditions of complete anonymity, to admit on a survey to having murdered or raped someone! This should help you see why many social scientists have concerns about the accuracy of self-report data. Serious offenses may be under-reported while trivial ones are often over-reported. Also, those who are unavailable to be surveyed (such as institutionalized populations or, in school surveys, absentees and drop-outs) probably have higher offending rates. Many social scientists view self-report studies as being best for measuring less serious and chronic offending. However, self-report surveys are good for testing associations between many personal characteristics, experiences, and crime—for example, connecting attitudes and family backgrounds with criminality.[4]

---

[4] I have made use of a nice overview of self-report surveys in Larry J. Siegel, 2002, *Criminology: The Core*, Belmont, Calif.: Wadsworth, pages 30–32.

Let's look at some delinquency recorded in the YRBS. We will also see the ability of self-report data to connect individual characteristics and offending behavior. You may recall from Exercise 5 that "social strain" theory predicts that those from groups that have historically experienced discrimination will be involved in crime more than others. Thus, African American and Hispanic students should be more likely to carry a weapon at school. Let's find out.

> ➤ Data File: **YRBS**
> ➤ Task: **Cross-tabulation**
> ➤ Row Variable: **8) WEAPSCHL**
> ➤ Column Variable: **2) RACE**
> ➤ Subset Variable: **2) RACE**
> ➤ Subset Category: **Exclude: Other**
> ➤ View: **Tables**
> ➤ Display: **Column %**

WEAPSCHL   by   RACE

Weight Variable: WEIGHT
Cramer's V: 0.023

		RACE			
		Black	Hispanic	White NHis	TOTAL
W E A P S C H L	Yes	16	12	119	146
		4.9%	4.3%	5.9%	5.6%
	No	299	267	1903	2469
		95.1%	95.7%	94.1%	94.4%
	Missing	4	3	16	23
	TOTAL	315	279	2021	2615
		100.0%	100.0%	100.0%	

The prediction was *not* supported. Few students of any type carried a weapon at school, and the percentages for African Americans, non-Hispanic whites, and Hispanics were very similar (V = 0.023).

Do beliefs about crime match reality? Let's see to what extent the public have "caught on" to the substantial decline in the crime rate since the early 1990s. We'll look at answers to an NES question that asks how the crime rate has or has not changed since 1992.

> ➤ Data File: **ELECTION**
> ➤ Task: **Univariate**
> ➤ Primary Variable: **44) CRIME RATE**
> ➤ View: **Pie**

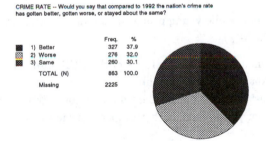

CRIME RATE -- Would you say that compared to 1992 the nation's crime rate has gotten better, gotten worse, or stayed about the same?

		Freq.	%
■	1) Better	327	37.9
▨	2) Worse	276	32.0
▨	3) Same	260	30.1
	TOTAL (N)	863	100.0
	Missing	2225	

Most of the public got it wrong! About 38% gave the right answer, while fully 32% thought things had gotten worse, and 30% believed there had been no change in the crime rate.

Now. let's examine differences in being afraid to walk near home in the night. Since males and younger adults are actually more likely to be victims of violence, we would assume that they should be most likely to have such fears. We'll use the GSS.

➤ Data File:	**GSS**
➤ Task:	**Cross-tabulation**
➤ Row Variable:	**44) FEAR WALK**
➤ Column Variable:	**2) GENDER**
➤ View:	**Tables**
➤ Display:	**Column %**

FEAR WALK   by   GENDER
Cramer's V: 0.306 **

		GENDER		
		Male	Female	TOTAL
FEAR WALK	Yes	282	739	1021
		21.6%	51.2%	37.1%
	No	1024	705	1729
		78.4%	48.8%	62.9%
	Missing	1151	1681	2832
	TOTAL	1306	1444	2750
		100.0%	100.0%	

Well, perceptions are counter to reality.[5] Females are more than twice as likely as males to be afraid to walk near their homes at night (V = 0.306**). Let's see if our hunch that younger adults will be more afraid to walk at night is true.

Data File:	**GSS**
Task:	**Cross-tabulation**
Row Variable:	**44) FEAR WALK**
➤ Column Variable:	**1) AGE**
➤ View:	**Tables**
➤ Display:	**Column %**

FEAR WALK   by   AGE
Cramer's V: 0.083 **

		AGE					
		<30	30-49	50-64	65 and Up	Missing	TOTAL
FEAR WALK	Yes	198	388	209	222	4	1017
		37.8%	33.8%	36.2%	45.0%		37.1%
	No	326	761	368	271	3	1726
		62.2%	66.2%	63.8%	55.0%		62.9%
	Missing	532	1230	578	477	15	2832
	TOTAL	524	1149	577	493	22	2743
		100.0%	100.0%	100.0%	100.0%		

Nope, while young people should have been more fearful than older persons, the opposite was true (V = 0.083**).

One of the big advantages of the UCR data is that it allows us to compare the crime rates of localities. Not only does this enable us to examine geographic distributions in crime, but we can also use this to test macro theories. Let's do both now. First, we'll test social strain theory again. Do areas with more poor people have higher property crime rates?[6]

➤ Data File:	**STATES**
➤ Task:	**Scatterplot**
➤ Dependent Variable:	**57) PROPCRIM01**
➤ Independent Variable:	**48) %POOR00**
➤ View:	**Reg. Line**

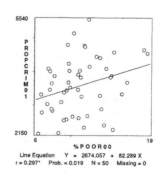

---

[5] Unless for some reason females really are more likely to live in unsafe neighborhoods or just to be victimized close to home. Neither of these factors is likely to account for this big gender difference, however.

[6] Cf. Mooney et al., op cit., page 97 on the social strain theory prediction of greater crime among the poor.

While we need to remember that correlation does not establish cause and that this r could be spurious,[7] strain theory is supported here ($r = 0.297*$), though weakly. On average, areas with more poor people have slightly higher property crime rates.

Another major theory of crime, clearly a "consensus" explanation and often applied at the macro level, is **social control theory**. Generally, theorists of this school hold that strong social bonds enhance conformity to social norms (that is, create "social control"), whereas weak ones are associated with greater violations of these rules, including more criminality.[8] To the extent that breakdowns in social relationships that facilitate social control are seen as a cause of crime, this theory shares at least some ideas with **social disorganization theory** (which is another macro consensus theory). Social disorganization theorists believe that, among a number of factors, breakdowns in institutions that promote social control (such as schools, churches, families, and cohesive neighborhoods) lead to greater crime.[9]

Both theories would predict that states in which people are more residentially stable would tend to have lower property crime rates. After all, changes of residence are tied to disrupted or weakened relationships in schools, churches, kinship networks, and so on.[10] Why don't we find out by looking at the correlation between property crime rates and the percentage of people who have lived in the same house since the previous year?

Data File: **STATES**
Task: **Scatterplot**
Dependent Variable: **57) PROPCRIM01**
➤ Independent Variable: **65) %SMHOUSE00**
➤ View: **Reg. Line**

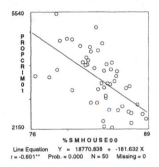

This hypothesis is powerfully supported ($r = -0.601**$). As the percentages of households that have *not* moved in the previous year increase, property crime rates decrease.

Let's look at one more ecological relationship and general idea about crime causation. Feminist theoreticians, operating within a general conflict perspective, would tend to argue that male domination of women is correlated with sexual aggression. You may recall from Exercise 3 that Guttentag and Secord's theory of sex ratios also predicts that the more males there are relative to females, the more such gender domination there will be.[11] Putting these ideas together would lead us to predict that the higher the ratio of males to females, the higher the forcible rape rates will be. We'll test this now.

---

[7] See Exercise 3.

[8] Perhaps *the* major single statement of this theory is Travis Hirschi, 1969, *Causes of Delinquency*, Berkeley: University of California Press.

[9] The expression of this theory that is probably best known is Clifford R. Shaw and Henry D. McKay, 1929, *Delinquency Areas*, Chicago: University of Chicago Press.

[10] It is also associated with other social disorganization factors related to population turnover.

[11] Op cit.

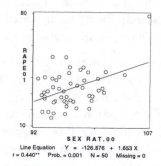

Data File: **STATES**
Task: **Scatterplot**
➤ Dependent Variable: **59) RAPE01**
➤ Independent Variable: **6) SEX RAT.00**
➤ View: **Reg. Line**

Bingo! There is a positive, moderate relationship between the ratio of males to females and rape ($r = 0.440$**). This hypothesis (and the theories underlying it) is supported here.

We've seen a lot of crime. Now let's turn our attention to punishment. We'll look at trends in two areas: imprisonment, and the "ultimate punishment" of execution.

➤ Data File: **TRENDS**
➤ Task: **Historical Trends**
➤ Variable: **85) #PRISONERS**

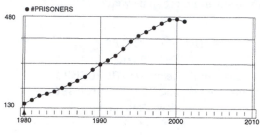

Number of inmates

It appears that punishment for crime in America has been getting stiffer for years, though there was some decline in the number of prisoners between 2000 and 2001. How do Americans feel about this? To find out, we'll look at information from the GSS to see whether Americans feel court treatment of criminals is too harsh or not harsh enough.

➤ Data File: **GSS**
➤ Task: **Univariate**
➤ Primary Variable: **42) COURTS?**
➤ View: **Pie**

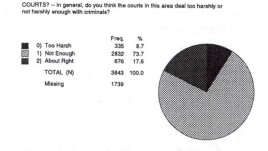

Americans clearly support tougher penalties for crime. In fact, despite increasing incarcerations levels and lower crime, 74% want punishment harsher still!

Investigating Social Problems

A very controversial issue in criminal justice today is the death penalty—the "ultimate punishment." What has been the trend in executions?

➤ *Data File:* **TRENDS**
   ➤ *Task:* **Historical Trends**
➤ *Variable:* **88) #EXECUTED**

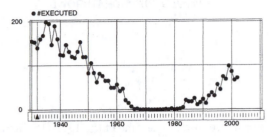

Number of executions

Here again, though there was generally some drop after 1999, the trend has been toward increasing harshness. The recent high in executions was reached in 1999 with 99 of them, and there were 71 in 2002. You may have noticed that executions disappeared completely in the late 1960s. After none for some time, there was one in 1977, and then they began picking up again in the 1980s and especially in the 1990s. In fact, in 1972 the U.S. Supreme Court decision ruled that the death penalty was unconstitutional, largely because they decided that it was being applied in a manner that discriminated against minorities and the poor. Executions could not take place in America until state statutes were redrafted to pass Constitutional muster.[12]

So, how do Americans feel about executions? Let's examine the trend in support for sentencing those convicted of murder to death, as measured by the GSS since 1972.

Data File: **TRENDS**
   Task: **Historical Trends**
➤ *Variable:* **89) SUPPEXEC**

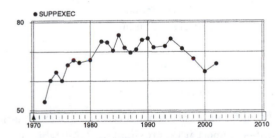

Percent supporting the death penalty for those convicted of murder

Support for the death penalty is strong and has grown since 1972. And though declining somewhat since 1994, it went up a little again between 2000 and 2002. In 2002, about 66% of GSS respondents supported it. Now, how about the important charge that the death penalty is applied in a racially discriminatory fashion? Let's look at the trend in what percentage of people under sentence of death is African American.

---

[12] Stark, op cit., page 221.

Data File: **TRENDS**
Task: **Historical Trends**
➤ *Variable:* **87) %DEATHROWB**

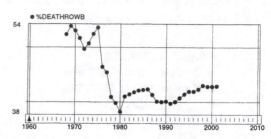

Percent of prisoners on death row that are African American

You can see that at the time of the 1972 U.S. Supreme Court decision banning executions, about half or more of all death-row inmates were African American. (Only about 12% to 13% of the U.S. population was African American at the time.) Notice, however, that as the effects of this court decision have taken hold, the percentage of African Americans under sentence of death has decreased. Still, this percentage has remained well above the proportion of the U.S. population that is African American.[13] It was about 43% as of 2001.

Given these facts, one might expect that the death penalty might have less support among African Americans than among Whites or the population as a whole. Let's see.

➤ *Data File:* **GSS**
➤ *Task:* **Cross-tabulation**
➤ *Row Variable:* **40) EXECUTE?**
➤ *Column Variable:* **3) RACE**
➤ *View:* **Tables**
➤ *Display:* **Column %**

EXECUTE? by RACE
Cramer's V: 0.234 **

		RACE			
		White	Black	Missing	TOTAL
EXECUTE?	Favor	2283	246	134	2529
		73.7%	43.7%		69.1%
	Oppose	814	317	79	1131
		26.3%	56.3%		30.9%
	Missing	1316	271	122	1709
	TOTAL	3097	563	335	3660
		100.0%	100.0%		

The difference between white and African American views on the death penalty is enormous. Most whites support it (approximately 74%), while most African Americans (about 56%) *oppose* executions. Of course, this difference is statistically significant (V = 0.234**).

There's still so much we can learn about crime and punishment in America. Even though you'll still only be scratching the surface, why not continue to look at the facts and perceptions in this important and interesting social problems area on your own?

---

[13] Whether or not the proportion of African Americans on death row is racially discriminatory, or justified by disproportionate involvement in capital offenses, is a raging and complicated controversy I will *not* try to settle here!

NAME:

COURSE:

DATE:

REVIEW QUESTIONS

Based on the first part of this exercise, answer True or False to the following items:

Crime categorized as "violent" in the UCR always involves the use, or threat of, force.   T   F

Crime estimates from the NCVS are generally higher than corresponding crime estimates from the UCR.   T   F

UCR data show crime violent crime decreasing since the early 1990s, but NCVS data do not show this decrease in violent crime.   T   F

The risk of violent crime victimization appears to be disproportionately high for males and young adults.   T   F

Most social scientists are convinced of the accuracy of self-report data for detecting serious, chronic criminal offenses.   T   F

Most Americans know that the crime rate has declined since 1992.   T   F

Social control and social disorganization theorists agree that the breakdown of institutions that promote social control will generally be associated with greater amounts of crime.   T   F

Feminist theorists argue that the greater the level of male domination of females, the higher the rate of rape will be.   T   F

Punishment for crimes has increased in recent decades, but it is clear that most Americans do not support these harsher penalties for crime.   T   F

The percentages of African Americans on death row have been much higher than the percentages of Americans who are African American.   T   F

Most African American GSS respondents for the years 2000 and 2002 combined did not support the death penalty.   T   F

EXPLORIT QUESTIONS

1. We'll start by comparing the *pattern of change* in two violent crimes, as measured by the UCR. (That is, to what extent do rates of these crimes rise, or fall, around the same times?)

    a. Open the TRENDS data set and examine the variable descriptions for 73) UCRROB and 75) UCRASSAULT.

b. Look at the Historical Trends chart for 73) UCRROB and 75) UCRASSAULT. Then, answer the following questions about what you see there.

> ➤ *Data File:* **TRENDS**
>   ➤ *Task:* **Historical Trends**
> ➤ *Variables:* **73) UCRROB**
>   **75) UCRASSAULT**

c. Overall, do you think that the pattern of change in the rate of these two crimes has been very similar, somewhat similar, or not at all similar? (Circle one.)

                                                     Very Similar

                                                Somewhat Similar

                                                Not At All Similar

2. How about rape? How has the rape rate changed in recent years? Let's compare NCVS and UCR forcible rape trends.

a. Carefully examine the variable description for 71) UCRRAPE.

b. Print the Historical Trends chart for 71) UCRRAPE, and look at it carefully.

>   *Data File:* **TRENDS**
>   *Task:* **Historical Trends**
> ➤ *Variable:* **71) UCRRAPE**

c. Examine the variable description for 72) NCVSRAPE.

d. Print the Historical Trends chart for 72) NCVSRAPE, and look at it carefully.

>   *Data File:* **TRENDS**
>   *Task:* **Historical Trends**
> ➤ *Variable:* **72) NCVSRAPE**

e. Overall, do you think that the *pattern of change* in the rate of rape from these two sources <u>*for 1990 through 2001 only*</u> was very similar, somewhat similar, or not at all similar? (Circle one.)

                                                     Very Similar

                                                Somewhat Similar

                                                Not At All Similar

f. Overall, do you think that the *pattern of change* in the rate of rape
    from these two sources *from 1973 to 1990* was very similar, somewhat
    similar, or not at all similar? (Circle one.)

Very Similar

Somewhat Similar

Not At All Similar

g. In your own words, summarize how the trends for rape from the NCVS and the UCR have been
    similar, and different, from 1973 to 2001. To the extent that the rates from these two sources have
    been different, what do you think are the reasons for these differences?

3. There have been a number of well-publicized incidents of violence involving weapons in schools in
    recent years, such as the horrible shootings at Columbine High School in Littleton, Colorado, in 1999.
    Let's use the YRBS to look at the issue of kids having weapons at school in more detail, starting with
    a simple overview. (Remember, our YRBS data set consists of high school seniors only.)

    a. Open the YRBS data set and carefully examine the variable description for 8) WEAPSCHL.

    b. Look at the percentage that said they had recently carried a weapon to school. Then, fill in that
        percentage below.

> *Data File:* **YRBS**
> *Task:* **Univariate**
> *Primary Variable:* **8) WEAPSCHL**
> *View:* **Pie**

Yes: _____%

4. People generally believe that urban high schools are more dangerous than suburban or rural ones.
    And social disorganization theorists would tend to agree. Let's find out. We will continue to use the
    YRBS. Our hypothesis is: *seniors in urban or suburban high schools will be more likely than those in
    rural high schools to have carried weapons in school.*

    a. Carefully examine the variable description for 5) METRO.

    b. Cross-tabulate 8) WEAPSCHL with 5) METRO. Then, fill in the percentages indicating that they
        had recently carried a weapon to school.

Data File: **YRBS**
➤ Task: **Cross-tabulation**
➤ Row Variable: **8) WEAPSCHL**
➤ Column Variable: **5) METRO**
➤ View: **Tables**
➤ Display: **Column %**

	URBAN	SUBURBAN	RURAL
YES	_____%	_____%	_____%

Now, get the Cramer's V and the significance level for these two variables.

c. Record the value of Cramer's V for this table. (Include asterisks, if any.)   V = _____

d. Is the relationship between METRO and WEAPSCHL statistically significant? (Circle one.)   Yes   No

e. Was the hypothesis supported? (Circle one.)   Yes   No

5. We just looked at self-report data. Now let's look at a corresponding victimization item from the YRBS. Our hypothesis is: *seniors in rural high schools will be less likely than those in urban or suburban high schools to have been threatened with a weapon in school.* And to see how often 12th graders claim to have been threatened with a weapon at school <u>overall</u>, we'll simply look at the "Totals" column in the cross-tabulation this time, rather than running a separate pie chart. (The "Totals" column in a cross-tabulation provides the same percentages for a row variable as you would get looking at the latter using the UNIVARIATE function to draw a pie chart.)

a. Carefully examine the variable description for 10) THREATWEAP.

b. Cross-tabulate 10) THREATWEAP with 5) METRO. Then, fill in the percentages indicating that they had not been threatened by a weapon at school.

Data File: **YRBS**
Task: **Cross-tabulation**
➤ Row Variable: **10) THREATWEAP**
➤ Column Variable: **5) METRO**
➤ View: **Tables**
➤ Display: **Column %**

	URBAN	SUBURBAN	RURAL	TOTAL
NONE	_____%	_____%	_____%	_____%

Now, carefully examine the Cramer's V and the significance level for these two variables.

c.   Is the relationship between METRO and THREATWEAP statistically significant?
(Circle one.)   Yes   No

d.   Was the hypothesis supported? (Circle one.)   Yes   No

e.   Looking at the "Totals" column, what percentage of students overall had not
been recently threatened with a weapon in school?   _____%

6.   All of this data on weapons brings the whole passionate issue of gun control to mind. To what extent
do Americans overall support or oppose stricter gun control? And, do men and women differ much in
their views on this issue? Let's find out. We'll use cross-tabulation to look at both. With regard to gender, our hypothesis is: *women will be more likely than men to support laws that would make it more
difficult to purchase guns.*

a.   Open the ELECTION data set and carefully examine the variable description for 47) GUNS SUP.

b.   Cross-tabulate 47) GUNS SUP with 2) GENDER. Then, fill in the percentages indicating that they
support making it harder to buy a gun.

> ➤ *Data File:* **ELECTION**
> ➤ *Task:* **Cross-tabulation**
> ➤ *Row Variable:* **47) GUNS SUP**
> ➤ *Column Variable:* **2) GENDER**
> ➤ *View:* **Tables**
> ➤ *Display:* **Column %**

	MALE	FEMALE	TOTAL
M DIFFIC	_____%	_____%	_____%

Now, carefully examine the Cramer's V and the significance level for these two variables.

c.   Is the relationship between GENDER and GUNS SUP weak,
moderate, strong, or not significant? (Circle one.)   Weak

Moderate

Strong

Not Significant

d.   Was the hypothesis supported? (Circle one.)   Yes   No

e.   Did most <u>men</u> want to make it harder to buy a gun? (Circle one.)   Yes   No

f.   Did most <u>women</u> want to make it harder to buy a gun? (Circle one.)   Yes   No

g. (Answer this question only if there were significant gender differences in views on gun control.) What do you think are the reasons why men and women differ in their support for tougher gun control?

7. How about the death penalty? Do men and women differ much in their views on this issue? Let's find out. Our hypothesis is: *women will be less likely than men to support the death penalty.* This time, we'll look at responses in the NES (rather than the GSS death penalty question we used earlier).

a. Carefully examine the variable description for 46) DEATH PEN.

b. Cross-tabulate 46) DEATH PEN with 2) GENDER. Then, fill in the percentages that support the death penalty.

Data File:	**ELECTION**
Task:	**Cross-tabulation**
➤ Row Variable:	**46) DEATH PEN**
➤ Column Variable:	**2) GENDER**
➤ View:	**Tables**
➤ Display:	**Column %**

	MALE	FEMALE
FAVOR	_____%	_____%

Now, carefully examine the Cramer's V and the significance level for these two variables.

c. Is the relationship between GENDER and DEATH PEN weak, moderate, strong, or not significant? (Circle one.)

Weak

Moderate

Strong

Not Significant

d. Was the hypothesis supported? (Circle one.)   Yes   No

e. Is the difference between male and female views small
    or large? (Circle one.)   Small   Large

8. Finally, let's look at ecological data in the STATES file to test some theories of crime. Both social dis-
    organization theory and social control theory predict that areas where there are more female-headed
    homes with children will have higher crime rates.[14] We'll test this hypothesis: *as the percentage of
    female-headed households with children increases, the violent crime rate will also increase.*

    a. Open the STATES data set.

    b. Construct a scatterplot that represents the association between 45) F HEAD/C00 and
        56) VIOLCRIM01.

        ➤ Data File: **STATES**
              ➤ Task: **Scatterplot**
        ➤ Dependent Variable: **56) VIOLCRIM01**
        ➤ Independent Variable: **45) F HEAD/C00**
              ➤ View: **Reg. Line**

    c. Provide Pearson's *r* (including asterisks, if any, and the direction sign, if any)   *r* = _____

    d. Is this correlation significant *and* negative, significant *and* positive,
        or *not* significant? (Circle one.)   Significant *and* Negative

                                                                     Significant *and* Positive

                                                                     Not Significant

    e. Is the correlation between VIOLCRIM01 and F HEAD/C00 weak, moderate,
        or strong? (Circle one.)   Weak

                                                                            Moderate

                                                                             Strong

    f. Was the hypothesis supported? (Circle one.)   Yes   No

9. You may recall that feminist social scientists link male domination to rape. One indicator of the extent
    to which men and women live in more patriarchal conditions is a high fertility rate. Putting these ideas
    together enables us to construct this hypothesis: *as fertility rates increase, rape rates will also
    increase.*

    a. Construct a scatterplot that represents the association between 27) FERTIL00 and 59) RAPE01.

---

[14] The reasons given for this prediction are many and complex. Theorists who make this prediction do not necessari-
ly assume that single-parent families, on average, do a worse job of raising children than two-parent families.

Data File: **STATES**
Task: **Scatterplot**
➤ *Dependent Variable:* **59) RAPE01**
➤ *Independent Variable:* **27) FERTIL00**
➤ *View:* **Reg. Line**

Carefully examine Pearson's *r* (Including asterisks and the direction sign, if any.)

b. Is this correlation significant *and* negative, significant *and* positive,
or *not* significant? (Circle one.)

Significant *and* Negative

Significant *and* Positive

Not Significant

c. Is this correlation between RAPE01 and FERTIL00 weak, moderate, strong,
or not significant? (Circle one.)

Weak

Moderate

Strong

Not Significant

d. Was the hypothesis supported? (Circle one.)

Yes   No

◆ EXERCISE 7 ◆
MENTAL HEALTH PROBLEMS

Tasks: Historical Trends, Cross-tabulation, Scatterplot, Mapping
Data Files: TRENDS, YRBS, GSS, STATES, COUNTRIES

Someone you know has been experiencing problems. She is very sad, and her gloominess does not seem to be justified by her personal circumstances. Complaining that she cannot concentrate, she has been neglecting her studies. She has not had much of an appetite and, though listless, has been having trouble sleeping. She even told you recently that she had been toying with the possibility of committing suicide. What's wrong with her?

Most social and behavioral scientists would agree that your friend might be suffering from a ***mental disorder or illness***.[1] That is, her condition could be a "behavioral or psychological . . . pattern . . . associated with . . . a painful symptom (distress) or impairment in one or more important areas of functioning" which commonly requires professional help, and is not merely a conflict between her and other people.[2] If a licensed professional diagnoses her, he or she will almost inevitably do so according to the classification system set forth in the American Psychiatric Association's *Diagnostic and Statistical Manual of Mental Disorders-IV* (DSM-IV). Based on DSM-IV criteria, she may be diagnosed as having a type of "depression."

Usually, experts who view your friend's suffering in this way employ an implicit or explicit ***medical model***. That is, they view her problems as possible "symptoms" of a "disease" which may require "treatment." If she is classified as "mentally ill" and receives therapy, they may even refer to her as a "patient." However, some social scientists disagree with routinely viewing mental disorders as diseases. They claim that most people who are classified as "mentally ill" are simply treated by medical professionals and/or others *as if they had* medical diseases, because they have violated certain types of social norms.[3]

This kind of dissent from psychiatric orthodoxy is controversial. But these critics encourage us to consider how labeling the "mentally ill" may worsen their problems. Moreover, their writings draw attention to the ways in which our classification and treatment of those who appear to be psychologically disturbed can be affected by many things other than their objective condition and needs, such as social expectations and goals, the sufferers' family dynamics, and even the professional interests and biases of mental health professionals or government officials.

The symptoms used to render psychiatric diagnoses are often vague and subject to multiple interpretations. Mental health professionals frequently classify people with the same symptoms differently.[4] Some studies

---

[1] Mental "disorders" are often distinguished from mental "illnesses." In the first, a person finds it "difficult or impossible . . . to cope with everyday life," while the latter" requires extensive [clinical] treatment" (Kendall, op cit., page 207; see also Parillo, op cit., page 324). However, for the sake of simplicity, here I will follow Kornblum and Julian (op cit., page 66) and many other social scientists in using these two terms interchangeably.

[2] Robert L. Spitzer and Janet B. W. Williams, 1982, "The Definition and Diagnosis of Mental Disorder," in Walter R. Gove (Ed.), *Deviance and Mental Illness*, pages 15–31, Beverly Hills, Calif.: Sage. Pages 19–20.

[3] Though their approaches differ in many ways, two of the best known critiques of this type are Thomas J. Scheff, 1966, *Being Mentally Ill*, Chicago: Aldine; and Thomas S. Szasz, 1974, *The Myth of Mental Illness (Revised Edition)*, New York: Harper & Row.

[4] Sullivan, op cit., pages 128–129.

have even shown race and gender bias in psychiatric categorization.[5] It would be unwise to conclude that diagnoses of mental illness are wholly inaccurate. And they may be improving.[6] However, data on the frequency and distribution of mental illness that are based on such classifications must be used with caution.

Such problems with the available data are compounded by the fact that most mental illnesses are not treated or reported. Meanwhile, many people without diagnosable mental disorders *do* use mental health services. In addition, accurate statistics on those treated in private practices are hard to get. Overall, variations in the official rates of mental disorders are affected by differences in access to and/or use of particular mental health services.[7]

Despite these difficulties, there is much that can be learned by examining official data on mental illness and mental health care. And we are not completely dependent on records and classifications associated with reported cases. A wealth of information is available from surveys in which respondents provide information about their own mental well-being and experience. We will use both types of data in this exercise.

How much mental illness and treatment is there in the United States? How has this changed over time? Let's start looking at this by exploring some data in your TRENDS file. First we will examine the *total number* of people who were admitted to mental health organizations to receive inpatient or outpatient treatment.

> *Data File:* **TRENDS**
> > *Task:* **Historical Trends**
> *Variable:* **109) #TREAT MH**

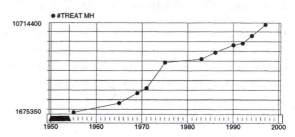

Number of patient care episodes and all mental health organizations combined

During the past three decades, the total number of Americans seeking mental health treatment has increased dramatically, from 1,675,350 to 10,714,400. Let's take a closer look at this issue by also looking at the *rate* per 100,000 people who are new patients to mental health care.

Data File: **TRENDS**
Task: **Historical Trends**
> *Variable:* **108) RATE MH**

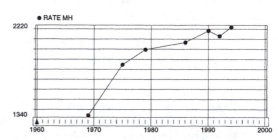

*Combined rate per 100,000 of all new additions to mental health organizations,
residential & 24-hour and less than 24 hour*

---

[5] Cf. the literature review and study reported in Marti Loring and Brian Powell ("Gender, Race, and DSM-III: A Study of the Objectivity of Psychiatric Diagnostic Behavior," *Journal of Health and Social Behavior 29: 1*, 1988, pages 1–22) on both serious unreliability, and race and gender bias, in diagnosis.

[6] Spitzer and Williams, op cit., pages 24–30; Kornblum and Julian, op cit., page 73.

[7] Kornblum and Julian, op cit., pages 73–74; Parillo, op cit., page 326.

It appears that both the total number and the proportion of Americans seeking mental health treatment have risen dramatically over the past several decades. We would expect this to be associated with a growth of personnel and dollars for mental health organizations. Let's look first at the spending per capita on mental health organizations.

> Data File: **TRENDS**
>   Task: **Historical Trends**
> ➤ Variable: **107) EXPENSE MH**

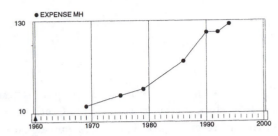

Expenditures per-capita on mental health organizations of all types

Spending on mental health organizations has risen steadily since the late 1960s. Let's now look at the growth of mental health personnel.

> Data File: **TRENDS**
>   Task: **Historical Trends**
> ➤ Variable: **113) #MH STAFF**

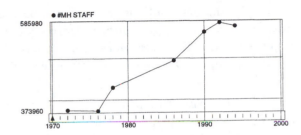

Number of full-time staff (professional and non-professional) in all mental-health organizations

The number of full-time staff at these organizations has risen since the 1970s. So far, we have seen steady, significant increases in the provision and utilization of mental health services. Does that mean the proportion of Americans suffering from mental disorders has been rising? Or do these trends only reflect growth in such things as access to psychiatric services, or people's recognition of and willingness to seek treatment for mental disorders?

It's hard to say. Reliable data showing changes in the true rates of mental disorders in the American population over time are hard to come by. There are some specific manifestations of some types of mental illness that we do have fairly good measures of, however. Among these are suicide rates. A National Institute of Mental Health (NIMH) bulletin states that "almost all people who kill themselves have a diagnosable mental or substance abuse[8] disorder or both . . . the majority have (depression)."[9] Certainly, the vast majority of people suffering from mental disorders do not commit suicide. But if most people who commit suicide are, for example, clinically depressed, and if depression has increased in recent years, then perhaps the suicide rate will have risen as well. Why don't we take a look?

---

[8] Many substance abuse problems are diagnosable mental disorders. However, we will not deal with substance abuse in this exercise, having already done so in Exercise 5.

[9] "Suicide Facts," National Institute of Mental Health, September 26, 1999, Bethesda, MD.

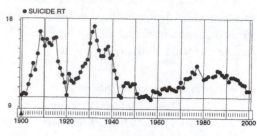

Suicides per 100,000

This trend chart shows some interesting things. Among them is the steep increase in suicide following the 1929 stock market crash into the Great Depression years. However, we do not see an increase in suicide in recent years. To be sure, suicide rose quite a bit from 1956 to 1977. But (despite some increase between 1980 and 1986), it has generally declined since then. Perhaps the increased use of mental health services during the last couple of decades has played a role in this drop in suicides. However, *if* suicide and depression rise together, these suicide rates do not suggest an increase in the overall true prevalence of depression.

Since 1972, the General Social Survey has asked respondents to rate their own level of happiness. Answering "not too happy" is hardly evidence that a respondent is clinically depressed! However, we might expect that if the percentage of Americans who are depressed has increased, then the percentage saying that they are unhappy should have risen as well.

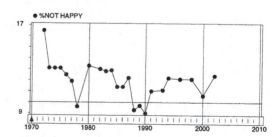

Percentage of GSS respondents indicating that they were "not too happy"

Unlike the provision or utilization of mental health services, the percentage of GSS respondents who say they are "not too happy" has not risen or fallen much overall since 1973. This percentage remained between about 9% and 13% from 1973 through 2002.

In a set of annual surveys, an agency of the Centers for Disease Control and Prevention (CDC) asks Americans how many days during the past month their "mental health, including stress, depression, and problems with emotions . . . was not good." Let's review some of these data.

Investigating Social Problems

Data File: **TRENDS**

Task: **Historical Trends**

➤ Variables: **115) %BADMH17**

116) %BADMH830

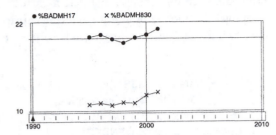

Percentage of respondents who indicated that their "mental health,"
including "stress, depression, and problems with emotions," was
"not good" for between 1 and 7, and 8 and 30 of the 30 days prior
to being surveyed

Although these data cover only the period since 1995, we don't see much of an increase in self-declared mental illness during that time. However, it is worth noting that in the year 2001, about 13% indicated poor mental health for a period of 8 or more days during the previous month, and another 21% suffered for up to one week. Like many studies, this suggests that Americans experience mental health problems more often than is commonly believed.

One of the most important developments in the treatment of mental disorders in the past several decades has been **deinstitutionalization**, in which (starting in the mid-1950s) a large number of patients in mental hospitals were released.[10] Much treatment for mental illness was shifted to community-based outpatient facilities. Let's see if we can graph this trend. We will compare, of the total persons admitted to receive professional mental health treatment, the percentages entering inpatient (residential) versus outpatient (ambulatory) care.

Data File: **TRENDS**

Task: **Historical Trends**

➤ Variables: **110) $ MHT RES**

111) % MHT N-RS

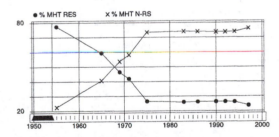

Of total people admitted to receive mental health treatment, percent of these
"patient care episodes" that were inpatient or outpatient

Wow! What a dramatic shift since 1955! In fact, the "market share" of inpatient and outpatient treatment has virtually become reversed. In 1955, about 77% of mental health admissions were inpatient, versus about 23% that were outpatient. In 1997, about 24% were inpatient and about 76% were outpatient.

Disparities between males and females in mental disorders are important. Feminist scholars argue that these variations reflect gender role socialization and women's restricted position in society. Some argue that hormonal sex differences are also partly responsible.[11] One key area in which women are thought to have greater difficulty than men is **depression**. As we have seen, this disorder involves

---

[10] Cf. Kornblum and Julian, op cit., page 86; Palen, op cit., page 419; Curran and Renzetti, op cit., pages 353–354.

[11] Cf. Kendall, op cit., pages 211–212; Kornblum and Julian, op cit., pages 78–79; Parillo, op cit., pages 327–328.

problems such as sadness, disinterest in life and its pleasures, increases or decreases in eating or sleeping, disruptions of energy and concentration, and thoughts of death. Let's look at some survey data to find out if we can detect gender differences in depression.

➤ *Data File:* **GSS**
  ➤ *Task:* **Cross-tabulation**
➤ *Row Variable:* **51) HAPPY?**
➤ *Column Variable:* **2) GENDER**
  ➤ *View:* **Tables**
  ➤ *Display:* **Column %**

HAPPY?   by   GENDER
Cramer's V: 0.026

		GENDER		
		Male	Female	TOTAL
HAPPY?	Happy	1672	2011	3683
		89.7%	88.1%	88.8%
	Not Happy	191	272	463
		10.3%	11.9%	11.2%
	Missing	594	842	1436
	TOTAL	1863	2283	4146
		100.0%	100.0%	

We don't see here that women are any more likely than men to say they are "not too happy" (V = 0.026). Percentages are about 12% and 10%, respectively. However, as we have noted, this item is certainly not a precise measure of depression! Let's turn to the YRBS to look at something more specific. This survey asked respondents such questions as whether or not they had seriously considered suicide, and whether they had been "so sad or hopeless almost every day for two weeks or more that (they) stopped doing some physical activities."

➤ *Data File:* **YRBS**
  ➤ *Task:* **Cross-tabulation**
➤ *Row Variable:* **13) SAD**
➤ *Column Variable:* **1) GENDER**
  ➤ *View:* **Tables**
  ➤ *Display:* **Column %**

SAD   by   GENDER
Weight Variable: WEIGHT
Cramer's V: 0.144 **

		GENDER			
		Female	Male	Missing	TOTAL
SAD	Yes	485	287	2	772
		33.2%	20.5%		27.0%
	No	973	1114	3	2087
		66.8%	79.5%		73.0%
	Missing	4	5	0	9
	TOTAL	1458	1401	5	2859
		100.0%	100.0%		

Among these 12th graders, more females (about 33%) than males (about 20.5%) had been sad for two weeks (V = 0.144**). Notice the large percentage overall who struggled with the "blues" to this extent (27%).

Data File: **YRBS**
Task: **Cross-tabulation**
➤ Row Variable: **14) CDRSUICIDE**
➤ Column Variable: **1) GENDER**
➤ View: **Tables**
➤ Display: **Column %**

CDRSUICIDE by GENDER
Weight Variable: WEIGHT
Cramer's V: 0.071 **

		GENDER			
		Female	Male	Missing	TOTAL
CDRSUICIDE	Yes	277	192	0	469
		18.9%	13.7%		16.4%
	No	1184	1209	4	2393
		81.1%	86.3%		83.6%
	Missing	1	5	0	7
	TOTAL	1461	1401	5	2862
		100.0%	100.0%		

As for seriously considering suicide, females were also more likely to do this than males (about 19% versus 14%, V = 0.071**). Again, notice the alarmingly high percentage of seniors who had had such suicidal ideation (about 16%).

Another area of mental disorder in which women are thought to be over-represented is eating disorders. These include two disorders that often occur together: ***anorexia nervosa*** (extreme fear of being obese leading to self-starvation) and ***bulimia nervosa*** (episodic binge eating combined with extreme means to prevent weight gain such as excessive exercise or "purging" by such means as vomiting and laxative abuse). The YRBS asks respondents if they have ever used vomiting or laxatives to control weight. Let's take a look.

Data File: **YRBS**
Task: **Cross-tabulation**
➤ Row Variable: **37) VOMITDIET**
➤ Column Variable: **1) GENDER**
➤ View: **Tables**
➤ Display: **Column %**

VOMITDIET by GENDER
Weight Variable: WEIGHT
Cramer's V: 0.110 **

		GENDER			
		Female	Male	Missing	TOTAL
VOMITDIET	Yes	102	32	0	134
		7.0%	2.3%		4.7%
	No	1353	1359	4	2712
		93.0%	97.7%		95.3%
	Missing	8	15	0	23
	TOTAL	1455	1391	5	2846
		100.0%	100.0%		

The predicted gender difference is definitely here! Among 12th graders, females were more than four times as likely as males to "purge" diet (about 7% versus 2%; V = 0.110**).

Many social scientists over the years have noted that as social class increases, the rate of mental disorders—particularly the most serious types that result in hospitalization—decreases. Explanations for this include the social strain approach we have considered elsewhere, which asserts that pressures associated with poverty produce higher rates of mental disorders. Others rely on a ***social drift*** explanation to claim that people who are mentally ill are, for many reasons, more likely to become poor. We won't settle that issue, but we can see if poverty is associated with various measures of mental illness. We'll turn to your STATES data set to do so.

> *Data File:* **STATES**
> *Task:* **Scatterplot**
> *Dependent Variable:* **76) MENT RES00**
> *Independent Variable:* **48) %POOR00**
> *View:* **Reg. Line**

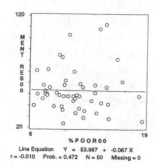

This analysis does not show a significant relationship between the percent poor and the proportion living in facilities for the mentally ill ($r = -0.010$). How about the percentage of people who claimed to be mentally ill for at least 8 days during a month prior to being surveyed?

> *Data File:* **STATES**
> *Task:* **Scatterplot**
> *Dependent Variable:* **72) %BAD MH**
> *Independent Variable:* **48) %POOR00**
> *View:* **Reg. Line**

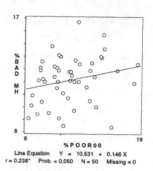

Here we do find the expected relationship. As the percentage who are poor increases, the percentage claiming to be mentally ill for a significant period of time also rises, though not a great deal ($r = 0.238*$). Finally, what about suicide, a very serious sign of distress?

> *Data File:* **STATES**
> *Task:* **Scatterplot**
> *Dependent Variable:* **66) SUICIDE 99**
> *Independent Variable:* **48) %POOR00**
> *View:* **Reg. Line**

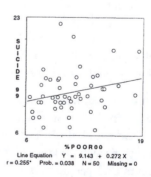

Again, poverty is associated with higher suicide rates ($r = 0.255*$). Though statistically significant, however, the relationship is not exceptionally powerful.

There is still much we can explore about mental disorders, related phenomena, and their variation across different subgroups. Why don't you continue doing so now, on your own?

Investigating Social Problems

REVIEW QUESTIONS

Based on the first part of this exercise, answer True or False to the following items:

To have a "mental disorder," a person must have received professional treatment for her or his problem(s). T F

Almost all social scientists agree that mental disorders are best understood as types of medical illnesses. T F

Studies have sometimes found psychiatric diagnosis to be biased. T F

One can easily determine the true level of mental disorders in the population by looking at levels of treatment for these disorders. T F

Rates of and spending on mental health treatment have risen in recent years. T F

American suicide rates have risen since 1986. T F

In the year 2001, over 10% of Americans surveyed indicated they had had poor mental health for at least 8 days in the previous month. T F

These days, most mental health care is provided "outpatient." T F

Among high school seniors, males are more likely than females to consider suicide. T F

Among high school seniors, females are more likely than males to be sad for about two weeks and to "purge" diet. T F

Among American states, the higher the percentage who are poor, the higher the rate of residency in residential treatment for mental illness. T F

Among American states, the higher the percentage who are poor, the higher the suicide rate. T F

EXPLORIT QUESTIONS

1. Let's continue our exploration of suicide rates. We'll start by looking at gender differences. It is commonly noted that while females are more likely both to be depressed and to *attempt* suicide, males are more likely to actually complete the act. Using TRENDS, we'll see if U.S. suicide rates are higher for males.

    a. Open the TRENDS data set and look carefully at the variable descriptions for 91) SUICIDE ML and 92) SUICIDE FM.

    b. Look at the Historical Trends chart for 91) SUICIDE ML and 92) SUICIDE FM. Then answer the following questions about what you see there.

➤ *Data File:* **TRENDS**
　➤ *Task:* **Historical Trends**
➤ *Variable:* **91) SUICIDE ML**
　　　　　　　92) SUICIDE FM

c. Males are _____ likely than females to commit suicide?
(Circle the one best answer that fills in the blank.)

A Lot More

Somewhat More

No More

Somewhat Less

A Lot Less

d. Between 1970 and 1990, do you think that the pattern of change in suicide
rates for males and females has been very similar, somewhat similar, or not
at all similar? (Circle one.)

Very Similar

Somewhat Similar

Not At All Similar

e. How would you describe the pattern of change in suicide rates for males and
females since 1990? (Circle one.)

Both Declined

Both Increased

Both Remained Level

One Declined but the Other Increased

2. We saw before that overall suicide rates have declined since 1977, and especially since 1986. But
many social scientists have expressed concern over more recent suicide rates for children and young
adults.

a. Look carefully at the variable description for 97) SUICIDE514.

b. Look at the Historical Trends chart for 97) SUICIDE514. Then answer the following questions
about what you see there.

　　　Data File: **TRENDS**
　　　　　Task: **Historical Trends**
➤ *Variable:* **97) SUICIDE514**

c. In your own words, briefly describe what happened to suicide rates for 5- to 14-year-old children
between 1950 and 2000.

d. Look carefully at the variable description for 98) SUICIDE1524.

e. Look at the Historical Trends chart for 98) SUICIDE1524. Then answer the following questions about what you see there.

>   *Data File:* **TRENDS**
>   *Task:* **Historical Trends**
> ➤ *Variable:* **98) SUICIDE1524**

f. In your own words, briefly describe what happened to suicide rates for 15- to 24-year-old people between 1950 and 2000.

g. <u>Comparing 1995 to 2000</u>, did the suicide rates for 5- to 14-year-olds and 15- to 24-year-olds year olds increase, decline, or remain about the same during this period? (Circle one.)

Increased

Declined

Remained about the Same

3. We saw that suicide rates are somewhat higher in states that have more poor people. What about unemployment? Let's test this hypothesis: *higher unemployment rates will be associated with higher suicide rates.*

a. Open the STATES data set and look carefully at the variable description for 52) UNEMP 01.

b. Draw two maps. One should show unemployment rates, and the other should show suicide rates.

> ➤ *Data File:* **STATES**
> ➤   *Task:* **Mapping**
> ➤ *Variable 1:* **52) UNEMP 01**
> ➤ *Variable 2:* **66) SUICIDE 99**
> ➤   *View:* **Maps**

c. Provide Pearson's *r* (including asterisks, if any, and the direction sign, if any).   *r* = _____

d. Is this correlation between UNEMP 01 and SUICIDE 99 significant *and* negative, significant *and* positive, or *not* significant? (Circle one.)

Significant *and* Negative

Significant *and* Positive

Not Significant

e. Was the hypothesis supported? (Circle one.)

Yes   No

4. Now let's test this hypothesis: *higher unemployment rates will be associated with higher percentages of people saying they've suffered from bad mental health for 8 days or longer.*

a. Draw maps of both 52) UNEMP 01 and 72) %BAD MH. Then look carefully at Pearson's *r.*

> Data File: **STATES**
> Task: **Mapping**
> Variable 1: **52) UNEMP 01**
> ➤ Variable 2: **72) %BAD MH**
>   ➤ View: **Maps**

b. Is this correlation between UNEMP 01 and %BAD MH significant *and* negative, significant *and* positive, or *not* significant? (Circle one.)

Significant *and* Negative

Significant *and* Positive

Not Significant

c. Was the hypothesis supported? (Circle one.)

Yes   No

5. If poverty is associated with (modestly) higher suicide rates, perhaps this is true for *nations* too. Let's use the COUNTRIES data set to test this hypothesis: *as the wealth per capita of nations increases, their suicide rates decrease.*

a. Does this hypothesis predict a negative, or a positive, correlation? (Circle one.)

Negative

Positive

b. Open the COUNTRIES data set and look carefully at the variable descriptions for 25) GDP/CAP and 55) SUICIDE.

c. Construct a scatterplot that represents the association between 25) GDP/CAP and 55) SUICIDE. Then, look carefully at Pearson's r.

> ➤ Data File: **COUNTRIES**
> ➤ Task: **Scatterplot**
> ➤ Dependent Variable: **55) SUICIDE**
> ➤ Independent Variable: **25) GDP/CAP**
>   ➤ View: **Reg. Line**

d. Is this correlation significant *and* negative, significant *and* positive, or *not* significant? (Circle one.)

Significant *and* Negative

Significant *and* Positive

Not Significant

e. Was the hypothesis supported? (Circle one.)

Yes   No

f. What do you think are the reasons for these results?

6. Could it be that money makes people happy? Let's use the GSS to find out. Our hypothesis is: *the higher a person's relative family income, the more likely they will be to say that they are happy.*

a. Open the GSS data set.

b. Cross-tabulate 51) HAPPY? with 16) $FAMRANK. Then, fill in the percentages indicating that they are happy.

> *Data File:* **GSS**
> *Task:* **Cross-tabulation**
> *Row Variable:* **51) HAPPY?**
> *Column Variable:* **16) $FAMRANK**
> *View:* **Tables**
> *Display:* **Column %**

	BELOW	AVERAGE	ABOVE
HAPPY	_____%	_____%	_____%

Now, get the Cramer's V and the significance level for these two variables.

c. Record the value of Cramer's V for this table. (Include asterisks, if any.)

V = _____

d. Is the relationship between $FAMRANK and HAPPY? statistically significant? (Circle one.)

Yes   No

e. Was the hypothesis supported? (Circle one.)

Yes   No

f. What do you think? Does having more money lead to (cause) great happiness and less unhappi-ness? Why or why not?

7. We saw that among 12th graders, females were more likely to "purge" diet than males. Maybe *females are also more likely than males to view themselves as overweight.* That will be our hypothesis.

a. Open the YRBS data set. Carefully read the variable description for 36) DESCWEIGHT.

b. Cross-tabulate 36) DESCWEIGHT with 1) GENDER. Then, fill in the percentages that say that they are overweight.

> *Data File:*   **YRBS**
> *Task:*   **Cross-tabulation**
> *Row Variable:*   **36) DESCWEIGHT**
> *Column Variable:*   **1) GENDER**
> *View:*   **Tables**
> *Display:*   **Column %**

	FEMALE	MALE
OVER	_____%	_____%

Now, examine the Cramer's V and the significance level for these two variables.

c. Is the relationship between GENDER and DESCWEIGHT statistically significant? (Circle one.)   Yes   No

d. Was the hypothesis supported? (Circle one.)   Yes   No

e. (If respondents of one gender were more likely to view themselves as overweight) how would you explain these gender differences in the self-perception of weight?

8. It is commonly believed that disorders such as bulimia are rooted at least partially in poor self-image. Perhaps *those who view themselves as overweight are more likely to "purge" diet than those who do not.* That will be our hypothesis.

   a. Cross-tabulate 37) VOMITDIET with 36) DESCWEIGHT. Then, fill in the percentages that indicated they took laxatives or vomited in order to lose or maintain weight.

Data File:	**YRBS**	
Task:	**Cross-tabulation**	
➤ Row Variable:	**37) VOMITDIET**	
➤ Column Variable:	**36) DESCWEIGHT**	
➤ View:	**Tables**	
➤ Display:	**Column %**	

	UNDER	**ABT RGHT**	**OVER**
YES	_____%	_____%	_____%

   Now, examine the Cramer's V and the significance level for these two variables.

   b. Is the relationship between DESCWEIGHT and VOMITDIET statistically significant? (Circle one.)   Yes   No

   c. Was the hypothesis supported? (Circle one.)   Yes   No

   d. Compare the percentage that had purge dieted who considered themselves under weight, with those who saw themselves as "about right." What do you notice here in comparing these two groups? What might be the reasons for these differences in purge dieting between those who are underweight versus those who see their weight as being about right?

9. Some people might assert that among those who feel overweight, males and females would be equally likely to take extreme measures, such as purge dieting, to lose weight. Thus, females are more likely to purge diet only because they are more likely to believe that they are overweight. However, feminists and others would argue that—given different cultural expectations for men and women—even among those who view themselves as overweight, females would be more likely to use purge dieting. Let's find out. Our hypothesis is: *among 12th graders who view themselves as overweight, females will be more likely than males to "purge" diet.*

a. Cross-tabulate 37) VOMITDIET with 1) GENDER, focusing only on those who see themselves as overweight. Then, fill in the percentages that indicated they took laxatives or vomited in order to lose or maintain weight.

> | | |
> |---|---|
> | Data File: | **YRBS** |
> | Task: | **Cross-tabulation** |
> | ➤ Row Variable: | **37) VOMITDIET** |
> | ➤ Column Variable: | **1) GENDER** |
> | ➤ Subset Variable: | **36) DESCWEIGHT** |
> | ➤ Subset Category: | **Include: Over** |
> | ➤ View: | **Tables** |
> | ➤ Display: | **Column %** |

	FEMALE	MALE
YES	_____%	_____%

Now, examine the Cramer's V and the significance level for these two variables.

b. Is the relationship between GENDER and VOMITDIET statistically significant? (Circle one.)   Yes   No

c. Was the hypothesis supported? (Circle one.)   Yes   No

d. (If respondents of one gender were more likely to purge diet) how would you explain these gender differences in purge dieting among those who view themselves as being overweight?

10. Formulate a hypothesis about what might be associated with variations in depression or suicide (ideation or rates). (This should be one we have not considered so far.) Test this hypothesis using GSS or YRBS (cross-tabulation), or COUNTRIES or STATES (scatterplot). Look at the relationship between two appropriate variables in the data set that you choose to use. Present your results below, including whether or not the hypothesis was supported, citing the appropriate measure of association, direction, and statistical significance in doing so. If cross-tabulation is used, be sure to present the appropriate percentages in discussing your results.

◆ EXERCISE 8 ◆

POVERTY AND CLASS INEQUALITY

Tasks: Historical Trends, Cross-tabulation, Mapping, Scatterplot
Data Files: TRENDS, GSS, COUNTRIES

Y ou may recall an old rhyme that children sometimes chant to keep themselves in step as they jump rope: "Rich Man, Poor Man, Beggar Man, Thief, Doctor, Lawyer, Indian Chief." We become conscious of the distinctions of power, honor, and wealth in the people around us early in life. It isn't long before we learn that, in many ways, the rich "do better" than the poor. We find out that our family occupies a position within this class structure too, "higher" than some and "lower" than others. Its rank may have given us advantages, but also limitations. Eventually, we may discover that larger social entities, such as racial, ethnic, and religious groups, can also occupy slots in such hierarchies. Perhaps we are taught that certain types of people are just "not as good" as others. Some of us notice that things like power and wealth even rank nations. Individuals, families, social groups, and nations may all be **stratified**. That is, valued resources, such as wealth and power, may be distributed unequally among them.

Throughout this workbook, we have dealt with poverty and social class[1] at many levels. For example, we looked at the unequal distribution of resources by race, ethnicity, and gender. We also explored the degree to which crime, mental illness, female-headed households, and political orientations varied by income level. These types of analyses will continue in subsequent exercises, as we examine the ways that poverty and wealth are associated with differences in areas such as health, age, and domestic violence.

In this exercise, however, we will focus exclusively on the phenomena of poverty and class inequality, in the United States and internationally. Our first undertaking will be to examine distributions of poverty, wealth, and class inequality across time and place. We will also look at some important correlates of these variables that are not considered elsewhere in this workbook. Some of these may affect, or be influenced by, levels of income and unequal distribution of resources. Let's start with the United States.

You may recall that in Exercise 3, we looked at differences among states in per capita income, median family, income, and the percent that are poor. We saw, for example, that on average, Southern states are less affluent and have a higher percentage of poor people than other parts of the country, while states in the Far West and Northeast tend to be wealthier.

Now, let's look at distribution of poverty in America over time. To do so, we will look at trends in the percentages of families categorized as "in poverty" by the U.S. Census. The Census determines the maximum amount of before-tax income a family of a particular size may have and still be considered poor. This is adjusted yearly to account for inflation. Any family whose income is at or below that income level—called the **poverty threshold**— is classified as "poor."[2] For example, in 2002, the poverty threshold for a family of

---

[1] We defined "social classes" in Exercise 2.

[2] Census calculations of poverty thresholds do not take into account differences in the cost of living from place to place, nor do they treat non-cash government benefits (such as food stamps, public housing, or Medicaid) as income. See Joseph Dalaker and Bernadette D. Proctor, U.S. Census Bureau, Current Population Reports, Series P60-210, *Poverty in the United States, 1999*, U.S. Government Printing Office, Washington, D.C.; as cited on the U.S. Census Bureau website "How the Census Bureau Calculates Poverty."

two adults and two children was $18,244 while in 1981 it was $9,218.[3] This means of measuring poverty is not perfect, and there are other poverty estimates. However, the Census is fine for our present purposes.

➤ *Data File:* **TRENDS**
   ➤ *Task:* **Historical Trends**
➤ *Variable:* **117) %POOR**

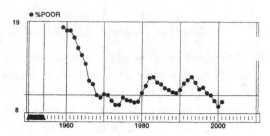

Percent of families (with and without children) that are below the official poverty level

Notice that the percentage of Americans who are poor declined significantly from 1959 (18.5%) through the mid-1970s. It rose from 1978 through 1983 (9.1% to 12.3%), and then fell until 1989 (10.3%) before rising again. The percentage of Americans who are poor declined from 1993 (12.3%) through 2000 (8.6%), but then rose slightly in 2001 (9.2%).

We have already seen that poverty is not distributed equally across different groups of people. For example, it is often said to disproportionately affect children.[4] Let's find out.

Data File: **TRENDS**
   Task: **Historical Trends**
➤ *Variable:* **117) %POOR**
        118) %POORCHLD

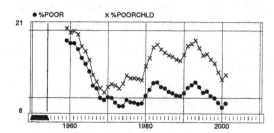

Percent of all families and percent of families with children under 18 that are below the official poverty level

As you can see, the percentage of families with children that are poor rises and falls at the same points as the overall poverty figures. However, each year, the percentages of households with kids that are poor are higher than the overall poverty rate. As you can see, this disparity became much greater after 1970.

In Exercise 2, we saw that African Americans and Hispanics are not generally as well off as whites. Let's look at whether or not this is reflected in official poverty percentages over time.

---

[3] Taken from 1981 and 2002 Current Population Survey, U.S. Census Bureau, as cited on the U.S. Census Bureau websites "Income and Poverty 1981 Thresholds" and "Income and Poverty 2002 Thresholds."

[4] Cf. Mooney et al., op cit., page 293.

Data File: **TRENDS**

Task: **Historical Trends**

➤ Variable: **119) %POORWH**

120) %POORBL

121) %POORHS

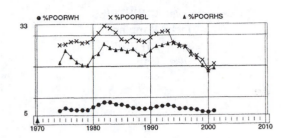

Percent of white (non-Hispanic) families, African American families,
and Hispanic families (with or without children under 18) that are
below the official poverty level

Generally, the percentages that are poor for these three groups follow the same pattern of change over time. However, figures for whites are much lower than those for Hispanics and African Americans. The latter two groups have been similar since 1993, when the percentage of African American poor began dropping sharply. In 2001, poverty percentages were 5.7%, 20.7%, and 19.4% for whites, African Americans, and Hispanics, respectively.

Finally, in the worksheets for Exercise 3 we saw that states with higher percentages of female-headed households with children also tended to have a greater proportion of poor people. Is this reflected in the official poverty rates for these households?

Data File: **TRENDS**

Task: **Historical Trends**

➤ Variable: **118) %POORCHLD**

122) %POORFH/CH

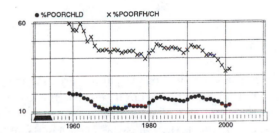

Percent of families and percent of female-headed (no husband present)
families with children with children under 18 that are below the official
poverty level

The percentage of female-headed households with children that are poor is consistently quite high—much greater than the percentage poor for households with children generally. In 2001, these figures were 33.6% and 13.4%, respectively.

We mentioned earlier that nations are also stratified. Let's turn to this now, starting by examining a variable we used briefly in the worksheets of the previous exercise—variations in gross domestic product (GDP) per capita, a measure of national wealth.

➤ *Data File:* **COUNTRIES**
➤ *Task:* **Mapping**
➤ *Variable 1:* **25) GDP/CAP**
➤ *View:* **Map**

GDP/CAP -- GROSS DOMESTIC PRODUCT PER CAPITA IN U.S. DOLLARS (TWF, 2001)

Notice the degree to which the poorer (lighter colored) nations are focused in Africa. Selecting the List: Rank view to look at the lowest ranked nations makes this fact even clearer.

Data File: **COUNTRIES**
Task: **Mapping**
Variable 1: **25) GDP/CAP**
➤ *View:* **List: Rank**

RANK	CASE NAME	VALUE
163	Eritrea	750
164	Burundi	730
165	Comoros	725
166	Rwanda	720
167	Cambodia	710
167	Congo, Dem. Republic	710
169	Somalia	600
170	Ethiopia	560
171	Tanzania	550
172	Sierra Leone	500

As you can see, the poorest nations are extremely deprived (with per capita GDP under $1,000) and disproportionately African. If you go to the top of this rank list, you will notice that the United States is the second richest nation by this measure ($33,900). Now, what about levels of *inequality*? One measure of this is the proportion of total national income received by the richest 10% of the population. Let's find out how this is distributed internationally. We will add it as a second map to the analysis of per capita GDP that we have been doing.

Data File: **COUNTRIES**
Task: **Mapping**
Variable 1: **25) GDP/CAP**
➤ *Variable 2:* **22) $ RICH 10%**
➤ *Views:* **Map**

GDP/CAP -- GROSS DOMESTIC PRODUCT PER CAPITA IN U.S. DOLLARS (TWF, 2001)

r = −0.503**

Investigating Social Problems

$ RICH 10% -- SHARE OF INCOME OR CONSUMPTION BY THE RICHEST 10% OF THE POPULATION (HDR, 2001)

Remember, just add Variable 2, 22) $ RICH 10%, in the appropriate slot, in the same way you added Variable 1. Don't clear or delete 25) GDP/CAP as Variable 1.

Many of the African nations are "missing" on $ RICH 10%. However, you will see that these two variables are strongly, negatively correlated (−0.503**). That is, among nations, as per capita GDP increases, the proportion of national income that is received by the richest 10% decreases. Looking at ranking on this last variable is also instructive.

Data File: **COUNTRIES**
Task: **Mapping**
Variable 1: **25) GDP/CAP**
Variable 2: **22) $ RICH 10%**
➤ *Views:* **List: Rank**

RANK	CASE NAME	VALUE
1	Luxembourg	34200
2	United States	33900
3	Singapore	27800
4	Switzerland	27100
5	Norway	25100

RANK	CASE NAME	VALUE
1	Swaziland	50.2
2	Nicaragua	48.8
3	Chile	46.9
3	Zimbabwe	46.9
5	Brazil	46.7

As you can see, in the highest ranked nation on this measure of inequality (Swaziland), fully 50.2% of all the national income is received by the richest 10% of the population. By contrast, in the lowest ranked nation (Slovak Republic), that figure is 18.2%. In the United States, the wealthiest 10% receive 30.5% of the total national income.

Social scientists have noted for years that moving from reliance on agriculture to becoming a more modern, industrialized country is strongly associated with both increased wealth and decreased inequality. If this is true, then as the percentage of GDP that is accounted for by agriculture *in*creases, per capita GDP should *de*crease, but the percentage of national income received by the richest 10% should *in*crease. Let's take a look.

Data File: **COUNTRIES**
➤ Task: **Scatterplot**
➤ Dependent Variable: **25) GDP/CAP**
➤ Independent Variable: **27) % AGRIC $**
➤ View: **Reg. Line**

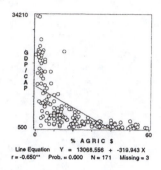

The first part of our prediction is strongly supported. The more a nation's economy depends on agriculture, the lower its per capita GDP (−0.650**). Now, let's look at the second part of our prediction.

Data File: **COUNTRIES**
Task: **Scatterplot**
➤ Dependent Variable: **22) $ RICH 10%**
➤ Independent Variable: **27) % AGRIC $**
➤ View: **Reg. Line**

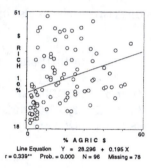

In fact, *both* predictions were supported. The greater the percentage of national income received by the richest 10%, the larger the percentage of GDP that is accounted for by agriculture (0.339**).

Among nations, ***industrialization*** (growth in the manufacturing and sale of goods) has historically been associated with increased prosperity. However, the most modern and wealthy countries today are ***post-industrial***. In these, the ***service sector*** (where services are provided, "including . . . producing, managing, and distributing services and information with the help of electronic technology, especially computers") is the largest portion of the economy.[5] Thus, as the percentage of the GDP that is accounted for by the service sector increases, the per capita GDP should also *increase*, while inequality should *decrease*. Let's see if this is true.

---

[5] Curran and Renzetti, op cit., pages 31–32.

Investigating Social Problems

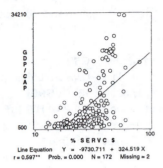

Data File: **COUNTRIES**
Task: **Scatterplot**
➤ Dependent Variable: **25) GDP/CAP**
➤ Independent Variable: **29) % SERVC $**
➤ View: **Reg. Line**

Supported on the first count! The larger the service sector, the higher the per capita GDP (0.597**).

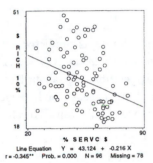

Data File: **COUNTRIES**
Task: **Scatterplot**
➤ Dependent Variable: **22) $ RICH 10%**
➤ Independent Variable: **29) % SERVC $**
➤ View: **Reg. Line**

The second count holds up too. When the percentage of GDP accounted for by the service sector increases, the percentage of income received by the richest 10% decreases (−0.345**).

In the worksheets, we'll look at some of the consequences of impoverishment among nations. For now, let's take a peek at one very important one—what the average person gets to eat! Our dependent variable is the number of calories available each day per person.

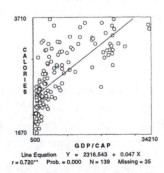

Data File: **COUNTRIES**
Task: **Scatterplot**
➤ Dependent Variable: **20) CALORIES**
➤ Independent Variable: **25) GDP/CAP**
➤ View: **Reg. Line**

Wow! This sad correlation is quite strong (0.720**). As countries get wealthier, the average person has access to a lot more food. Unfortunately, the opposite is true as well.

Well, it's time to return to the United States. Let's examine the extent to which the advantages of class are transferred from one generation to another. We'll start by analyzing the relationship of parents' occupational prestige levels to respondents' education. How are the children of parents with more prestigious (and generally, better-paid) jobs advantaged relative to others?

➤ *Data File:* **GSS**
➤ *Task:* **Cross-tabulation**
➤ *Row Variable:* **13) DEGREE**
➤ *Column Variable:* **22) PAR HIPRST**
➤ *View:* **Tables**
➤ *Display:* **Column %**

DEGREE   by   PAR HIPRST
Cramer's V: 0.223 **

		PAR HIPRST				
		Neither	One	Both	Missing	TOTAL
DEGREE	Not H.S.	205	26	8	600	239
		14.0%	3.5%	3.0%		9.7%
	H.S.	874	363	109	1640	1346
		59.9%	49.4%	40.4%		54.6%
	Jr. Col.	111	92	11	194	214
		7.6%	12.5%	4.1%		8.7%
	4 Yr Deg	181	184	84	429	449
		12.4%	25.0%	31.1%		18.2%
	Grad Deg	89	70	58	231	217
		6.1%	9.5%	21.5%		8.8%
	Missing	5	2	1	15	23
	TOTAL	1460	735	270	3109	2465
		100.0%	100.0%	100.0%		

This relationship is as predicted. Respondents whose parents had higher prestige jobs tended to be better educated themselves (V = 0.223**). For example, among respondents with two parents who had high-prestige occupations, about 53% had obtained a college degree (4-year or graduate), as had 34.5% of those with one parent who had such a job. But only 18.5% of respondents who had no parent with a high prestige job had obtained a college degree.

Now let's examine another aspect of the advantage of class. Let's see if there is a relationship between parents' occupational prestige levels and the respondent's income.

Data File: **GSS**
Task: **Cross-tabulation**
➤ *Row Variable:* **16) $FAMRANK**
➤ *Column Variable:* **22) PAR HIPRST**
➤ *View:* **Tables**
➤ *Display:* **Column %**

$FAMRANK   by   PAR HIPRST
Cramer's V: 0.109 **

		PAR HIPRST				
		Neither	One	Both	Missing	TOTAL
$FAMRANK	Below	315	99	40	752	454
		29.1%	18.6%	18.7%		24.8%
	Average	540	269	98	1093	907
		49.9%	50.5%	45.8%		49.6%
	Above	227	165	76	472	468
		21.0%	31.0%	35.5%		25.6%
	Missing	383	204	57	792	1436
	TOTAL	1082	533	214	3109	1829
		100.0%	100.0%	100.0%		

Again, as predicted. Respondents from families where the parents had higher prestige jobs also have higher family incomes (V = 0.109**). In fact, when both parents had higher prestige jobs, 35.5% of respondents had above average incomes as compared to 21% of those who came from families where neither parent had a high prestige job.

Now, let's briefly consider the consequences of poverty and inequality in a key area of American life—political participation. Drawing generally on the insights of conflict sociology, it makes sense to suspect that Americans of lower class will often feel they have not been treated equitably by society and that government is more responsive to the interests of the upper classes than to their own needs. Thus, activities such as voting may be seen as "making little difference." If true, then we would expect those in the upper classes would be more likely to vote than those in the lower classes. We can find out using the GSS, and we will start by seeing if there is a relationship between voting and family income rank.

Data File: **GSS**
Task: **Cross-tabulation**
➤ Row Variable: **45) VOTE96**
➤ Column Variable: **16) $FAMRANK**
➤ View: **Tables**
➤ Display: **Column %**

VOTE96 by $FAMRANK
Cramer's V: 0.140 **

		$FAMRANK				
		Below	Average	Above	Missing	TOTAL
VOTE96	Yes	665	1211	714	881	2590
		62.9%	68.8%	80.5%		69.9%
	No	392	549	173	342	1114
		37.1%	31.2%	19.5%		30.1%
	Missing	149	240	53	213	655
	TOTAL	1057	1760	887	1436	3704
		100.0%	100.0%	100.0%		

Self-identified family income rank is strongly associated with whether or not the respondent voted in the 1996 presidential election (V = 0.140**). About 37% of those with below average family income had *not* voted in that election, versus roughly 31% of those with average, and only 19.5% of those with above average family income. Let's see if self-identified class rank is also associated with likelihood to vote.

Data File: **GSS**
Task: **Cross-tabulation**
Row Variable: **45) VOTE96**
➤ Column Variable: **15) CLASS?**
➤ View: **Tables**
➤ Display: **Column %**

VOTE96 by CLASS?
Cramer's V: 0.190 **

		CLASS?					
		Lower	Working	Middle	Upper	Missing	TOTAL
VOTE96	Yes	142	1367	1795	148	19	3452
		55.3%	62.6%	78.8%	80.4%		70.4%
	No	115	816	484	36	5	1451
		44.7%	37.4%	21.2%	19.6%		29.6%
	Missing	52	328	247	18	10	655
	TOTAL	257	2183	2279	184	34	4903
		100.0%	100.0%	100.0%	100.0%		

Sure enough, class rank is also strongly associated with whether or not the respondent voted in the 1996 election (V = 0.190**). Of those who identified themselves as lower class, fully about 45% had *not* voted in the last presidential election. Corresponding percentages for working, middle, and upper class respondents were roughly 37%, 21%, and 20%, respectively. The disadvantaged in America are less involved in the political process.

Now it's time for you to continue these analyses on your own. You will continue to look at the correlates of poverty and class inequality in the United States and internationally, including what may be causes or consequences of both. Dig in!

REVIEW QUESTIONS

Based on the first part of this exercise, answer True or False to the following items:

Southern states tend to be poorer than other states.	T	F
The percentage of poor families in the United States has been rising since 1996.	T	F
In the United States, families with children are no more likely to be poor than are families without children.	T	F
African American and Hispanic families are much more likely to be poor than are white families.	T	F
Female-headed households with children are more likely to be poor than are households with children overall.	T	F
South American countries are more likely than African countries to be poor.	T	F
Countries that are wealthy tend to have more inequality in the distribution of wealth than countries that are poor.	T	F
The more a nation's economy consists of agriculture, the poorer and more unequal in distribution of wealth it tends to be.	T	F
The service sector makes up the largest percentage of the economies of post-industrial countries.	T	F
People whose parents had more prestigious jobs tend to be more educated and to have higher family incomes as adults than people whose parents did not have high prestige jobs.	T	F
In the United States, lower class people are just as likely to vote as others.	T	F

EXPLORIT QUESTIONS

1. Let's start by testing some hypotheses that have to do with possible disadvantages of living in poorer countries. We'll start with this one: *the wealthier nations are, the lower their rate of women who die during childbirth will tend to be.*

   a. Does this hypothesis predict a negative or a positive correlation? (Circle one.)   Negative

      Positive

   b. Open the COUNTRIES data set and look carefully at the variable description for 11) MOM MORTAL.

c. Construct a scatterplot that represents the association between 25) GDP/CAP and 11) MOM MORTAL.

> *Data File:* **COUNTRIES**
> *Task:* **Scatterplot**
> *Dependent Variable:* **11) MOM MORTAL**
> *Independent Variable:* **25) GDP/CAP**
> *View:* **Reg. Line**

d. Provide Pearson's *r* (including asterisks, if any, and the direction sign, if any).   *r* = _____

e. Is this correlation significant *and* negative, significant *and* positive,
   or *not* significant? (Circle one.)

                                       Significant *and* Negative

                                       Significant *and* Positive

                                       Not Significant

f. Is the hypothesis supported? (Circle one.)   Yes   No

g. Compared to wealthier nations, in poorer nations, women are _____
   likely to die during childbirth. (Circle one.)   More   Less

2. Now, for this hypothesis: *the wealthier nations are, the higher their literacy rate will tend to be.*

a. Carefully examine the variable description for 32) LITERACY.

b. Construct a scatterplot that represents the association between 25) GDP/CAP and 32) LITERACY.

> *Data File:* **COUNTRIES**
> *Task:* **Scatterplot**
> *Dependent Variable:* **32) LITERACY**
> *Independent Variable:* **25) GDP/CAP**
> *View:* **Reg. Line**

Examine Pearson's *r*.

c. Is this correlation significant *and* negative, significant *and* positive,
   or *not* significant? (Circle one.)

                                         Significant *and* Negative

                                         Significant *and* Positive

                                         Not Significant

d. Is this correlation weak, moderate, or strong? (Circle one.)

                                           Weak

                                        Moderate

                                          Strong

e. Is the hypothesis supported? (Circle one.)   Yes   No

f. Increasingly, being educated is associated with the ability to succeed in the modern world. What does the information that you see in this scatterplot tell you about the capacity of people in poorer, less developed nations to compete effectively for prosperity in the modern world?

3. Cirrhosis of the liver is a serious disease that is associated with things like alcohol abuse, nutritional deficits, and hepatitis. This hypothesis seems reasonable: *the wealthier nations are, the lower their rates of death from cirrhosis will tend to be.*

a. Carefully examine the variable description for 54) CIRRHOSIS.

b. Construct a scatterplot that represents the association between 25) GDP/CAP and 54) CIRRHOSIS.

> Data File: **COUNTRIES**
> Task: **Scatterplot**
> ➤ Dependent Variable: **54) CIRRHOSIS**
> ➤ Independent Variable: **25) GDP/CAP**
> ➤ View: **Reg. Line**

Examine Pearson's r.

c. Is this correlation significant *and* negative, significant *and* positive, or *not* significant? (Circle one.)

                                   Significant *and* Negative

                                   Significant *and* Positive

                                       Not Significant

d. Is the hypothesis supported? (Circle one.)

4. Much conflict theory would lead us to believe that in poor countries, many people would want to see radical social change, while where people are generally more prosperous, less people would support such change. To look into this question, we will use an item included in the World Values Survey, which was conducted in 43 nations that comprise about 70% of the world population. Summaries of the percentage in these countries that support radical social change are included in your COUNTRIES file. Here is our hypothesis: *the wealthier nations are, the lower the percentage that supports radical social change will be.*

    a. Carefully examine the variable description for 64) REVOLUTION.

    b. Construct a scatterplot that represents the association between 25) GDP/CAP and 64) REVOLUTION.

    > Data File: **COUNTRIES**
    > Task: **Scatterplot**
    > ➤ Dependent Variable: **64) REVOLUTION**
    > ➤ Independent Variable: **25) GDP/CAP**
    > ➤ View: **Reg. Line**

    Examine Pearson's *r*.

    c. Is this correlation significant *and* negative, significant *and* positive, or *not* significant? (Circle one.)

    Significant *and* Negative

    Significant *and* Positive

    Not Significant

    d. Is this correlation weak, moderate, or strong? (Circle one.)

    Weak

    Moderate

    Strong

    e. Is the hypothesis supported? (Circle one.)

    Yes   No

    f. What does this scatterplot suggest about the probable success of revolutionary political movements in prosperous versus poorer countries?

5. Let's consider inequality directly, focusing again on the proportion of the national income received by the richest 10%. It seems that where people have a lot of political freedom, they will use this to resist extreme inequality. Meanwhile, where a small portion of the population hold a greatly disproportionate share of the wealth, they may use their resources to prevent others from gaining political freedoms which might threaten their privileges. If so, this hypothesis may be supported: *the greater the proportion of nations' wealth that is received by the richest 10%, the lower the degree of individual political freedoms the people will have.*

    a. Carefully examine the variable description for 67) DEMOCRACY.

    b. Draw two maps, one showing national variation in the proportion of income received by the richest 10%, and the other showing variations in the extent of individual political freedom. When you have done so, look at Pearson's *r*.

Data File:	**COUNTRIES**
➤ *Task:*	**Mapping**
➤ *Variable 1:*	**67) DEMOCRACY**
➤ *Variable 2:*	**22) $ RICH 10%**
➤ *View:*	**Maps**

    Examine Pearson's *r*.

    c. Is this correlation significant *and* negative, significant *and* positive, or *not* significant? (Circle one.)

    Significant *and* Negative

    Significant *and* Positive

    Not Significant

    d. Is this correlation weak, moderate, or strong? (Circle one.)

    Weak

    Moderate

    Strong

    e. Is the hypothesis supported? (Circle one.)   Yes   No

    f. (Answer only if there was a significant relationship between these two variables.) Do you think that political freedom influences how much income inequality there is, or that the amount of income inequality affects the degree of political freedom that is allowed, or both? Explain your answer.

6. It seems that in nations where the degree of inequality is great, many people may distrust the political process for various reasons, including the perception that the government is controlled by the wealthy. If so, we would expect voter turnout to be affected. Let's test this hypothesis: *the greater the proportion of nations' wealth that is received by the richest 10%, the lower the voter turnout will tend to be.*

    a. Carefully examine the variable description for 66) %TURNOUT.

    b. Draw two maps, one showing national variation in the proportion of income received by the richest 10%, and the other showing variations in voter turnout. When you have done so, look at Pearson's *r*.

>   Data File: **COUNTRIES**
>   Task: **Mapping**
> ➤   Variable 1:   **66) %TURNOUT**
> ➤   Variable 2:   **22) $ RICH 10%**
> ➤   View: **Maps**

Examine Pearson's *r*.

    c. Is this correlation significant *and* negative, significant *and* positive, or *not* significant? (Circle one.)

                                                         Significant *and* Negative

                                                          Significant *and* Positive

                                                                  Not Significant

    d. Is the hypothesis supported? (Circle one.)   Yes   No

7. Time to return to the United States and to looking at individuals. We'll look again at the issue of the relative advantages of having parents who are better off in some way. Let's see how parental education is associated with obtaining a high prestige occupation. Our hypothesis is: *among those whose parents finished high school, those whose parents obtained four-year college degrees will be more likely to have obtained a high prestige job than those whose parents did not.*

    a. Open the GSS data set. Then, carefully examine the variable descriptions for 14) PAR DEGREE and 21) HIPRESTIGE.

    b. Cross-tabulate 21) HIPRESTIGE with 14) PAR DEGREE. Then, fill in the percentages that had a high prestige job.

> ➤   Data File: **GSS**
> ➤   Task: **Cross-tabulation**
> ➤   Row Variable: **21) HIPRESTIGE**
> ➤ Column Variable: **14) PAR DEGREE**
> ➤   View: **Tables**
> ➤   Display: **Column %**

	NEITHER	**ONE**	**BOTH**
YES	_____%	_____%	_____%

Now, get the Cramer's V and the significance level for these two variables.

c. Record the value of Cramer's V for this table. (Include asterisks, if any.)

V = _____

d. Is the relationship between PAR DEGREE and HIPRESTIGE statistically significant? (Circle one.)

Yes   No

e. Is the relationship between PAR DEGREE and HIPRESTIGE weak, moderate, strong, or not significant? (Circle one.)

Weak

Moderate

Strong

Not Significant

f. Was the hypothesis supported? (Circle one.)

Yes   No

8. Our hypothesis is: *among those whose parents finished high school, on average, those whose parents obtained four-year college degrees will have more education than those whose parents did not.*

a. Cross-tabulate 13) DEGREE with 14) PAR DEGREE. Then, fill in the designated percentages.

> Data File: **GSS**
> Task: **Cross-tabulation**
> ➤ Row Variable: **13) DEGREE**
> ➤ Column Variable: **14) PAR DEGREE**
> ➤ View: **Tables**
> ➤ Display: **Column %**

	NEITHER	**ONE**	**BOTH**
H.S.	_____%	_____%	_____%
4 YR DEG	_____%	_____%	_____%
GRAD DEG	_____%	_____%	_____%

Now, examine the Cramer's V and the significance level for these two variables.

b. Is the relationship between PAR DEGREE and DEGREE statistically significant? (Circle one.)

Yes   No

Exercise 8: Poverty and Class Inequality

c. Is the relationship between PAR DEGREE and DEGREE weak, moderate, or strong? (Circle one.)

Weak

Moderate

Strong

d. Was the hypothesis supported? (Circle one.)

Yes   No

e. Consider this last table, the table you created in question 7, and the analysis of the relationship of parental occupational prestige to children's income and educational attainments that we looked at earlier. Do you think that people in the United States inherit much class advantage or disadvantage? Why or why not?

9. In a well-known micro-sociological conflict theory, Randall Collins has asserted that people whose jobs require that they take more orders than they give will be more likely to be mistrustful.[6] Those who occupy lower and working class positions are more likely to have to take rather than give orders than middle or upper class persons. Our hypothesis is: *as social class rises, the percentage that says they generally trust others will also increase.*

a. Carefully examine the variable description for 52) MISTRUST.

b. Cross-tabulate 52) MISTRUST with 15) CLASS?. Then, fill in the percentages that say that most people can be trusted.

> Data File: **GSS**
> Task: **Cross-tabulation**
> ➤ Row Variable: **52) MISTRUST**
> ➤ Column Variable: **15) CLASS?**
> ➤ View: **Tables**
> ➤ Display: **Column %**

	LOWER	WORKING	MIDDLE	UPPER
CAN TRUST	_____%	_____%	_____%	_____%

---

[6] Randall Collins, 1975, *Conflict Sociology: Toward an Explanatory Science*, New York: Academic Press, page 74.

Now, examine the Cramer's V and the significance level for these two variables.

c. Is the relationship between CLASS? and MISTRUST statistically significant? (Circle one.)

Yes   No

d. Is the relationship between CLASS? and MISTRUST weak, moderate, strong, or not significant? (Circle one.)

Weak

Moderate

Strong

Not Significant

e. Was the hypothesis supported? (Circle one.)

Yes   No

10. Randall Collins has also asserted that those whose jobs require that they take rather than give orders will be more likely to be concerned with working as a means to some end (such as money), rather than because they find their work itself to be satisfying.[7] Keeping in mind that, like the last item, this is an imperfect test of Collins' proposition, let's test this hypothesis: *as social class falls, the percentage who would work even if they did not need to earn money will decrease.*

a. Carefully examine the variable description for 53) WORK IF $$.

b. Cross-tabulate 53) WORK IF $$ with 15) CLASS?. Then, fill in the percentages that indicated they would work even if they did not need the money.

> Data File: **GSS**
> Task: **Cross-tabulation**
> ➤ Row Variable: **53) WORK IF $$**
> ➤ Column Variable: **15) CLASS?**
> ➤ View: **Tables**
> ➤ Display: **Column %**

	LOWER	WORKING	MIDDLE	UPPER
WORK	_____%	_____%	_____%	_____%

Now, examine the Cramer's V and the significance level for these two variables.

c. Is the relationship between CLASS? and WORK IF $$ statistically significant? (Circle one.)

Yes   No

---

[7] Ibid.

d. Is the relationship between CLASS? and WORK IF $$ weak, moderate, or strong? (Circle one.)

Weak

Moderate

Strong

e. Was the hypothesis supported? (Circle one.)

Yes   No

RACIAL AND ETHNIC PREJUDICE AND DISCRIMINATION

Tasks: Historical Trends, Cross-tabulation, Univariate, Mapping, Scatterplot
Data Files: TRENDS, ELECTION, GSS, COUNTRIES

Problems associated with racial and ethnic conflict and inequality have been with the human race for millennia, and with the United States from its earliest years. It is probably fair to say that few if any societies have ever been entirely unacquainted with these phenomena. And while prejudice and discrimination are not the only factors that create or perpetuate disparities and tensions among people of different backgrounds and color in the United States and across the world, historically, they have certainly played a major role in these difficulties.

We have already dealt with race and ethnicity, as well as inequities and other variations related to them, to some extent in this workbook. In Exercise 2, we defined "races" and "ethnic groups." We have already seen that in the United States people of different racial and ethnic groups do not possess valued resources to the same extent. In comparing African Americans and whites, we saw differences in areas such as the chance of being executed, infant mortality, and political views. In later exercises we will look at other important areas of disparity and disagreement between people of different races and ethnicities. However, in this exercise, we will concentrate particularly on racial and ethnic prejudice and discrimination.

Both of these may take on "positive" forms (for example, showing unfair partiality toward certain types of people).[1] However, here, following Gordon Allport's classic discussion, we will deal only with unfavorable opinions toward, and treatment of, others. Drawing on his work, we will define ***racial and ethnic prejudice*** as dislike of a racial or ethnic group, or of individuals because they are members of this group, which is based upon "faulty and inflexible generalization."[2] Prejudice is closely tied to ***ethnocentrism***, in which the supposed virtues of one's own group are extolled while those of other groups are disparaged.[3] In ***racial and ethnic discrimination***, people deny equal treatment to others because they are members of a racial or ethnic group.[4] Note that while prejudice has to do with beliefs and attitudes, discrimination involves action.

Let's begin our exploration of this critical issue by examining the distribution of various types of prejudice, and support for discrimination, in the United States across time by looking at shifts in responses to certain GSS items. First, we'll see how the percentages of whites that believe housing discrimination should be allowed have changed over time.

---

[1] Cf. Gordon W Allport., 1958, *The Nature of Prejudice*, Garden City: Doubleday, page 7, on "positive" prejudice.

[2] Ibid., page 10.

[3] Richard D. Alba, op cit., page 844.

[4] Ibid.; Allport, op cit., pages 15, 50–51.

> *Data File:* **TRENDS**
> > *Task:* **Historical Trends**
> > *Variable:* **124) RACE SEG**

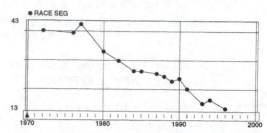

Percent of white GSS respondents who agreed "White people have a right to keep (Blacks/African Americans) out of their neighborhoods if they want to, and (Blacks/African Americans) should respect that right."

White support for this kind of overt residential segregation has fallen quite a bit since 1972. From about 42% in 1978, the percentages that believed whites "have a right to keep African Americans out of their neighborhoods" fell to roughly 13% in 1996. How about white support for this idea: "African Americans shouldn't push themselves where they're not wanted"?

> *Data File:* **TRENDS**
> > *Task:* **Historical Trends**
> > *Variable:* **123) RACE PUSH**

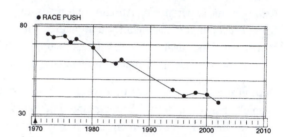

Percent of white GSS respondents who agreed that "(Blacks/African Americans) shouldn't push themselves where they're not wanted."

The proportion of whites supporting this statement has also dropped a great deal since 1972, from about 76% that year, to roughly 38% in 2002. It is interesting, however, that about 2 out of 5 whites continue to affirm this sentiment. Now, both of these last examples focused on support for racial *discrimination*. Let's look at a *prejudicial* belief, namely, that African Americans are disadvantaged because "Blacks have less in-born ability to learn."

> *Data File:* **TRENDS**
> > *Task:* **Historical Trends**
> > *Variable:* **126) RACE DIF**

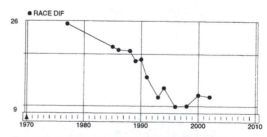

Percentage of white GSS respondents affirming that African Americans "have worse jobs, income, and housing than white people" because "Blacks have less in-born ability to learn."

Among whites, agreement with this prejudiced belief has dropped since the 1970s, though it has risen a bit in recent years. In 1977, about 26% affirmed this prejudicial belief, down to a low of roughly 10% in 1996 but back up to about 12% in 2000 and 2002.

Investigating Social Problems

Let's look now at differences among American racial and ethnic groups themselves in prejudice and support for discrimination. First, we'll analyze the extent to which African American and white respondents feel "warm," "neutral," or "cold" toward Hispanic or Asian people. To do so, open your ELECTION data set.

> *Data File:* **ELECTION**
> *Task:* **Cross-tabulation**
> *Row Variable:* **52) ASIA THERM**
> *Column Variable:* **8) RACE**
> *View:* **Tables**
> *Display:* **Column %**

ASIA THERM by RACE
Cramer's V: 0.017

		RACE			
		White	Black	Missing	TOTAL
ASIA THERM	COLD	37	6	5	43
		3.3%	4.1%		3.4%
	NEUTRAL	581	73	60	654
		51.6%	49.7%		51.4%
	WARM	507	68	80	575
		45.1%	46.3%		45.2%
	Missing	1359	213	99	1671
	TOTAL	1125	147	244	1272
		100.0%	100.0%		

There were no differences between whites and African Americans in these feelings toward Asians (V = 0.017). For example, the percentages in the "warm" range were about 45% and 46% for the two races, respectively.

Data File: **ELECTION**
Task: **Cross-tabulation**
> *Row Variable:* **53) HISP THERM**
> *Column Variable:* **8) RACE**
> *View:* **Tables**
> *Display:* **Column %**

HISP THERM by RACE
Cramer's V: 0.113 **

		RACE			
		White	Black	Missing	TOTAL
HISP THERM	COLD	52	9	5	61
		4.5%	6.0%		4.7%
	NEUTRAL	618	54	56	672
		53.9%	36.2%		51.9%
	WARM	476	86	82	562
		41.5%	57.7%		43.4%
	Missing	1338	211	101	1650
	TOTAL	1146	149	244	1295
		100.0%	100.0%		

These two groups did significantly differ in their feeling toward Hispanics (V = 0.113**). African Americans were much more likely to rate themselves in the "warm" range (about 58%), and less likely to be "cold" (roughly 6%), toward Hispanics than whites (whose percentages on these categories were approximately 41.5% and 4.5%, respectively). Let's take a peek at African American "thermometer" feelings about whites.

Data File: **ELECTION**
> *Task:* **Univariate**
> *Primary Variable:* **54) WH THERM**
> *Subset Variable:* **8) RACE**
> *Subset Category:* **Include: Black**
> *View:* **Pie**

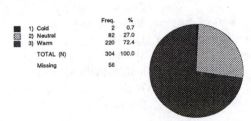

WH THERM -- Respondent's ratings of whites on a thermometer. Lower scores equal a negative feeling.

	Freq.	%
1) Cold	2	0.7
2) Neutral	82	27.0
3) Warm	220	72.4
TOTAL (N)	304	100.0
Missing	56	

[Subset]

Notice that about 72% of African American respondents placed themselves in the "warm" range toward whites, and less than 1% (2 people) were "cold." How did white respondents feel about African Americans?

Data File: **ELECTION**
Task: **Univariate**
➤ Primary Variable: **55) BL THERM**
➤ Subset Variable 1: **8) RACE**
➤ Subset Category 1: **Include: White**
➤ View: **Pie**

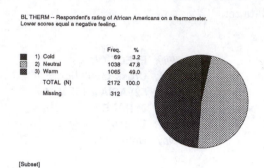

BL THERM -- Respondent's rating of African Americans on a thermometer.
Lower scores equal a negative feeling.

		Freq.	%
■	1) Cold	69	3.2
▨	2) Neutral	1038	47.8
▨	3) Warm	1065	49.0
	TOTAL (N)	2172	100.0
	Missing	312	

[Subset]

Whites were much less likely to rate themselves in the "warm" range toward African Americans than the latter had toward whites. Only 49% did so.

We might suspect that younger people are more "liberal minded" on racial and ethnic matters than older people. Let's find out if younger and older whites vary in what they say their reaction would be if a "close relative married a black person."

➤ Data File: **GSS**
➤ Task: **Cross-tabulation**
➤ Row Variable: **57) MARRY BLK**
➤ Column Variable: **1) AGE**
➤ Subset Variable: **3) RACE**
➤ Subset Category: **Include: White**
➤ View: **Tables**
➤ Display: **Column %**

MARRY BLK   by   AGE

Cramer's V: 0.234 **

		AGE					
		<30	30-49	50-64	65 and Up	Missing	TOTAL
MARRY BLK	Favor	171	266	89	64	4	590
		37.3%	25.7%	16.7%	13.5%		23.6%
	Neither	204	488	188	123	2	1003
		44.5%	47.1%	35.3%	25.9%		40.1%
	Oppose	83	282	255	287	4	907
		18.1%	27.2%	47.9%	60.5%		36.3%
	Missing	322	772	425	378	6	1903
	TOTAL	458	1036	532	474	16	2500
		100.0%	100.0%	100.0%	100.0%		

It does appear that the older white Americans are, the less likely they are to be comfortable with a close relative marrying someone who is African American (V = 0.234**). For example, 60.5% of those 65 and older would oppose such a marriage, compared to about 48% of the 50 to 64 group, 27% of those 30 to 49, and only 18% of the "under 30 crowd." How about the item we looked at earlier, namely, believing that African Americans are innately inferior?

Data File: **GSS**
Task: **Cross-tabulation**
➤ Row Variable: **65) RACE DIF**
➤ Column Variable: **1) AGE**
➤ Subset Variable: **3) RACE**
➤ Subset Category: **Include: White**
➤ View: **Tables**
➤ Display: **Column %**

RACE DIF   by   AGE

Cramer's V: 0.179 **

		AGE					
		<30	30-49	50-64	65 and Up	Missing	TOTAL
RACE DIF	Yes	26	76	61	89	0	252
		6.8%	8.7%	13.5%	23.5%		12.1%
	No	356	802	391	290	9	1839
		93.2%	91.3%	86.5%	76.5%		87.9%
	Missing	398	930	505	473	7	2313
	TOTAL	382	878	452	379	16	2091
		100.0%	100.0%	100.0%	100.0%		

Again, the older whites were, the more likely they were to give what most would regard as a racially prejudiced response (V = 0.179**). Of those 65 and older, 23.5% believed that African Americans were innately inferior, contrasted with 13.5% of those 50 to 64, about 9% of those between 30 and 49, and 7% of those less than 30. Happily, these age differences suggest that such beliefs are dying out among white Americans.

As I indicated early in this exercise, prejudicial attitudes toward those of other races and ethnic groups are hardly restricted to Americans. Now, we'll examine some international variations in prejudice. You may recall that in the worksheets of Exercise 8, we learned that something called the World Values Survey (WVS) has been administered in 43 countries comprising about 70% of the world's population. Summaries of percentages in these nations who indicated on the WVS that they would not like having certain types of people as neighbors are included in your COUNTRIES data set. Let's look at variations in the percentages of those who would prefer not living near someone of another race.

> *Data File:* **COUNTRIES**
> *Task:* **Mapping**
> *Variable 1:* **69) RACISM**
> *View:* **Map**

RACISM -- PERCENT WHO WOULD NOT WANT MEMBERS OF ANOTHER RACE AS NEIGHBORS (WVS)

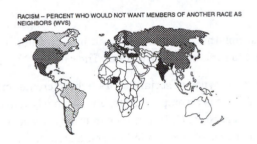

It appears that the nations with the greatest proportion of people expressing these prejudicial views are located heavily in Eastern Europe. Let's see.

Data File: **COUNTRIES**
Task: **Mapping**
Variable 1: **69) RACISM**
> *View:* **List: Rank**

RANK	CASE NAME	VALUE
1	South Korea	58
2	India	44
3	Slovenia	40
4	Bulgaria	39
5	Turkey	34
5	Nigeria	34
5	Slovak Republic	34
8	Czech Republic	28
8	Romania	28
10	Finland	25

Ranks appear to confirm that the nations of Eastern Europe grade high in this type of expressed prejudice, though South Korea and India have the highest percentage of those who would not want members of another race as neighbors (58% and 44%, respectively). At 10%, the United States has a rank of 24 out of 39 countries on this variable.

Do nations in which many people don't want to live near people of other races tend to also be places where many would not wish to have foreigners as neighbors? Let's see.

Data File: **COUNTRIES**
Task: **Mapping**
Variable 1: **69) RACISM**
➤ *Variable 2:* **68) ANTI-FORGN**
➤ *View:* **List: Rank**

RANK	CASE NAME	VALUE
1	South Korea	58
2	India	44
3	Slovenia	40
4	Bulgaria	39
5	Turkey	34

RANK	CASE NAME	VALUE
1	South Korea	53
2	India	48
3	Slovenia	40
4	Czech Republic	34
4	Bulgaria	34

It seems that nations that rank high in the percentages having one type of prejudicial attitudes also tend to rank high on the other. The *r* (0.899**) is powerful, significant and positive.

So, what types of social factors help to create and sustain racial and ethnic prejudice and discrimination? This is a complex issue, and obviously, a detailed look at this question is well beyond the scope of this workbook! However, we can briefly consider a few key factors that appear to be among the important causes of such prejudice and discrimination. Gordon Allport dealt with each of these in his classic work on *The Nature of Prejudice*.[5] These social factors are not mutually exclusive, but are interrelated.

One factor is *socialization*. You may recall that in Exercise 5, we pointed out that this includes the learning of one's cultures, including values and norms. The idea is that youngsters often learn from their elders to think of, and treat, people of particular racial and ethnic groups badly.[6] The other two factors are *inequality* (of things such as status, power, and material resources), and "*competition* over scarce resources," of groups that have come into contact with each other.[7] When people of different statuses interact, for example, the dominance of the one and submission of the other, with all the behaviors and attitudes that typically accompany this, is constantly reinforced. Moreover, when one group seems to pose a threat to resources valued by another group (as in situations such as competition over jobs, pay, and promotions), hostility between them tends to develop. One group may try to retain and/or exploit their advantages while the other attempts to "gain ground" against the resistance of the first.[8] Not a happy mix.

To consider the socialization issue, let's look at a related hypothesis advanced by Allport—that those parents who are stricter or more authoritarian are more likely to produce prejudiced children.[9] While we don't have the data to examine this directly, we can look at whether or not such parents are more

---

[5] Op cit.

[6] See Curran and Renzetti, op cit., pages 185–186; also Allport, op cit., pages 276–295.

[7] Ibid., pages 186–187. See also the discussion in Stark, op cit., pages 294–295, 300–306.

[8] Very succinctly explained in ibid., pages 300–301, and by Allport, op cit., pages 222–228.

[9] Op cit., pages 283–284.

Investigating Social Problems

prejudiced themselves (and thus more likely to pass on such beliefs and attitudes to their own children). We'll use the GSS to see if white parents who embrace spanking are more likely to believe that African Americans tend to be "lazy."

> ➤ Data File: **GSS**
> ➤ Task: **Cross-tabulation**
> ➤ Row Variable: **69) BLACK WORK**
> ➤ Column Variable: **73) SPANKING**
> ➤ Subset Variable: **3) RACE**
> ➤ Subset Category: **Include: White**
> ➤ View: **Tables**
> ➤ Display: **Column %**

BLACK WORK   by   SPANKING

Cramer's V: 0.125 **

		SPANKING			
		Agree	Disagree	Missing	TOTAL
BLACK WORK	Wrk. Hard	249	138	87	387
		16.6%	24.7%		18.8%
	Neutral	651	266	168	917
		43.5%	47.6%		44.6%
	Lazy	598	155	126	753
		39.9%	27.7%		36.6%
	Missing	59	25	1891	1975
	TOTAL	1498	559	2272	2057
		100.0%	100.0%		

About 40% of whites who agreed that children sometimes need a "hard spanking" claimed that African Americans tend to be lazy, while 28% of those who did not agree with spanking held this belief. The difference is significant (V = 0.125**). Are white children raised in (often stricter) religiously fundamentalist homes more likely to hold this belief? Let's see.

Data File: **GSS**
Task: **Cross-tabulation**
Row Variable: **69) BLACK WORK**
➤ Column Variable: **24) R.RUND@16**
➤ Subset Variable: **3) RACE**
➤ Subset Category: **Include: White**
➤ View: **Tables**
➤ Display: **Column %**

BLACK WORK   by   R.FUND@16

Cramer's V: 0.058 **

		R.FUND@16				
		Fundam.	Moderate	Liberal	Missing	TOTAL
BLACK WORK	Wrk. Hard	109	218	127	20	454
		16.6%	21.0%	19.5%		19.4%
	Neutral	273	460	311	41	1044
		41.6%	44.4%	47.8%		44.5%
	Lazy	275	359	213	32	847
		41.9%	34.6%	32.7%		36.1%
	Missing	517	838	530	90	1975
	TOTAL	657	1037	651	183	2345
		100.0%	100.0%	100.0%		

Whites raised in fundamentalist homes are significantly more likely to believe that African Americans tend to be "lazy" (V = 0.058**), though the association is rather weak. About 42% hold this belief, versus 35% of those from religiously moderate, and about 33% of those from liberal, homes. Note that about 36% of white GSS respondents overall held this belief.

Now, let's move on to considering the role of inequality and competition (especially the latter) as social factors that stimulate prejudice and discrimination. We'll consider whether or not whites who think that "a white person won't get a job or promotion while an equally or less qualified black person gets one instead" will be more likely to be prejudiced, or support discrimination, against African Americans.

Data File:	**GSS**
Task:	**Cross-tabulation**
Row Variable:	**69) BLACK WORK**
➤ Column Variable:	**66) REV.DISCRM**
➤ Subset Variable:	**3) RACE**
➤ Subset Category:	**Include: White**
➤ View:	**Tables**
➤ Display:	**Column %**

BLACK WORK by REV.DISCRM

Cramer's V: 0.092 **

	REV.DISCRM				
BLACK WORK		Vry Likely	Sm Likely	Not Likely	Missing	TOTAL
	Wrk. Hard	41	122	95	216	258
		14.3%	18.2%	23.9%		19.1%
	Neutral	106	306	169	504	581
		37.1%	45.7%	42.5%		42.9%
	Lazy	139	242	134	364	515
		48.6%	36.1%	33.7%		38.0%
	Missing	181	390	236	1168	1975
	TOTAL	286	670	398	2252	1354
		100.0%	100.0%	100.0%		

Among whites who believed it is "very likely" that whites will be disadvantaged in this way in job competition with African Americans, about 49% thought the latter tend to be "lazy," while among whites who believed it is "somewhat likely," roughly 36% held these beliefs. As for whites who were not concerned about such racial disadvantage, the percentage was 34%. These differences are significant (V = 0.092**), though not very strong. Let's look at this same issue using a different measure of prejudice, how respondents would feel about a close relative marrying a black person.

Data File:	**GSS**
Task:	**Cross-tabulation**
➤ Row Variable:	**57) MARRY BLK**
➤ Column Variable:	**66) REV.DISCRM**
➤ Subset Variable:	**3) RACE**
➤ Subset Category:	**Include: White**
➤ View:	**Tables**
➤ Display:	**Column %**

MARRY BLK by REV.DISCRM

Cramer's V: 0.121 **

	REV.DISCRM				
MARRY BLK		Vry Likely	Sm Likely	Not Likely	Missing	TOTAL
	Favor	61	170	104	259	335
		20.6%	24.9%	25.2%		24.0%
	Neither	83	283	187	452	553
		28.0%	41.4%	45.3%		39.7%
	Oppose	152	231	122	406	505
		51.4%	33.8%	29.5%		36.3%
	Missing	171	376	221	1135	1903
	TOTAL	296	684	413	2252	1393
		100.0%	100.0%	100.0%		

The results here are very similar. Among whites who believe reverse discrimination is "very likely," 51.4% would be opposed to a close relative marrying an African American, while 33.8% of those who believe reverse discrimination is "somewhat likely" and 29.5% of those who thought it was "not likely" held the same opposition. Again, these differences are significant (V = 0.121**), but not strong.

The idea that competition between racial or ethnic groups over valued resources that are seen as scarce stimulates prejudice and discrimination suggests that more "economic growth and development" will be associated with less racial and ethnic prejudice.[10] Let's return to the COUNTRIES data set and WVS prejudice items to look into this.

---

[10] Curran and Renzetti, op cit., page 187. As the latter point out, this is true if the growing wealth is more widely enjoyed than restricted to dominant groups. As we saw in the previous exercise, this is nowhere close to perfect, but it seems to be true more often in developed than in less developed nations.

Investigating Social Problems

> *Data File:* **COUNTRIES**
> *Task:* **Scatterplot**
> *Dependent Variable:* **69) RACISM**
> *Independent Variable:* **25) GDP/CAP**
> *View:* **Reg. Line**

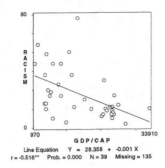

Line Equation   Y = 28.358 + -0.001 X
r = -0.516**   Prob. = 0.000   N = 39   Missing = 135

The scatterplot supports this idea. As GDP per capita increases, the percentage that would be unwilling to live near someone of another race decreases ($r = -0.516$**). Let's also examine this idea by looking at the percentage that would be willing to live next to someone from another country.

Data File: **COUNTRIES**
Task: **Scatterplot**
> *Dependent Variable:* **68) ANTI-FORGN**
> *Independent Variable:* **25) GDP/CAP**
> *View:* **Reg. Line**

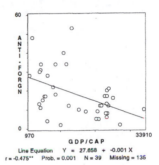

Line Equation   Y = 27.658 + -0.001 X
r = -0.475**   Prob. = 0.001   N = 39   Missing = 135

Although this relationship is not quite as strong as the RACISM variable ($r = -0.475$**), this idea is still upheld. An increase in GDP per capita is related to a decrease in the percentage that would be unwilling to have a neighbor from another country.

Obviously, we have only begun to scratch the surface regarding the distribution of, and explanations for, racial and ethnic prejudice and discrimination. Why don't you explore this a bit more on your own? Your turn!

REVIEW QUESTIONS

Based on the first part of this exercise, answer True or False to the following items:

Racial and ethnic prejudice, as we chose to define it here, always involves unfavorable opinions about other groups.   T   F

The GSS indicates that among white Americans, overt racial and ethnic prejudice has decreased considerably since the 1970s.   T   F

In the 2000/2002 GSS, about 2 out of 5 whites agreed that African Americans "shouldn't push themselves where they're not wanted."   T   F

The percentage of whites who rated themselves as "warm" toward African Americans was greater than the percentage of African Americans who rated themselves as "warm" toward whites.   T   F

The GSS items we looked at showed that among whites, racial prejudice increased as age increased.   T   F

Eastern European countries tend to rank high in the percentage of WVS respondents in them who would not want foreigners or those of another race as neighbors.   T   F

Social scientists agree that while prejudice leads to racial inequality, racial inequality cannot lead to prejudice.   T   F

Socialization and inter-group competition over scarce resources are both often cited as social factors that tend to increase racial and ethnic prejudice and discrimination.   T   F

The GSS data we examined suggests that people raised in religiously fundamentalist homes tend to be more likely than others to believe that African Americans tend to be "lazy."   T   F

Based on WVS data, people in wealthier nations appear to be less likely to be willing to have someone who is a foreigner or of another race as a neighbor than people in poorer countries.   T   F

EXPLORIT QUESTIONS

1. Let's compare the views of whites and African Americans on having a close relative marry someone of the other of these two races.

    a. Open the GSS data set.

b. Look at the percentages of whites who would oppose having a close relative marry an African American. Then, fill in that percentage below.

> *Data File:* **GSS**
> *Task:* **Univariate**
> *Primary Variable:* **57) MARRY BLK**
> *Subset Variable:* **3) RACE**
> *Subset Category:* **Include: White**
> *View:* **Pie**

OPPOSE: _____%

c. Now, look at the percentages of African Americans who would oppose having a close relative marry a white. Then, fill in that percentage below.

> **Remember that, after using the [↺] button to return to the variable selection screen, you must click the "Clear All" button before proceeding with this next pie chart. This will enable you to re-enter the Subset Variable, 3) RACE, and change the Subset Category to "Include: Black."**

> *Data File:* **GSS**
> *Task:* **Univariate**
> *Primary Variable:* **60) MARRY WHT**
> *Subset Variable:* **3) RACE**
> *Subset Category:* **Include: Black**
> *View:* **Pie**

OPPOSE: _____%

d. Fill in the blanks: _____% of whites said they would be opposed to a   _____%
close relative marrying an African American, while _____% of African
Americans said they would be opposed to a close relative marrying a white.   _____%

e. Are whites and African Americans very different in their view on this matter? If so, what do you think are the reasons for this difference in African American and white views on this matter?

2. Now, let's compare the views of whites and African Americans on whether or not people in the other of these two races tend to be "hardworking" or "lazy." We will remain in the GSS.

    a. Look at the percentages of whites who indicated African Americans were either hardworking or lazy. Then, fill in the percentage for each category below.

    > Data File: **GSS**
    > Task: **Univariate**
    > ➤ Primary Variable: **69) BLACK WORK**
    > ➤ Subset Variable: **3) RACE**
    > ➤ Subset Category: **Include: White**
    > ➤ View: **Pie**

    WRK HARD: _____%

    LAZY: _____%

    b. Now, look at the percentages of African Americans that indicated whites were either hardworking or lazy. Then, fill in the percentage for each category below.

    > Data File: **GSS**
    > Task: **Univariate**
    > ➤ Primary Variable: **67) WHITE WORK**
    > ➤ Subset Variable: **3) RACE**
    > ➤ Subset Category: **Include: Black**
    > ➤ View: **Pie**

    WRK HARD: _____%

    LAZY: _____%

    c. Fill in the blanks: _____% of whites said that African Americans tend   _____%
        to be lazy, while _____% of African Americans said that whites tend to
        be lazy.   _____%

    d. Are whites and African Americans very different in their view on this matter? If so, what do you think are the reasons for this difference in African American and white views on this matter?

3. One area of controversy in race relations these days is whether policies of preferences in hiring to alleviate the effects of past discrimination are justified or wrong. Let's see if and how African Americans and whites differ on this matter. We'll use the ELECTIONS data set to do so.

    a. Open the ELECTION data set and carefully examine the variable description for 49) AFFIRM.ACT.

    b. Cross-tabulate 8) RACE with 49) AFFIRM.ACT. Then, fill in the percentages supporting preferential hiring and promotion of African Americans

> Data File: **ELECTION**
> Task: **Cross-tabulation**
> Row Variable: **49) AFFIRM.ACT**
> Column Variable: **8) RACE**
> View: **Tables**
> Display: **Column %**

	WHITE	BLACK
FOR	_____%	_____%

Now, get the Cramer's V and the significance level for these two variables.

    d. Record the value of Cramer's V for this table. (Include asterisks, if any.)   V = _____

    e. Is the relationship between AFFIRM.ACT and RACE statistically significant? (Circle one.)   Yes   No

    f. Is the relationship between AFFIRM.ACT and RACE weak, moderate, strong, or not significant? (Circle one.)

                                                                            Weak

                                                                         Moderate

                                                                          Strong

                                                                     Not Significant

    g. Fill in the blanks: _____% of whites supported affirmative action (as it   _____%
        was described in this item), while _____% of African Americans did so.
                                                                                            _____%

4. Now let's compare the views of non-Hispanic whites and Hispanics on affirmative action (again, as it is described in this NES item). We're still in ELECTION.

    a. Cross-tabulate 49) AFFIRM.ACT with 9) HISPANIC. Then, fill in the percentages supporting preferential hiring and promotion of African Americans.

Data File: **ELECTION**
Task: **Cross-tabulation**
Row Variable: **49) AFFIRM.ACT**
➤ Column Variable: **9) HISPANIC**
➤ View: **Tables**
➤ Display: **Column %**

	YES	**NO**
FOR	_____%	_____%

Now, examine the Cramer's V and the significance level for these two variables.

b. Is the relationship between AFFIRM.ACT and HISPANIC statistically
    significant? (Circle one.)   Yes   No

c. Is the relationship between AFFIRM.ACT and HISPANIC weak,
    moderate, strong, or not significant? (Circle one.)   Weak

                                                                                    Moderate

                                                                                      Strong

                                                                               Not Significant

d. Fill in the blanks: _____% of Hispanics supported affirmative action (as   _____%
    it was described in this item), while _____% of non-Hispanic whites did
    so.   _____%

e. Are Hispanics and non-Hispanic whites very different in their view on this matter? If so, what do
    you think are the reasons for this difference in Hispanic and non-Hispanic white views on this
    matter?

5. I don't know about you, but I found the idea that stricter parents may be more likely to be prejudiced, and thus perhaps more likely to pass on such attitudes and beliefs to their children, kind of interesting. Let's revisit this. Our hypothesis: *non-Hispanic people who agree that it is sometimes necessary to discipline a child with a spanking will be more likely than other non-Hispanic people to oppose living in a neighborhood with many Hispanics.*

   a. Open the GSS data set and carefully examine the variable description for 62) LIVE HISP.

   b. Cross-tabulate 62) LIVE HISP with 73) SPANKING, while excluding Hispanics. Then, fill in the percentages opposed to living in a heavily Hispanic neighborhood.

> ➤ *Data File:* **GSS**
> ➤ *Task:* **Cross-tabulation**
> ➤ *Row Variable:* **62) LIVE HISP**
> ➤ *Column Variable:* **73) SPANKING**
> ➤ *Subset Variable:* **4) HISPANIC**
> ➤ *Subset Category:* **Include: No**
> ➤ *View:* **Tables**
> ➤ *Display:* **Column %**

	AGREE	DISAGREE
OPPOSE	_____%	_____%

Now, examine the Cramer's V and the significance level for these two variables.

   c. Is the relationship between LIVE HISP and SPANKING statistically significant? (Circle one.)   Yes   No

   d. Is the relationship between LIVE HISP and SPANKING weak, moderate, strong, or not significant? (Circle one.)

                                                          Weak

                                                      Moderate

                                                      Strong

                                             Not Significant

   e. Is the hypothesis supported? (Circle one.)   Yes   No

6. Next hypothesis: *whites who agree that it is sometimes necessary to discipline a child with a spanking will be more likely than others to oppose living in a neighborhood with many African Americans. We're still using the GSS.*

    a. Cross-tabulate 61) LIVE BLACK with 73) SPANKING, while excluding African Americans. Then, fill in the percentages opposed to living in a heavily African American neighborhood.

Data File:	**GSS**
Task:	**Cross-tabulation**
➤ *Row Variable:*	**61) LIVE BLACK**
➤ *Column Variable:*	**73) SPANKING**
➤ *Subset Variable:*	**3) RACE**
➤ *Subset Category:*	**Include: White**
➤ *View:*	**Tables**
➤ *Display:*	**Column %**

	AGREE	**DISAGREE**
OPPOSE	_____%	_____%

    Now, examine the Cramer's V and the significance level for these two variables.

    b. Is the relationship between LIVE BLACK and SPANKING statistically significant? (Circle one.)   Yes   No

    c. Is the relationship between LIVE BLACK and SPANKING weak, moderate, strong, or not significant? (Circle one.)

        Weak

        Moderate

        Strong

        Not Significant

    d. Is the hypothesis supported? (Circle one.)   Yes   No

7. The idea that competition might stimulate racial and ethnic prejudice suggests that the most vulnerable workers may feel most threatened by competition from other racial or ethnic groups, and thus be most prone to prejudice. This would suggest that those with less income might be most prejudiced (though this may depend on various other historical and economic circumstances). Let's see if this is true with regard to some recent GSS items. Since many recent immigrants to the country (and thus potential new competitors) are Asian, we will look at anti-Asian prejudice. Our hypothesis: *the lower the family income rank, the more respondents will say they would oppose living in a neighborhood with many Asians.*

    a. Cross-tabulate 63) LIVE ASIAN with 16) $FAMRANK. Then, fill in the percentages opposed to living in a heavily Asian neighborhood.

Exercise 9: Racial and Ethnic Prejudice and Discrimination   171

Data File: **GSS**
Task: **Cross-tabulation**
➤ Row Variable: **63) LIVE ASIAN**
➤ Column Variable: **16) $FAMRANK**
➤ Subset Variable: **3) RACE**
➤ Subset Category: **Include: White, Black**
➤ View: **Tables**
➤ Display: **Column %**

(By including "White" and "Black" on Race, this excludes those "missing" on the Race item, thus excluding all Asian American respondents.)

	BELOW	AVERAGE	ABOVE
OPPOSE	_____%	_____%	_____%

Now, examine the Cramer's V and the significance level for these two variables.

b. Is the relationship between LIVE ASIAN and $FAMRANK statistically significant? (Circle one.)

Yes   No

c. Is the relationship between LIVE ASIAN and $FAMRANK weak, moderate, strong, or not significant? (Circle one.)

Weak

Moderate

Strong

Not Significant

d. Is the hypothesis supported? (Circle one.)

Yes   No

e. Do these results surprise you? Why or why not?

8. Both socialization and "competition over scarce resources/economic threat" arguments could be made to suggest that the more educated people are, the less racially or ethnically prejudiced or supportive of discrimination they should be. Our hypothesis: *among whites, the more educated they are, the less likely they are to say they would oppose a close relative marrying an African American.*

a. Cross-tabulate 57) MARRY BLACK with 13) DEGREE. Then, fill in the percentages of whites who would oppose a close relative marrying an African American.

> Data File: **GSS**
> Task: **Cross-tabulation**
> ➤ Row Variable: **57) MARRY BLACK**
> ➤ Column Variable: **13) DEGREE**
> ➤ Subset Variable: **3) RACE**
> ➤ Subset Category: **Include: White**
> ➤ View: **Tables**
> ➤ Display: **Column %**

	NOT H.S.	H.S.	JR. COL	4 YR DEG	GRAD DEG
OPPOSE	_____%	_____%	_____%	_____%	_____%

Now, examine the Cramer's V and the significance level for these two variables.

b. Is the relationship between MARRY BLACK and DEGREE statistically significant? (Circle one.)   Yes   No

c. Is the relationship between MARRY BLACK and DEGREE weak, moderate, strong, or not significant? (Circle one.)

                                                                     Weak

                                                                     Moderate

                                                                     Strong

                                                                     Not Significant

d. Is the hypothesis supported? (Circle one.)   Yes   No

e. What do you think are the reasons for this particular relationship (or lack of relationship, as the case may be) among whites between level of education and reaction to a close relative marrying an African American?

9. We'll finish by continuing to look at the idea that prejudice decreases as economic wealth and development increases. You may recall from Exercise 8 that the most developed nations tend to also have a large proportion of the economy in the service sector. Let's explore this hypothesis: *among nations, as the percentage of the GDP accounted for by the service sector increases, the percentage that would not want a neighbor of another race will decrease.*

    a. Open the COUNTRIES data set.

    b. Construct a scatterplot that represents the association between 29) % SERVC $ and 69) RACISM.

> ➤ *Data File:* **COUNTRIES**
> ➤ *Task:* **Scatterplot**
> ➤ *Dependent Variable:* **69) RACISM**
> ➤ *Independent Variable:* **29) % SERVC $**
> ➤ *View:* **Reg. Line**

    c. Provide Pearson's *r* (including asterisks, if any, and the direction sign, if any).   *r* = _____

    d. Is this correlation significant *and* negative, significant *and* positive, or *not* significant? (Circle one.)

        Significant *and* Negative

        Significant *and* Positive

        Not Significant

    e. Is this correlation weak, moderate, or strong? (Circle one.)

        Weak

        Moderate

        Strong

    f. Is the hypothesis supported? (Circle one.)   Yes   No

10. Anti-Muslim prejudice is not only a religious, but also an ethnic, prejudice. Among nations, does it also decrease with economic development? Let's explore this hypothesis: *among nations, as the GDP per capita underlineincreases, the percentage that would not want a Muslim neighbor will decrease.*

    a. Construct a scatterplot that represents the association between 25) GDP/CAP and 71) ANTI-MUSLM.

> *Data File:* **COUNTRIES**
> *Task:* **Scatterplot**
> ➤ *Dependent Variable:* **71) ANTI-MUSLIM**
> ➤ *Independent Variable:* **25) GDP/CAP**
> ➤ *View:* **Reg. Line**

Examine Pearson's *r*.

b. Is this correlation significant *and* negative, significant *and* positive,
    or *not* significant? (Circle one.)

Significant *and* Negative

Significant *and* Positive

Not Significant

c. Is this correlation weak, moderate, or strong? (Circle one.)

Weak

Moderate

Strong

d. Is the hypothesis supported? (Circle one.)

Yes   No

GENDER INEQUALITY

Tasks: Cross-tabulation, Historical Trends, Mapping, Scatterplot
Data Files: GSS, ELECTION, TRENDS, COUNTRIES

In previous exercises, we have looked carefully at the issue of social inequality, particularly examining variations in the degree to which people possess wealth, prestige, or power. We have seen that many things are correlated with such disparities, including factors that may be causes or consequences of them. It has been obvious that with regard to social class[1] and the things associated with it, some groups are disadvantaged relative to others (such as African Americans and Hispanics versus non-Hispanic whites). We have also already seen some evidence of **gender[2] inequality**. That is, on average, the **socioeconomic status** (or **SES**, meaning social class level) of women is lower than that of men.

In the previous exercise we saw that two of the reasons for racial and ethnic inequality are *prejudice* and *discrimination*.[3] This is also true for gender inequality. Women are often the target of attitudes or beliefs characterized by negative "faulty and inflexible generalizations."[4] And they are also frequently subjected to "unequal treatment" simply because they are female.[5]

The term **sexism** frequently comes up in discussions of prejudice and discrimination against women, and of gender inequality generally. While definitions of *sexism* vary, a simple one that appears to capture its basic meaning is this: the domination of females by males, justified by the belief that males are inherently superior to females.[6]

In this exercise, we will look at variations across time, place, and group in gender inequality, attitudes toward women, and the social roles and identities that are considered appropriate for males and females.[7] This will include some consideration of possible causes and effects of these variations. Let's start by examining female participation in the labor force. First, we'll look at a trend chart that compares single and married women.

---

[1] You may recall we defined "social class" in Exercise 2.

[2] We also defined "gender" in Exercise 2.

[3] Both of these terms are defined, relative to race and ethnicity, in Exercise 9.

[4] Allport, op cit., page 10; as cited in Exercise 9. This is "prejudice."

[5] Alba, op cit., page 844; Allport, op cit., pages 15, 50–51; both cited in Exercise 9. This is "discrimination."

[6] Here, I have particularly combined Kendall, op cit., page 64, and Sullivan, op cit., page 224. To get an idea of the range of definitions of "sexism," compare both of the latter with other "social problems" sources such as Kornblum and Julian, op cit., page 298; Mooney et al., op cit., page 221; Palen, op cit., page 122; and Curran and Renzetti, op cit., page 193, to name a few.

[7] Again, see the definition of "gender" in Exercise 2.

> ➤ *Data File:* **TRENDS**
> ➤ *Task:* **Historical Trends**
> ➤ *Variable:* **130) F.LAB. SING**
>   **131) F.LAB. MAR**

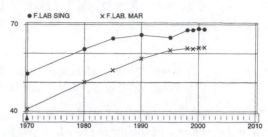

Percent of single women in labor force age 16 and over and percent of married women in labor force

As you can see, female participation in the labor force has increased dramatically since 1970. While the involvement of single females in paid work has remained greater than that of married women, this gap appears to have narrowed considerably in recent years. Since 1981, most married females have been in the labor force. In 2001, the percentage of single versus married women who were employed was about 68% versus 62%, respectively.

However, notice that here, "single women" included females 16 and up. Younger women are more likely to be single and less likely to be working! If only older women were included, the percentage of single women who are working would be larger, and there would be a bigger gap between the employment of single and married females. Second, not all of these women who were in the labor force were employed full-time. Finally, we could not distinguish women who were divorced or separated. Let's use the GSS to get a clearer idea of the relative degree of *full-time* employment for adult women of different marital statuses (not including widows).

> ➤ *Data File:* **GSS**
> ➤ *Task:* **Cross-tabulation**
> ➤ *Row Variable:* **18) FULL TIME?**
> ➤ *Column Variable:* **8) MARITAL**
> ➤ *Subset Variable:* **2) GENDER**
> ➤ *Subset Category:* **Include: Female**
> ➤ *Subset Variable:* **8) MARITAL**
> ➤ *Subset Category:* **Exclude: Widowed**
> ➤ *View:* **Tables**
> ➤ *Display:* **Column %**

FULL TIME?   by   MARITAL

Cramer's V: 0.123 **

		MARITAL			
		Married	Div/Sep	Nev Mar	TOTAL
FULL TIME?	Yes	587	381	383	1351
		43.8%	58.0%	53.6%	49.8%
	No	753	276	331	1360
		56.2%	42.0%	46.4%	50.2%
	TOTAL	1340	657	714	2711
		100.0%	100.0%	100.0%	

You may recall that you can use more than one Subset Variable. After selecting your Row and Column Variables, choose 2) GENDER as your first Subset Variable, and when the "Subset By Categories" box comes up, select "Female" as your subset category. Leave the [Include] option selected, and then click [OK]. Before proceeding with the table, choose 8) MARITAL as your second Subset variable, and when the "Subset By Categories" box comes up, select "Widowed" as your subset category. This time, be sure the check the [Exclude] option-not [Include]! Then, click [OK], and click [OK] again when the Cross-tabulation box reappears. Now, your table includes only females who are not widows.

Among 2000/2002 non-widowed female GSS respondents, about 44% of those who were married were employed full-time, compared to 58% of divorced or separated women and roughly 54% of never-married women. The differences in full-time employment for women of different marital statuses were statistically significant (V = 0.123**).

To really directly deal with gender inequality, of course, we need to compare males and females. How do men and women differ in full-time employment?

Data File: **GSS**
Task: **Cross-tabulation**
Row Variable: **18) FULL TIME?**
➤ Column Variable: **2) GENDER**
➤ View: **Tables**
➤ Display: **Column %**

FULL TIME?   by   GENDER
Cramer's V: 0.187 **

		GENDER		
		Male	Female	TOTAL
FULL TIME?	Yes	1560	1396	2956
		63.5%	44.7%	53.0%
	No	897	1729	2626
		36.5%	55.3%	47.0%
	TOTAL	2457	3125	5582
		100.0%	100.0%	

We can see that males are much more likely than females to work full-time (63.5% versus about 45%; V = 0.187**). However, more critical to the question of gender inequality is the issue of whether or not, and to what extent, the *income* or occupational *prestige* of men and women who *are* working full-time is different. Using GSS, we saw in Exercise 2 that indeed, among those who work full-time, on average women make less money than men. But we also learned that women are a little more likely to hold high prestige jobs! Could it be that women who have high prestige occupations make less money than men who have such prestigious jobs? Let's see. Of course, we will only compare those who are working full-time.

Data File: **GSS**
Task: **Cross-tabulation**
➤ Row Variable: **17) OWN INCOME**
➤ Column Variable: **2) GENDER**
➤ Subset Variable: **18) FULL TIME?**
➤ Subset Category: **Include: Yes**
➤ Subset Variable: **21) HIPRESTIGE**
➤ Subset Category: **Include: Yes**
➤ View: **Tables**
➤ Display: **Column %**

OWN INCOME   by   GENDER

Cramer's V: 0.137 **

		GENDER		
		Male	Female	TOTAL
OWN INCOME	0-14.9	19	19	38
		6.7%	6.3%	6.5%
	15-24.9	14	39	53
		4.9%	12.8%	9.0%
	25+	250	246	496
		88.3%	80.9%	84.5%
	Missing	41	40	81
	TOTAL	283	304	587
		100.0%	100.0%	

Among those with high prestige jobs, women were *more* likely to make *less* than $25,000 (some simple addition shows their percentage at about 19%, versus roughly 12% of men). And they are *less* likely to make $25,000 or more (approximately 81%, versus 88% for men). These differences are significant (V = 0.137**). What about those with lower prestige jobs?

			Data File:	GSS
			Task:	Cross-tabulation
			Row Variable:	17) OWN INCOME
			Column Variable:	2) GENDER
			Subset Variable:	18) FULL TIME?
			Subset Category:	Include: Yes
	➤	Subset Variable:	20) PRESTIGE
	➤	Subset Category:	Include: Lower Half
		➤	View:	Tables
		➤	Display:	Column %

OWN INCOME   by   GENDER

Cramer's V: 0.301 **

| | | GENDER | | |
		Male	Female	TOTAL
OWN INCOME	0-14.9	92	171	263
		14.4%	32.8%	22.7%
	15-24.9	159	187	346
		25.0%	35.8%	29.9%
	25+	386	164	550
		60.6%	31.4%	47.5%
	Missing	83	79	162
	TOTAL	637	522	1159
		100.0%	100.0%	

After using the [[↻]] button to return to the variable selection screen, do not click "Clear All." Just use your mouse to click on the Subset Variable 21) HIPRESTIGE. Then, hit the "Delete" button on your keyboard. Now, add 20) PRESTIGE as your second Subset Variable. When the "Subset By Categories" box comes up, select "Lower Half" as your subset category, and keep the [Include] option. Then click [OK] and continue. Your table will now only include those working full-time with job prestige in the lower half.

Gender income disparity is *much* greater for full-time workers with lower job prestige (V = 0.301**). Among these respondents, women were much *more* likely to have incomes *below* $25,000 (addition shows this to be roughly 69%, versus 39% for men). And again, they are much *less* likely to make $25,000 or more (approximately 31%, versus 61% for men).

Perhaps women make less money because they are, on average, less educated than men. First, we'll compare the educational attainment of men and women. Let's switch to the ELECTION data set to complete these analyses.

	➤	Data File:	ELECTION
	➤	Task:	Cross-tabulation
	➤	Row Variable:	4) EDUCATION
	➤	Column Variable:	2) GENDER
	➤	View:	Tables
	➤	Display:	Column %

EDUCATION   by   GENDER
Cramer's V: 0.080 **

| | | GENDER | | |
		Male	Female	TOTAL
EDUCATION	No HS	153	196	349
		11.3%	11.4%	11.3%
	HS Deg	353	552	905
		26.0%	32.2%	29.4%
	College	684	813	1497
		50.3%	47.4%	48.7%
	Adv Degree	170	155	325
		12.5%	9.0%	10.6%
	Missing	5	7	12
	TOTAL	1360	1716	3076
		100.0%	100.0%	

Gender differences in education attainment are significant (V = 0.080**), but not large. Females (32.2%) are more likely than males (26%) to have completed only high school and less likely to have finished a four-year college (about 47% versus 50%) or graduate degree (9% versus 12.5%). Now let's see if male and female full-time workers with the same education (here, college degrees) make the same amount of money.

Data File:	**ELECTION**		
Task:	**Cross-tabulation**		
➤ *Row Variable:*	**6) PERS INCOME**		
➤ *Column Variable:*	**2) GENDER**		
➤ *Subset Variable:*	**12) WORK FT**		
➤ *Subset Category:*	**Include: Yes**		
➤ *Subset Variable:*	**4) EDUCATION**		
➤ *Subset Category:*	**Include: College**		
➤ *View:*	**Tables**		
➤ *Display:*	**Column %**		

PERS INCOM   by   GENDER

Cramer's V: 0.384 **

		GENDER		
		Male	Female	TOTAL
PERS INCOM	<15,000	27	50	77
		15.9%	32.7%	23.8%
	15-24.9	19	39	58
		11.2%	25.5%	18.0%
	25-49.9	69	55	124
		40.6%	35.9%	38.4%
	50-74.9	33	6	39
		19.4%	3.9%	12.1%
	75+	22	3	25
		12.9%	2.0%	7.7%
	Missing	288	286	574
	TOTAL	170	153	323
		100.0%	100.0%	

Clearly the fact that among those employed full-time, women make less money than men is *not* just because they are less educated. Among those with just college degrees, women tend to have significantly lower incomes (V = 0.384**). For example, about 33% of these females made less than $15,000, compared to 16% of males. And only about 4% of women made between $50,000 and $74,999, and 2% earned $75,000 or more, compared to percentages of 19% and 13% at these income levels, respectively, for men.

What about differences in gender inequality among nations? One valuable way of measuring this is the **gender empowerment measure (GEM)** presented in the United Nation's *Human Development Report*. A GEM score is a good estimate of the degree to which, in any given country, the socioeconomic status (SES) of women is less than that of men. Factors considered in calculating a nation's GEM score include female incomes, as well as the percentage of political and business leaders, and professional and technical workers, that are women.[8] This provides some idea of the extent to which women participate in economic and political decision-making, or control economic resources. A GEM score of 1.00 means perfect gender equality. The lower the score, the lower the SES of women relative to men.

➤ *Data File:*	**COUNTRIES**
➤ *Task:*	**Mapping**
➤ *Variable 1:*	**42) GEM**
➤ *View:*	**Map**

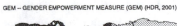
GEM -- GENDER EMPOWERMENT MEASURE (GEM) (HDR, 2001)

In the nations of North America and Western Europe, gender *in*equality is not as great as in the other regions shown on this map (though much of Africa, Asia, and South America is missing). Does the

---

[8] *Human Development Report 2001*, United Nations Development Programme (UNDP), New York: Oxford University Press, page 217. GEM scores used here are from the 1998 report, which included more nations.

relative SES of women improve as nations become more modern? Let's find out if GEM scores tend to increase with per capita gross domestic product (GDP).

Data File: **COUNTRIES**
➤ Task: **Scatterplot**
➤ Dependent Variable: **42) GEM**
➤ Independent Variable: **25) GDP/CAP**
➤ View: **Reg. Line**

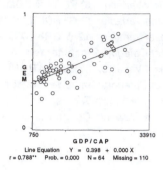

It certainly appears that as nations become wealthier, they tend to become more gender equal, at least as measured by GEM scores ($r = 0.788**$). What about the relative amount of education received by men and women? Is male and female schooling more equal in wealthier countries? Let's find out.

Data File: **COUNTRIES**
Task: **Scatterplot**
➤ Dependent Variable: **41) M/F EDUC.**
➤ Independent Variable: **25) GDP/CAP**
➤ View: **Reg. Line**

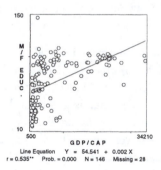

Obviously, as nations become wealthier, the amount of education that females receive relative to males increases ($r = 0.535**$). Is this type of educational equality in schooling also tied to greater relative political and economic status and empowerment for women?

Data File: **COUNTRIES**
Task: **Scatterplot**
➤ Dependent Variable: **42) GEM**
➤ Independent Variable: **41) M/F EDUC.**
➤ View: **Reg. Line**

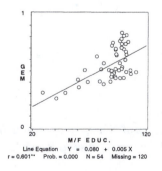

As the amount of education received by females and males becomes more equal, so does the GEM ($r = 0.601$**).

So far, we have looked at the concrete attainments and resources of women in such areas as occupation, income, education, and (as part of the GEM measure) power in economic and political decisions. However, we have not yet examined attitudes toward gender roles and identities, including people's views about gender socioeconomic equality. Let's do so now. Since we already have the COUNTRIES data set open, we'll start by looking at national variations in the percentages who indicated, in the World Values Survey (WVS), that they believed what "women really want is a home and children."

Data File: **COUNTRIES**
➤ Task: **Mapping**
➤ Variable 1: **44) HOME&KIDS**
➤ View: **Map**

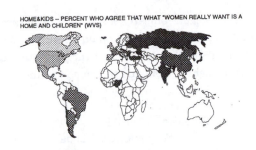

HOME&KIDS -- PERCENT WHO AGREE THAT WHAT "WOMEN REALLY WANT IS A HOME AND CHILDREN" (WVS)

Respondents were more likely to agree with this statement in Asia than they were in Western Europe or North America. Perhaps nations where more people agree that what "women really want is a home and children" also tend to have lower GEM scores (that is, the SES of females is lower relative to males). Let's find out if such a negative correlation exists.

Data File: **COUNTRIES**
➤ Task: **Scatterplot**
➤ Dependent Variable: **42) GEM**
➤ Independent Variable: **44) HOME&KIDS**
➤ View: **Reg. Line**

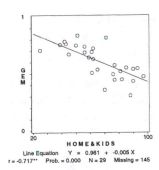

HOME&KIDS

Line Equation   Y = 0.961 + -0.005 X
r = -0.717**   Prob. = 0.000   N = 29   Missing = 145

Yes indeed! As the percentage that affirmed this traditional view of male and female roles increased, GEM scores tended to decrease a great deal ($r = -0.717$**).

How about attitudes in the United States? Let's use the TRENDS data set to look at changes over time in the degree to which people indicated they were willing to vote for a woman for president.

➤ *Data File:* **TRENDS**
   ➤ *Task:* **Historical Trends**
➤ *Variable:* **127) %FEM PRES**

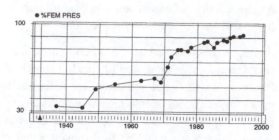

Percent who would vote for a woman for president

This trend graph indicates a strong shift toward a more gender-equal view of women over time. The percentages indicating they would be willing to vote for a woman for president rose from 34% in 1937 to 92% in 1994. Now let's look at the percentage of GSS respondents who agreed that it is better if "the man is the achiever outside the home and the woman takes care of the home and family."

Data File: **TRENDS**
   Task: **Historical Trends**
➤ *Variable:* **133) WIFE@HOME**

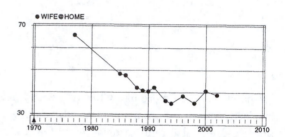

Percent of GSS respondents who agreed that "It is much better for everyone concerned if the man is the achiever outside the home and the woman takes care of the home and family."

Again we see a strong shift toward a more gender-equal view of women. The percentages indicating it is better for women to focus on the home and for men to achieve things outside the home dropped from about 66% in 1977 to 39% in 2002.

Finally, let's look at variations in the degree to which different types of GSS respondents agreed with the latter item affirming traditional gender roles. It makes sense that those who are female will be less likely to agree with this statement. Let's see.

➤ *Data File:* **GSS**
   ➤ *Task:* **Cross-tabulation**
➤ *Row Variable:* **78) WIFE@HOME**
➤ *Column Variable:* **2) GENDER**
   ➤ *View:* **Tables**
   ➤ *Display:* **Column %**

WIFE@HOME   by   GENDER
Cramer's V: 0.030

		GENDER		
		Male	Female	TOTAL
	Agree	489	594	1083
		41.8%	38.8%	40.1%
	Disagree	682	937	1619
		58.2%	61.2%	59.9%
	Missing	1286	1594	2880
	TOTAL	1171	1531	2702
		100.0%	100.0%	

Investigating Social Problems

Well, we were wrong. There is not a significant difference between men and women on this item (about 42% versus 39%, respectively; V = 0.030). Perhaps those with more education will be less likely to agree with this viewpoint.

Data File: **GSS**
Task: **Cross-tabulation**
Row Variable: **78) WIFE@HOME**
➤ Column Variable: **13) DEGREE**
➤ View: **Tables**
➤ Display: **Column %**

WIFE@HOME   by   DEGREE
Cramer's V: 0.217 **

		Not H.S.	H.S.	Jr. Col.	4 Yr Deg	Grad Deg	Missing	TOTAL
WIFE@HOME	Agree	246	610	54	122	46	5	1078
		60.3%	41.4%	29.2%	28.6%	23.2%		40.1%
	Disagree	162	864	131	304	152	6	1613
		39.7%	58.6%	70.8%	71.4%	76.8%		59.9%
	Missing	431	1512	223	452	250	12	2880
	TOTAL	408	1474	185	426	198	23	2691
		100.0%	100.0%	100.0%	100.0%	100.0%		

As we expected, generally, the *less* educated respondents were, the *more* likely they were to agree that it is better if men are the achievers "outside the home" while women take "care of the home and family" (V = 0.217**). For example, among those who had not completed high school, about 60% agreed with this statement, but this figure was roughly 41% for high school graduates, 29% for those with bachelor's degrees, and 23% for respondents with advanced degrees.

Finally, you may recall the culture wars debate in Exercise 4. Proponents of the idea that the United States is in the midst of a culture war would predict that among Protestants, fundamentalists would be more likely than moderates or liberals to affirm traditional gender roles. Let's test this.

Data File: **GSS**
Task: **Cross-tabulation**
Row Variable: **78) WIFE@HOME**
➤ Column Variable: **23) R.FUND/LIB**
➤ Subset Variable: **25) RELIGION**
➤ Subset Category: **Include: Protestant**
➤ View: **Tables**
➤ Display: **Column %**

WIFE@HOME   by   R.FUND/LIB
Cramer's V: 0.155 **

		Fundam.	Moderate	Liberal	Missing	TOTAL
WIFE@HOME	Agree	403	106	132	11	641
		52.1%	34.4%	39.4%		45.3%
	Disagree	370	202	203	25	775
		47.9%	65.6%	60.6%		54.7%
	Missing	788	348	363	30	1529
	TOTAL	773	308	335	66	1416
		100.0%	100.0%	100.0%		

The differences in this table are significant (V = 0.155**) and as predicted. The key distinction here is between fundamentalists on the one hand (about 52% of whom agreed) versus moderates and liberals on the other hand (for whom agreement was similar—roughly 34% and 39%, respectively). It is noteworthy, however, that despite what is commonly believed about fundamentalists, about half did not agree with this statement.

I'd like you to pursue all of these various lines of analysis having to do with gender inequality, attitudes, and beliefs in the following worksheets. In other words, it's your turn.

REVIEW QUESTIONS

Based on the first part of this exercise, answer True or False to the following items:

Normally, the term "sexism" refers only to *negative* beliefs about women.	T F
Since 1970, the labor force participation of both married and single women has increased steadily.	T F
Women who are divorced or separated are more likely than married women to be employed full-time.	T F
On average, the pay of women and men in low prestige jobs is about the same.	T F
Among those who are employed full-time and have college degrees, the personal incomes of women and men are about the same.	T F
The *gender empowerment measure* (GEM) score takes into account both women's political and economic status relative to men.	T F
GEM scores tend to be higher in wealthy nations than in poor ones.	T F
Among nations, GEM scores are not significantly correlated to levels of gender equality in educational attainment.	T F
Nations where more respondents agree that what "women really want is a home and children" tend to have higher GEM scores.	T F
About one-third of GSS respondents in recent years have indicated that they would not be willing to vote for a woman for president.	T F
Women are significantly *less* likely than men to agree that men should be the achievers "outside the home" while women "take care of the home and family."	T F

EXPLORIT QUESTIONS

1. I wonder what the recent labor force participation trends have been for married women with young children. I am also curious as to how this has been different from labor force participation for married women overall. My suspicion is that married women with young children will be less likely to have been involved in the labor force than married women overall. Why don't we take a look?

    a. Open the TRENDS data set and carefully examine the variable description for 132) MOM LABOR.

    b. Look at the Historical Trends chart for 131) F.LAB. MAR and 132) MOM LABOR. Then answer the following questions about what you see there.

➤ *Data File:* **TRENDS**
➤ *Task:* **Historical Trends**
➤ *Variable:* **131) F.LAB. MAR**
132) MOM LABOR

c. From 1970 to 1980, was the labor force participation percentage mostly higher for married women overall, or for married women with young children? Or were both about equal during those years? (Circle one.) (Treat differences of what appear to be less than 3% as "about equal.")

Married Women

Married Women With Young Children

Both About Equal

d. From 1981 to 2001, was the labor force participation percentage mostly higher for married women overall, or for married women with young children? Or were both about equal during those years? (Circle one.) (Treat differences of what appear to be less than 3% as "about equal.")

Married Women

Married Women With Young Children

Both About Equal

2. Let's continue to pursue this last issue of employment by married women with or without children, focusing on *full-time* employment only. We'll turn to the GSS. Our hypothesis will be: *among married women, the more children they have, the less likely they will be employed full-time.*

a. Open the GSS data set.

b. Cross-tabulate 18) FULL TIME? with 10) #CHILDREN for married women only. Then, fill in the percentages employed full time.

➤ *Data File:* **GSS**
➤ *Task:* **Cross-tabulation**
➤ *Row Variable:* **18) FULL TIME?**
➤ *Column Variable:* **10) #CHILDREN**
➤ *Subset Variable:* **8) MARITAL**
➤ *Subset Category:* **Include: Married**
➤ *Subset Variable:* **2) GENDER**
➤ *Subset Category:* **Include: Female**
➤ *View:* **Tables**
➤ *Display:* **Column %**

	NONE	ONE	TWO	3–4	>4
YES	_____%	_____%	_____%	_____%	_____%

Investigating Social Problems

Now, get the Cramer's V and the significance level for these two variables.

c. Record the value of Cramer's V for this table. (Include asterisks, if any.)   V = _____

d. Is the relationship between FULL TIME? and #CHILDREN statistically significant? (Circle one.)   Yes   No

e. Is the relationship between FULL TIME? and #CHILDREN weak, moderate, strong, or not significant? (Circle one.)

Weak

Moderate

Strong

Not Significant

f. Was the hypothesis supported? (Circle one.)   Yes   No

g. The majority of married women with which of the following number(s) of children were employed full-time? (*Circle **each** that applies!*)

None

One

Two

Three or Four

Greater Than Four

3. We touched on the culture war thesis again in this exercise just before starting these worksheets. Let's see if the religious differences we looked at are related to the employment patterns of married women. (We will not restrict ourselves to Protestants here.) Our hypothesis will be: *among married women, fundamentalists will be less likely than moderates or liberals to be employed full-time.*

a. Cross-tabulate 18) FULL TIME? with 23) R.FUND/LIB for married women only. Then, fill in the percentages employed full-time.

> | | |
> | ---: | :--- |
> | Data File: | **GSS** |
> | Task: | **Cross-tabulation** |
> | Row Variable: | **18) FULL TIME?** |
> | ➤ Column Variable: | **23) R.FUND/LIB** |
> | ➤ Subset Variable: | **8) MARITAL** |
> | ➤ Subset Category: | **Include: Married** |
> | ➤ Subset Variable: | **2) GENDER** |
> | ➤ Subset Category: | **Include: Female** |
> | ➤ View: | **Tables** |
> | ➤ Display: | **Column %** |

	FUNDAM.	**MODERATE**	**LIBERAL**
YES	_____%	_____%	_____%

Now, examine the Cramer's V and the significance level for these two variables.

b. Is the relationship between FULL TIME? and R.FUND/LIB statistically
    significant? (Circle one.)   Yes   No

c. Was the hypothesis supported? (Circle one.)   Yes   No

d. Do these results surprise you? Why or why not?

4. In Exercises 3 and 6, we mentioned that higher fertility rates are commonly believed to be associated
    with greater allegiance to traditional gender roles and hence greater gender inequality. Let's look at
    this more directly, by exploring this hypothesis: *among nations, as the fertility rates increase, GEM
    scores will tend to decrease.* We'll use the COUNTRIES data set.

    a. Open the COUNTRIES data set.

    b. Construct a scatterplot that represents the association between 42) GEM and 8) FERTILITY.

    > *Data File:* **COUNTRIES**
    > *Task:* **Scatterplot**
    > *Dependent Variable:* **42) GEM**
    > *Independent Variable:* **8) FERTILITY**
    > *View:* **Reg. Line**

    c. Provide Pearson's *r* (including asterisks, if any, and the direction sign, if any).   *r* = _____

    d. Is this correlation significant *and* negative, significant *and* positive,
        or *not* significant? (Circle one.)

                                                                        Significant *and* Negative

                                                                        Significant *and* Positive

                                                                        Not Significant

e. Is this correlation weak, moderate, or strong? (Circle one.)

           Weak

           Moderate

           Strong

f. Is the hypothesis supported? (Circle one.)

           Yes   No

g. Does this scatterplot show that increases in fertility lead to (cause) increases in GEM scores? Why or why not? (It may be helpful here to review the rules for establishing cause and effect that were presented in Exercise 3.)

5. If women having a lot of children is associated with traditional gender roles, then perhaps nations where more people want large families will tend to have more gender inequality. Let's explore this hypothesis: *among nations, as the percentage desiring three or more children increases, GEM scores will tend to decrease.*

a. Construct a scatterplot that represents the association between 42) GEM and 9) LARGE FAML.

> | | |
> | ---: | :--- |
> | Data File: | **COUNTRIES** |
> | Task: | **Scatterplot** |
> | Dependent Variable: | **42) GEM** |
> | ➤ Independent Variable: | **9) LARGE FAML** |
> | ➤ View: | **Reg. Line** |

Examine Pearson's *r*.

b. Is this correlation significant *and* negative, significant *and* positive, or *not* significant? (Circle one.)

           Significant *and* Negative

           Significant *and* Positive

           Not Significant

c. Is the hypothesis supported? (Circle one.)

           Yes   No

d. How do these results compare with those of question 4? Do they appear to point to the same basic realities or to contradict each other? If the latter, how might you reconcile or explain this apparent contradiction?

6. One thing that may hold many married women with children back from being as involved in their careers as they might otherwise be is the belief that children suffer from having a working mother. Why don't we see how different types of people feel about this? Let's start with this hypothesis: *men will be more likely than women to believe that preschool children will suffer if their mothers work.*

   a. Open the GSS data set and carefully examine the variable description for 80) PRESCH.WRK.

   b. Cross-tabulate 80) PRESCH.WRK with 2) GENDER. Then, fill in the percentages that believe that preschool children are likely to suffer if their mothers work.

> Data File: **GSS**
> Task: **Cross-tabulation**
> Row Variable: **80) PRESCH.WRK**
> Column Variable: **2) GENDER**
> View: **Tables**
> Display: **Column %**

	MALE	FEMALE	TOTAL
AGREE	_____%	_____%	_____%

Now, examine the Cramer's V and the significance level for these two variables.

   c. Is the relationship between PRESCH.WRK and GENDER statistically significant? (Circle one.)   Yes   No

   d. Is the relationship between PRESCH.WRK and GENDER weak, moderate, strong, or not significant? (Circle one.)

                                                        Weak

                                               Moderate

                                                 Strong

                                       Not Significant

   e. Is the hypothesis supported? (Circle one.)   Yes   No

   f. Look at the TOTAL column and fill in the blank on the following: _____% of GSS respondents in 2000 and 2002 (combined) believed that "a preschool child is likely to suffer if his or her mother works."   _____%

7. Next hypothesis: *among married women, those who work full-time are less likely than those who do not work full-time to believe that preschool children will suffer if their mothers work.*

    a. Cross-tabulate 80) PRESCH.WRK with 18) FULL TIME? for married women only. Then, fill in the percentages that believe preschool children are likely to suffer if their mothers work.

Data File:	**GSS**
Task:	**Cross-tabulation**
Row Variable:	**80) PRESCH.WRK**
➤ Column Variable:	**18) FULL TIME?**
➤ Subset Variable:	**8) MARITAL**
➤ Subset Category:	**Include: Married**
➤ Subset Variable:	**2) GENDER**
➤ Subset Category:	**Include: Female**
➤ View:	**Tables**
➤ Display:	**Column %**

	YES	NO	TOTAL
AGREE	_____%	_____%	_____%

    Now, examine the Cramer's V and the significance level for these two variables.

    b. Is the relationship between PRESCH.WRK and FULL TIME? statistically significant? (Circle one.)

    Yes   No

    c. Is the relationship between PRESCH.WRK and FULL TIME? weak, moderate, strong, or not significant? (Circle one.)

    Weak

    Moderate

    Strong

    Not Significant

    d. Is the hypothesis supported? (Circle one.)

    Yes   No

    e. Look at the TOTAL column and fill in the blank on the following:
    _____% of GSS respondents in 2000 and 2002 (combined) who were married women, believed that "a preschool child is likely to suffer if his or her mother works."

    _____%

8. Finally, let's see how different types of people feel about the "women's movement." We'll move to the ELECTION data set. Let's start with this hypothesis: *men will be less likely than women to feel "warm," and more likely to be "cold," toward the women's movement.*

    a. Open the ELECTION data set and carefully examine the variable description for 58) WLIB THERM.

b. Cross-tabulate 58) WLIB THERM with 2) GENDER. Then, fill in the percentages that are "cold" and "warm" toward the women's movement.

> ➤ Data File: **ELECTION**
> ➤ Task: **Cross-tabulation**
> ➤ Row Variable: **58) WLIB THERM**
> ➤ Column Variable: **2) GENDER**
> ➤ View: **Tables**
> ➤ Display: **Column %**

	MALE	FEMALE	TOTAL
COLD	_____%	_____%	_____%
WARM	_____%	_____%	_____%

Now, examine the Cramer's V and the significance level for these two variables.

c. Is the relationship between WLIB THERM and GENDER statistically significant? (Circle one.)   Yes   No

d. Is the relationship between WLIB THERM and GENDER weak, moderate, strong, or not significant? (Circle one.)

Weak

Moderate

Strong

Not Significant

e. Is the hypothesis supported? (Circle one.)   Yes   No

f. Look at the TOTAL column and fill in the blank on the following: _____%
_____% of NES respondents in 1998 and 2000 (combined) felt <u>warm</u> toward the women's movement.

g. Look at the TOTAL column and fill in the blank on the following: _____%
_____% of NES respondents in 1998 and 2000 (combined) felt <u>cold</u> toward the women's movement.

9. Next hypothesis: *among women, those who are employed full-time will be more likely than those who do not work full-time to feel "warm" toward the women's movement.*

    a. Cross-tabulate 58) WLIB THERM with 12) WORK FT for women. Then, fill in the appropriate column percentages that are "warm" toward the women's movement.

Data File:	**ELECTION**
Task:	**Cross-tabulation**
Row Variable:	**58) WLIB THERM**
➤ *Column Variable:*	**12) WORK FT**
➤ *Subset Variable:*	**2) GENDER**
➤ *Subset Category:*	**Include: Female**
➤ *View:*	**Tables**
➤ *Display:*	**Column %**

	YES	NO	TOTAL
WARM	_____%	_____%	_____%

Now, examine the Cramer's V and the significance level for these two variables.

    b. Is the relationship between WLIB THERM and WORK FT statistically significant? (Circle one.)   Yes   No

    c. Is the relationship between WLIB THERM and WORK FT weak, moderate, strong, or not significant? (Circle one.)

                                                               Weak

                                                           Moderate

                                                             Strong

                                                     Not Significant

    d. Is the hypothesis supported? (Circle one.)   Yes   No

    e. Do these results surprise you? Why or why not?

10. Final hypothesis—from the "culture wars" debate again: *born-again Christians will be less likely than others to feel "warm," and more likely to feel "cold," toward the women's movement.*

a. Cross-tabulate 58) WLIB THERM with 19) BORN AGAIN. Then, fill in the percentages that feel "warm" and "cold" towards the women's movement.

> Data File: **ELECTION**
> Task: **Cross-tabulation**
> Row Variable: **58) WLIB THERM**
> ➤ Column Variable: **19) BORN AGAIN**
> ➤ View: **Tables**
> ➤ Display: **Column %**

	YES	NO
COLD	_____%	_____%
WARM	_____%	_____%

Now, examine the Cramer's V and the significance level for these two variables.

b. Is the relationship between WLIB THERM and BORN AGAIN statistically significant? (Circle one.)   Yes   No

c. Is the relationship between WLIB THERM and BORN AGAIN weak, moderate, strong, or not significant? (Circle one.)

Weak

Moderate

Strong

Not Significant

d. Is the hypothesis supported? (Circle one.)   Yes   No

AGING IN AMERICA

Tasks: Cross-tabulation, Historical Trends, Mapping, Scatterplot
Data Files: GSS, ELECTION, TRENDS, STATES

Some years ago, I had the privilege of sitting through a presentation by Stephen Crystal on aging and the elderly in America.[1] I found his talk to be eye opening, and I came away from it with a new appreciation for the importance of a couple of general truths.

First, I was impressed by the extent to which the elderly population has swelled both in absolute numbers and as a percentage of the population, and by some of the implications of these changes. Certainly, as we shall see, the relative size of the population that is 65 and over did not grow between 1990 and 2001 (following decades of climbing steadily). But in the near future, we can expect the proportion of Americans who are elderly to burgeon again, especially as large numbers of "baby boomers"[2] begin reaching retirement age in 2011, less than ten years from now. Increases in the relative and absolute size of the elderly population have already led to numerous social changes and challenges, and there are many more to come.

Second, Crystal's lecture helped me begin to see some of the many important ways that Americans—be they policy makers or "everyday citizens"—typically misunderstand the material situations, life experiences, abilities, and viewpoints of the elderly. Crystal emphasized the connection between certain misperceptions and public policies designed to help the aged that may actually be useless, or even harmful, to them and others.

We could also point out that, in terms of distorted perceptions and wrong action, sometimes the elderly may even be the target of *ageism*. That is, they may be subjected to prejudice and discrimination[3] because of their age.[4]

In this exercise we will look, first, at differences in the size of the elderly population across different localities and time periods, and at some things that are associated with these variations. Then we will compare some of the life situations, experiences, habits, and viewpoints of older Americans with those of people of other ages.[5] In the process I hope to challenge, or at least qualify, some common myths and stereotypes about elderly people and their lives.

Let's begin, as we often have, by examining some important historical trends related to the "aging of America." We'll start with total numbers of the elderly population.

---

[1] This lecture included main ideas from his book, *America's Old Age Crisis* (New York: Basic Books, 1982).

[2] That is, people born during the period of very high birth rates that extended from immediately after World War II in 1946 into the early 1960s.

[3] See Exercise 9 for full definitions of "prejudice" and "discrimination."

[4] Cf. Kendall, op cit., page 86. Some sociologists say that "ageism" may be directed against any age group (as in ibid.), whereas others use the term only for prejudice and/or discrimination against the elderly (cf. Palen, op cit., page 304; Kornblum and Julian, op cit., page 327; Mooney et al., op cit., page 160).

[5] We have already touched on this in previous exercises. For example, we looked at whether or not there were age differences in concerns about health-related social problems (Exercise 1); moral beliefs about premarital sex and the frequency of sex among the never-married (Exercise 4); victimization by, and fears of, crime (Exercise 6); and racial prejudice (Exercise 9). However, here we will, of course, focus more on comparing the elderly to younger populations, and do so in a lot more depth.

> *Data File:* **TRENDS**
>> ➤ *Task:* **Historical Trends**
> ➤ *Variable:* **146) #65&UP**

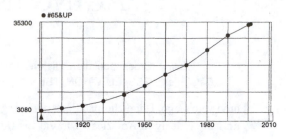

Population age 65 and over in thousands

The number of elderly in America has risen steadily throughout the 20th century. But has the *percentage* of elderly in the population also increased? Or is the increase in the number due to a general increase in the number of people?

Data File: **TRENDS**
Task: **Historical Trends**
➤ *Variable:* **147) %65&UP**

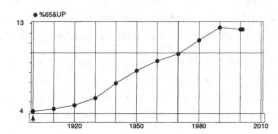

Percent of population 65 and over

Indeed, the proportion of elderly in the American population has also increased. The 1990 U.S. Census recorded a high of 12.6% over 65 years of age, with a slightly lower percentage (12.4%) in 2001.

The "typical" American is also getting older. Let's look at changes in the median age.

Data File: **TRENDS**
Task: **Historical Trends**
➤ *Variable:* **149) MEDIAN AGE**

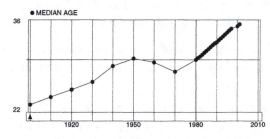

Median age of population

In 1900, the median age was 22.9. By 2001, it had risen to 35.6. It decreased only for a couple of decades following World War II, due to the baby boom (more on this below).

Two key trends that help account for the "aging of America" are increases in the length of people's lives and decreases in the number of births. That is, generally, people are living longer and having fewer children. Let's take a look, starting with life expectancies.

Investigating Social Problems

Data File: **TRENDS**

Task: **Historical Trends**

➤ Variable: **143) LIFE EXP**

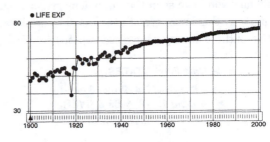

Expectation of life at birth

As you can see, the trend in life expectancies has been upward. In 1900, the average was 47.3 years, but by 2000 it was 76.9. What a difference!

Data File: **TRENDS**

Task: **Historical Trends**

➤ Variable: **144) LIFE EXP65**

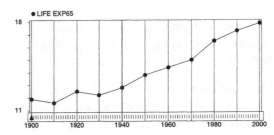

Expectation of life (number of years left) at age 65

As for people who have already lived to age 65, in 1900 they could expect to live another 11.9 years on average. By 2000, the average person who lived to be 65 could expect to live to be 83. It appears that the health of older Americans is improving. Now, how about birth rates?

Data File: **TRENDS**

Task: **Historical Trends**

➤ Variable: **139) BIRTH RATE**

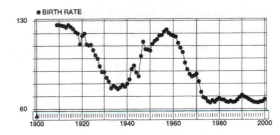

Birth rate per 1,000 women 15-44 years old

Birth rates present a very interesting picture. Overall, they decreased a great deal during the 20th century. In 1909, there were 126.8 babies born for every 1,000 women aged 15 to 44. But this rate was 67.5 (about half of the 1909 rate) in 2000. On the other hand, notice the huge "Baby Boom" from the mid-1940s into the 1960s! It is this group that will especially swell the ranks of the elderly very shortly, as we indicated earlier. But as you can see from the relatively low birth rates since the early 1970s, these "Baby Boomers" and *their* children have not been having as many children as parents did during the first two decades after World War II.[6]

---

[6] The contributions of low fertility and the upcoming Baby Boom elderly to the long-term projected accelerated aging of America are ably discussed by Crystal, op cit., pages 24–26.

So now you have seen the main demographic reasons for previous increases in the elderly population, and why this latter trend is expected to accelerate over the next few decades. How about the distribution of these elderly people *geographically*? We'll turn to the STATES data file to look into this.

> ➤ *Data File:* **STATES**
> ➤ *Task:* **Mapping**
> ➤ *Variable 1:* **78) %65 & OVER**
> ➤ *View:* **List: Rank**

RANK	CASE NAME	VALUE
1	Florida	17.6
2	Pennsylvania	15.6
3	West Virginia	15.3
4	Iowa	14.9
5	North Dakota	14.7
6	Rhode Island	14.5
7	Maine	14.4
8	South Dakota	14.3
9	Arkansas	14.0
10	Connecticut	13.8

As the ranked listing makes especially clear, the highest percentages of elderly persons are in Florida (17.6%), Pennsylvania (15.6%), and West Virginia (15.3%). The lowest ranked states are Georgia (9.6%), Utah (8.5%), and especially Alaska (5.7%).

I have commonly bumped into the misperception that elderly persons tend to move to warmer states, swelling the relative size of the elderly population in them. While this appears to be true with Florida, a glance at the map shows that this is not generally true. Most of the states with the highest percentages of older people are not in sunny climes! However, it may be that the proportions of elderly are higher in states with low or negative growth—that is, those that fewer young people are choosing to remain in or relocate to. Let's check it out.

> *Data File:* **STATES**
> ➤ *Task:* **Scatterplot**
> ➤ *Dependent Variable:* **78) %65 & OVER**
> ➤ *Independent Variable:* **3) POP%GRO**
> ➤ *View:* **Reg. Line**

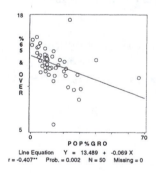

Line Equation   Y = 13.489 + -0.069 X
r = -0.407**   Prob. = 0.002   N = 50   Missing = 0

This hypothesis is supported by this scatterplot. As states' rate of growth increase, the percentage of their population that is 65 and older tends to decrease (r = –0.407**).

Now, let's consider the typical life experiences, views, and material situations of the elderly. First, we'll look at how well they are doing financially compared to younger age groups. It is difficult for elderly persons to accurately report their real incomes in dollars, given the diverse sources of revenue they typically have (assets, pensions, social security, earnings, and so on), some of which may be non-taxable. They also often have lower expenses than younger persons (for example, their houses may be paid off, they are probably no longer raising children, and so on), increasing their income *relative to their needs.*[7] But we can look at the *perceived* relative incomes of the elderly compared to those of others, as this gives us some idea of how well they *believe* they are doing financially overall relative to others. We'll use the GSS to do so.

➤ *Data File:* **GSS**
➤ *Task:* **Cross-tabulation**
➤ *Row Variable:* **16) $FAMRANK**
➤ *Column Variable:* **1) AGE**
➤ *View:* **Tables**
➤ *Display:* **Column %**

$FAMRANK by AGE
Cramer's V: 0.084 **

		AGE					
		<30	30-49	50-64	65 and Up	Missing	TOTAL
$FAMRANK	Below	239	494	237	233	3	1203
		30.6%	27.7%	27.8%	32.5%		29.1%
	Average	427	866	365	334	8	1992
		54.7%	48.6%	42.8%	46.6%		48.2%
	Above	114	422	250	150	4	936
		14.6%	23.7%	29.3%	20.9%		22.7%
	Missing	276	597	303	253	7	1436
	TOTAL	780	1782	852	717	22	4131
		100.0%	100.0%	100.0%	100.0%		

The elderly did differ from other age groups in their self-perceived general family incomes (V = 0.084**). Although the differences between the elderly and other age groups were relatively small, they were more likely than any other age group to identify themselves as "below average," and less likely than all but those under 30 to say they were "above average." Now, were they typically more or less *satisfied* than others with their financial situation?

Data File: **GSS**
Task: **Cross-tabulation**
➤ *Row Variable:* **88) SAT.$**
➤ *Column Variable:* **1) AGE**
➤ *View:* **Tables**
➤ *Display:* **Column %**

SAT.$ by AGE
Cramer's V: 0.114 **

		AGE					
		<30	30-49	50-64	65 and Up	Missing	TOTAL
SAT.$	Pretty Wel	179	457	298	305	5	1239
		22.7%	25.6%	34.9%	42.0%		29.8%
	More/Less	375	800	354	296	4	1825
		47.5%	44.8%	41.5%	40.7%		43.9%
	Not Satis.	235	530	202	126	6	1093
		29.8%	29.7%	23.7%	17.3%		26.3%
	Missing	267	592	301	243	7	1410
	TOTAL	789	1787	854	727	22	4157
		100.0%	100.0%	100.0%	100.0%		

Interestingly, the elderly were *more* likely to be satisfied with their incomes than younger age groups (V = 0.114**). For example, while about 30% of those less than 30, and even 24% of those between 50 and 64, were "not satisfied," only about 17% of those 65 and older felt this way. What about the relative financial situation of elderly men and elderly women?

---

[7] These well-known difficulties in truly determining the relative income and wealth of the elderly are discussed lucidly by Crystal (ibid., see especially pages x–xiii, 16–17, 28–32).

Data File: **GSS**

Task: **Cross-tabulation**

➤ Row Variable: **16) $FAMRANK**

➤ Column Variable: **2) GENDER**

➤ Subset Variable: **1) AGE**

➤ Subset Category: **Include: 65 and up**

➤ View: **Tables**

➤ Display: **Column %**

$FAMRANK   by   GENDER

Cramer's V: 0.166 **

		GENDER		
		Male	Female	TOTAL
$FAMRANK	Below	75	158	233
		26.3%	36.6%	32.5%
	Average	128	206	334
		44.9%	47.7%	46.6%
	Above	82	68	150
		28.8%	15.7%	20.9%
	Missing	95	158	253
	TOTAL	285	432	717
		100.0%	100.0%	

Here, we see that among those 65 and older, the self-perceived family income situation of women is worse than that of men (V = 0.166**). For example, about 37% of elderly females saw their income as below average, compared to roughly 26% of elderly men.

We saw in Exercise 9 that, by some measures, older Americans are more likely to be racially prejudiced. Are the elderly somehow unable to "keep up" with social changes because they are "out of touch"? I have often heard this stereotype expressed. We'll test this idea by considering whether or not older people are less likely than others to read the newspaper regularly—a key means of keeping in touch with modern events, trends, and viewpoints.

Data File: **GSS**

Task: **Cross-tabulation**

➤ Row Variable: **83) NEWSPAPER**

➤ Column Variable: **1) AGE**

➤ View: **Tables**

➤ Display: **Column %**

NEWSPAPER   by   AGE
Cramer's V: 0.181 **

		AGE					
		<30	30-49	50-64	65 and Up	Missing	TOTAL
NEWSPAPER	Daily	103	384	276	298	6	1061
		19.3%	31.9%	49.5%	62.9%		38.3%
	1-Few Wk	275	513	174	98	4	1060
		51.6%	42.6%	31.2%	20.7%		38.3%
	<Weekly	106	200	60	31	1	397
		19.9%	16.6%	10.8%	6.5%		14.3%
	Never	49	106	48	47	2	250
		9.2%	8.8%	8.6%	9.9%		9.0%
	Missing	523	1176	597	496	9	2801
	TOTAL	533	1203	558	474	22	2768
		100.0%	100.0%	100.0%	100.0%		

Surprise, surprise! Older Americans were actually a lot more likely to read the newspaper regularly (V = 0.181**). For example, about 63% said they do so "daily," compared to 49.5% of those 50 to 64, and only 19% of those under 30 years old. Of course, this may be because the elderly are usually retired and thus have more time to peruse the paper. Never-the-less, it does appear that most do keep up with current events.

People often suggest that the elderly are socially isolated in other ways, namely, being alone too much and lacking interaction with others. Let's find out.

Investigating Social Problems

Data File: **GSS**

Task: **Cross-tabulation**

➤ Row Variable: **85) SOC.KIN**

➤ Column Variable: **1) AGE**

➤ View: **Tables**

➤ Display: **Column %**

		AGE					
		<30	30-49	50-64	65 and Up	Missing	TOTAL
SOC.KIN	Alm. Daily	82	104	56	39	2	281
		15.4%	8.7%	10.1%	8.2%		10.2%
	1-2 Week	168	304	123	115	5	710
		31.6%	25.4%	22.2%	24.3%		25.8%
	1-Fw Month	172	462	193	157	1	984
		32.3%	38.6%	34 8%	33.2%		35.7%
	1-Fw Year	97	274	145	130	3	646
		18.2%	22.9%	26.2%	27.5%		23.4%
	Never	13	54	37	32	1	136
		2.4%	4.5%	6.7%	6.8%		4.9%
	Missing	524	1181	601	497	10	2813
	TOTAL	532	1198	554	473	22	2757
		100.0%	100.0%	100.0%	100.0%		

As we can see, elderly respondents are less likely than others to spend a social evening with relatives (V = 0.085**). Still, as you can see with some simple addition, most (about 66%) spend a social evening with a relative at least once a month.

Data File: **GSS**

Task: **Cross-tabulation**

➤ Row Variable: **87) SOC.FRIEND**

➤ Column Variable: **1) AGE**

➤ View: **Tables**

➤ Display: **Column %**

		AGE					
		<30	30-49	50-64	65 and Up	Missing	TOTAL
SOC.FRIEND	Alm. Daily	63	31	13	5	2	112
		11.9%	2.6%	2.3%	1.1%		4.1%
	1-2 Week	162	209	91	70	3	532
		30.5%	17.4%	16.3%	14.9%		19.3%
	1-Fw Month	215	578	236	164	4	1193
		40.5%	48.2%	42.4%	34.9%		43.3%
	1-Fw Year	68	300	166	137	3	671
		12.8%	25.0%	29.8%	29.1%		24.3%
	Never	23	80	51	94	0	248
		4.3%	6.7%	9.2%	20.0%		9.0%
	Missing	525	1181	598	500	10	2814
	TOTAL	531	1198	557	470	22	2756
		100.0%	100.0%	100.0%	100.0%		

Again, elderly respondents are less likely than others to spend a social evening with friends (V = 0.185**). About half (51%) spend a social evening with a friend outside their neighborhood at least once a month.

I have heard comments that imply elderly people are typically constantly obsessed with concerns about their health. Is this true?

Data File: **GSS**
Task: **Cross-tabulation**
➤ *Row Variable:* **90) HEALTH**
➤ *Column Variable:* **1) AGE**
➤ *View:* **Tables**
➤ *Display:* **Column %**

HEALTH   by   AGE
Cramer's V: 0.135 **

		AGE					
		<30	30-49	50-64	65 and Up	Missing	TOTAL
HEALTH	Excellent	295	578	261	130	6	1264
		36.2%	33.1%	29.7%	18.1%		30.4%
	Good	387	866	389	309	6	1951
		47.5%	49.6%	44.3%	42.9%		46.9%
	Fair	121	246	164	185	0	716
		14.8%	14.1%	18.7%	25.7%		17.2%
	Poor	12	56	64	96	0	228
		1.5%	3.2%	7.3%	13.3%		5.5%
	Missing	241	633	277	250	10	1411
	TOTAL	815	1746	878	720	22	4159
		100.0%	100.0%	100.0%	100.0%		

Respondents 65 and older were less likely than others to rate their own health highly (V = 0.135**). For example, only 18% viewed themselves in "excellent" health, compared to about 30% of those 50 to 64, and roughly 36% of the "under 30 crowd." Still, it is quite unfair to state that most elderly people *typically* see themselves in poor health. A little addition reveals that 61% of elderly respondents described their own health as "good" or "excellent."

Let's return to the TRENDS data file to consider one other popular supposition. This is that the elderly in the United States are being put into nursing homes to an ever-increasing degree.

➤ *Data File:* **TRENDS**
➤ *Task:* **Historical Trends**
➤ *Variables:* **151) NURS HM65**
152) NURS HM75
153) NURS HM85

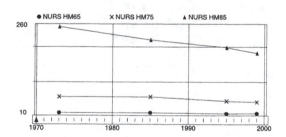

Nursing home residents per 1,000 population; 65-74 years old,
75-84 years old, and 85 years old and older

We can see a couple of things in this trend chart. First, as we would expect, the older that elderly people are, the more likely they are to be in nursing homes. If you could see the numbers underlying this chart, you would notice that in 1999, among those 85 and older, 182.5 of every 1,000 (about 18%) were in a nursing home, compared to only 10.8 of every 1,000 between 65 and 74 (about 1%). Second, you can see that as the general health of the elderly improves, and other options become increasingly available to care for them if they are sick, the rate of nursing-home residency for the elderly has been steadily, mildly *decreasing*, not increasing.

But this is not true for all sectors of society. Twenty years ago, Crystal noted that "other things equal, the poorer health" of African Americans *should* lead to "more nursing home use." However, he pointed out, they were actually *less* likely to be placed in nursing homes because of a variety of factors, including perhaps "discrimination in access to nursing homes . . . cultural preferences and greater likelihood of family care."[8] But some time has passed since he wrote these things. Does African American usage of

---

[8] Ibid., pages 73–75.

nursing homes still lag behind that of whites, and has it declined, as the rest of the population's has? Let's take a look.

Data File: **TRENDS**
Task: **Historical Trends**
➤ Variables: **156) NURS HMWH**
157) NURS HMBL

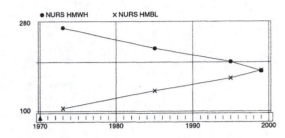

Nursing home residents per 1,000 population for whites 85 and over and for African Americans 85 and over

This graph charts significant changes in the patterns of nursing-home usage among African Americans and whites in the past few decades. While white use by those 85 years and older (the heaviest user group) has declined, African American nursing-home residence has steadily increased. In 1999, these two residency rates per 1,000 converged, with 181.8 for whites and 183.1 for African Americans. Crystal was right.

I know we've covered a lot, but there is still much to look at with regard to the elderly population in the United States. And you'll get to look into this further now, as you turn to the worksheets.

NAME:

COURSE:

DATE:

REVIEW QUESTIONS

Based on the first part of this exercise, answer True or False to the following items:

The term "ageism" always refers to prejudice, not discrimination.	T F
Both the total numbers and percentages of Americans who are 65 and older increased every decade between 1900 and 2000.	T F
Despite increases in percentages that are over 65 years old, the median age of Americans fell throughout the 20th century.	T F
At the beginning of the 20th century, the life expectancy was much lower, and the birth rate much higher, than at this century's end.	T F
The states with the largest elderly populations are mostly Southern.	T F
Elderly people were significantly more likely than other GSS respondents to regard their family incomes as "below average."	T F
GSS respondents over 65 years of age were more likely than younger respondents to be satisfied with their financial situation.	T F
About *half* of both elderly male and elderly female GSS respondents indicated that their family incomes were "below average."	T F
Evidence from the GSS suggests that the elderly are less likely than younger folk to spend a social evening with a relative or friends outside their own neighborhoods.	T F
It appears that elderly GSS respondents are no more likely than younger ones to feel that their health is generally "poor."	T F
The rate of nursing-home residency for older Americans generally has been declining, but it has been increasing for African Americans who are 85 and older.	T F

EXPLORIT QUESTIONS

1. Let's begin by pursuing this matter of nursing-home residency a bit further. It seems reasonable that rural people will have closer families and communities, and thus the aged in rural areas will not be as likely as those in urban areas to be living in a nursing home. If so, then this hypothesis makes sense: *among states, the greater their percentage that live in rural areas, the lower their rate of nursing-home residency will tend to be.*

   a. Open the STATES data set and then carefully examine the variable descriptions for 5) %RURAL00 and 79) NURSING HM.

b. Does this hypothesis predict a negative or a positive correlation? (Circle one.)   Negative

Positive

c. Construct a scatterplot that represents the association between 5) %RURAL00 and 79) NURSING HM.

> *Data File:* **STATES**
> *Task:* **Scatterplot**
> *Dependent Variable:* **79) NURSING HM**
> *Independent Variable:* **5) %RURAL00**
> *View:* **Reg. Line**

d. Provide Pearson's *r* (including asterisks, if any, and the direction sign, if any).   *r* = _____

e. Is this correlation significant *and* negative, significant *and* positive,
or *not* significant? (Circle one.)   Significant *and* Negative

Significant *and* Positive

Not Significant

f. Is the hypothesis supported? (Circle one.)   Yes   No

g. Suggest a few possible reasons for the correlation (or lack of correlation) that you just observed in this last scatterplot.

2. As long as we have the STATES data set open, let's look at another important issue related to aging, namely, Alzheimer's disease. This disease, which involves the progressive deterioration of brain cells, is usually found in elderly rather than younger people. This hypothesis seems almost self-evident: *among states, the greater their percentage that are 65 and older, the higher their rate of death from Alzheimer's disease will tend to be.*

a. Carefully examine the variable description for 75) ALZHEIMERS.

b. Construct a scatterplot that represents the association between 78) %65 & OVER and 75) ALZHEIMERS.

   Data File: **STATES**
   Task: **Scatterplot**
> *Dependent Variable:* **75) ALZHEIMERS**
> *Independent Variable:* **78) %65 & OVER**
> *View:* **Reg. Line**

c. Select [Find: Case]. When the "Select One Case" box pops up, select the state you are in right now. Then, fill in the values for the state you are in, for each of these variables, below. (Remember, the X axis is horizontal, and the Y axis is vertical.) When you are done filling in the percentages for your state (below), just click anywhere in the white area outside the scatterplot itself to make this special information disappear.

75) ALZHEIMERS _____ deaths per 100,000

78) %65 & OVER _____%

Examine Pearson's *r*.

d. Is this correlation significant *and* negative, significant *and* positive, or *not* significant? (Circle one.)

Significant *and* Negative

Significant *and* Positive

Not Significant

e. Is this correlation weak, moderate, strong, or not significant? (Circle one.)

Weak

Moderate

Strong

Not Significant

f. Is the hypothesis supported? (Circle one.)

Yes   No

3. We have already looked at trends in the percentage of Americans who are 65 and older. What about those who are sometimes described as the "very old," that is those 85 and older? Let's open TRENDS and look.

a. Open the TRENDS data set and carefully examine the variable description for 148) %85&UP.

b. Look at the Historical Trends chart for 148) %85&UP. Then, answer the following questions about what you see there.

> ➤ *Data File:* **TRENDS**
>   ➤ *Task:* **Historical Trends**
> ➤ *Variable:* **148) %85&UP**

c. Generally, over the course of the 20th century, did the percentage of Americans who are 85 and older increase, decrease, or stay about the same? (Circle one.)

Increased

Decreased

Stayed About the Same

d. You may recall that the percentage of Americans who are <u>65</u> and older did not rise between 1990 and 2001. How about the percentage <u>85</u> and older? Between 1990 and 2001, did it increase, decrease, or stay about the same? (Circle one.)

Increased

Decreased

Stayed About the Same

4. To what extent do older Americans continue to work (at least part-time)? How has this changed in the last several decades? Let's find out, using TRENDS.

a. Carefully examine the variable description for 150) WORK@70.

b. Look at the Historical Trends chart for 150) WORK@70. Then, use what you see there to indicate if the following statements are true or false.

> Data File: **TRENDS**
> Task: **Historical Trends**
> ➤ Variable: **150) WORK@70**

c. In 2001, over 10% of Americans age 70 and older participated in the labor force. (Circle one.)   T   F

d. The percentage of Americans age 70 and older participating in the labor force has declined in every decade since 1970. (Circle one.)   T   F

e. In 1963, almost 21% of Americans age 70 and older participated in the labor force. (Circle one.)   T   F

f. The percentage of Americans age 70 and older participating in the labor force generally rose from 1990 to 2001. (Circle one.)   T   F

g. In the next few decades, do you expect the percentage of Americans who are 70 and older and working to increase, decrease, or stay the same? Provide reasons for your answer.

5. How do males and females differ in the extent to which they are likely to live in a nursing home? We'll stick with TRENDS to find out.

   a. Carefully examine the variable descriptions for 154) NURS HMML and 155) NURS HMFM.

   b. Look at the Historical Trends chart for 154) NURS HMML and 155) NURS HMFM. Then, answer the following question about what you see there.

      > Data File: **TRENDS**
      > Task: **Historical Trends**
      > ➤ Variables: **154) NURS HMML**
      > **155) NURS HMFM**

   c. Among those 85 and older, are males or females more likely to live in nursing homes? (Circle one.)

      Males

      Females

      Both Are About Equal

6. Now let's get back to looking at the issue of whether or not the elderly tend to be "out of touch" in comparison to other age groups. If so, they might vote less than others. Do they? Social scientists and politicians say otherwise, that the elderly vote more than others. We will test this hypothesis: *people 65 and older will be more likely than younger people to have voted in 1996.* We'll use GSS.

   a. Open the GSS data set.

   b. Cross-tabulate 45) VOTE96 and 1) AGE. Then, fill in the percentages that voted in 1996.

      > ➤ Data File: **GSS**
      > ➤ Task: **Cross-tabulation**
      > ➤ Row Variable: **45) VOTE96**
      > ➤ Column Variable: **1) AGE**
      > ➤ View: **Tables**
      > ➤ Display: **Column %**

	<30	30–49	50–64	65 AND UP
YES	_____%	_____%	_____%	_____%

      Now, get the Cramer's V and the significance level for these two variables.

   c. Record the value of Cramer's V for this table. (Include asterisks, if any.)   V = _____

   d. Is the relationship between AGE and VOTE96 statistically significant? (Circle one.)   Yes   No

e. Is the relationship between AGE and VOTE96 weak, moderate, strong, or not significant? (Circle one.)

Weak

Moderate

Strong

Not Significant

f. Was the hypothesis supported? (Circle one.)   Yes   No

g. What do these results suggest about the political "clout" of the elderly compared to that of younger age groups? Might politicians be more or less likely to pay attention to the political opinions of the elderly? Why or why not?

7. Now, let's continue dealing with the "social isolation" issue with this hypothesis: *on average, people 65 and older will spend a social evening with a neighbor less often than younger people will.*

a. Carefully examine the variable description for 86) SOC.NEIGH.

b. Cross-tabulate 86) SOC.NEIGH and 1) AGE. Then, fill in the designated percentages.

> Data File: **GSS**
> Task: **Cross-tabulation**
> ➤ Row Variable: **86) SOC.NEIGH**
> ➤ Column Variable: **1) AGE**
> ➤ View: **Tables**
> ➤ Display: **Column %**

	<30	30–49	50–64	65 AND UP
ALM. DAILY	_____%	_____%	_____%	_____%
1–2 WEEK	_____%	_____%	_____%	_____%
1–FW MONTH	_____%	_____%	_____%	_____%

Now, examine the Cramer's V and the significance level for these two variables.

c. Is the relationship between AGE and SOC.NEIGH statistically significant? (Circle one.)   Yes   No

d. Is the relationship between AGE and SOC.NEIGH weak, moderate, strong, or not significant? (Circle one.)

Weak

Moderate

Strong

Not Significant

e. Was the hypothesis supported? (Circle one.)   Yes   No

f. Compare the percentage of elderly who visit with a neighbor almost daily with the percentage of those 30 to 64 years of age who do so. How are these percentages different? What do you think may be the reason(s) for these differences?

8. Do the elderly typically like the idea of living with their children? Try this hypothesis: *people 65 and older will be more likely than those who are younger to think it is a good idea for older people to share a home with their grown children.*

a. Carefully examine the variable description for 82) LIVE W KID.

b. Cross-tabulate 82) LIV W KID with 1) AGE. Then, fill in the percentages that think it is a good idea for older people to share a home with their grown children.

> Data File: **GSS**
> Task: **Cross-tabulation**
> ➤ Row Variable: **82) LIVE W KID**
> ➤ Column Variable: **1) AGE**
> ➤ View: **Tables**
> ➤ Display: **Column %**

	<30	30–49	50–64	65 AND UP
GOOD IDEA	_____%	_____%	_____%	_____%

Now, examine the Cramer's V and the significance level for these two variables.

c. Is the relationship between AGE and LIVE W KID statistically
    significant? (Circle one.)   Yes   No

d. Is the relationship between AGE and LIVE W KID weak,
    moderate, strong, or not significant? (Circle one.)   Weak

                                                                     Moderate

                                                                       Strong

                                                                 Not Significant

e. Was the hypothesis supported? (Circle one.)   Yes   No

f. Did you find these results surprising? Why or why not?

g. (Answer this item *only* if the above results were statistically significant.) Looking at the table in
    part b, compare the percentages that responded "Good Idea" who were under 30, and 30 to 49
    years old, with those who were 65 and older. What might be the main reasons for this difference
    between these age groups?

9. Switch to ELECTION and we'll look at another "social isolation" issue. Here is our hypothesis, which
    is rooted in the idea that older people might have more time to provide volunteer service: *people 65
    and older will be more likely than younger people to have done volunteer work recently.*

    a. Open the ELECTION data set and carefully examine the variable description for 62) VOLUNTR.

    b. Cross-tabulate 62) VOLUNTR with 3) AGE. Then, fill in the percentages that had performed vol-
        unteer work within the past year.

> *Data File:* **ELECTION**
> > *Task:* **Cross-tabulation**
> *Row Variable:* **62) VOLUNTR**
> *Column Variable:* **3) AGE**
> > *View:* **Tables**
> > *Display:* **Column %**

	<30	30–49	50–64	65 AND UP
YES	_____%	_____%	_____%	_____%

Now, examine the Cramer's V and the significance level for these two variables.

c. Is the relationship between AGE and VOLUNTR statistically significant? (Circle one.)

Yes   No

d. Is the relationship between AGE and VOLUNTR weak, moderate, strong, or not significant? (Circle one.)

Weak

Moderate

Strong

Not Significant

e. Was the hypothesis supported? (Circle one.)

Yes   No

f. (Answer this item *only* if the above results were statistically significant.) Looking at the above table, compare the percentages that responded "yes" who were 30 to 49 years old, with those who were 65 and up. What do you think might be the main reasons for this difference between these two age groups?

10. Now, let's compare the views of elderly people with those of other age groups on what many consider major, related social policy issues—the difficulties facing our Social Security and Medicare programs in the years ahead. Here's our hypothesis: *people 65 and older will be more likely than younger people to feel that most of any expected federal budget surplus should be used to protect Social Security and Medicare.*

a. Carefully examine the variable description for 60) SOCSEC SP.

b. Cross-tabulate 60) SOCSEC SP with 3) AGE. Then, fill in the percentages that think most of any federal budget surplus should be used to protect Social Security and Medicare.

> Data File: **ELECTION**
>
> Task: **Cross-tabulation**
>
> ➤ Row Variable: **60) SOCSEC SP**
>
> ➤ Column Variable: **3) AGE**
>
> ➤ View: **Tables**
>
> ➤ Display: **Column %**

	<30	30–49	50–64	65 AND UP
APPROVE	_____%	_____%	_____%	_____%

Now, examine the Cramer's V and the significance level for these two variables.

c. Is the relationship between AGE and SOCSEC SP statistically significant? (Circle one.)   Yes   No

d. Is the relationship between AGE and SOCSEC SP weak, moderate, strong, or not significant? (Circle one.)

Weak

Moderate

Strong

Not Significant

e. Was the hypothesis supported? (Circle one.)   Yes   No

f. Regardless of whether or not the differences in the above table were statistically significant, do those 65 and older, and those who are younger, appear to generally agree or disagree on whether or not most of any federal budget surplus should be used to protect Social Security and Medicare?

ABUSIVE INTIMATE RELATIONSHIPS

Tasks: Historical Trends, Cross-tabulation, Univariate, Mapping
Data Files: GSS, TRENDS, STATES, YRBS

"Y ou tend to hurt the ones you love," goes a well-known saying. Across America every year, it appears, millions of people experience this in ways far more ugly than lovers' quarrels. Abuse within intimate relationships is an enormous problem by any measure, though no one knows its true frequency and scope.

Abuse within intimate relationship includes actions between people who may not live together, such as ex-spouses, boyfriends and girlfriends. However, most of it involves forms of domestic abuse—that is, abuse within families and households. This includes *child abuse*, namely actions, or failures to take actions, that harm or are likely to harm children or put them at serious risk.[1] This in turn includes *neglect* (guardians failing to provide for their children's needs for food, clothing, shelter, safety, medical care, hygiene, and so forth), *physical abuse* (which includes such things as inflicting bodily harm to children or threatening to do so), *sexual abuse*, *abandonment*, some types of *psychological maltreatment*, and more.[2]

Of course, domestic abuse also occurs between spouses and between live-in partners. This may include not only physical beatings, but also such behaviors as rape, harmful psychological mistreatment, or even murder. The elderly are also often victims of domestic abuse beyond spousal abuse as when, for example, they are beaten, neglected, sexually abused, or psychologically mistreated by their adult children, other family members, or caregivers.

An important term that is frequently used by students of crime and domestic violence is *intimate partner violence*. It refers to "violent crimes . . . committed against persons by their current or former spouses, boyfriends or girlfriends."[3] This obviously includes relationships both within and outside families and households, while being restricted to acts of physical violence such as murder, rape, robbery, and assault.[4]

In this exercise, we will of course not be able to thoroughly look at all of these diverse aspects and types of abuse within intimate relationships. However, we will examine abuse directed toward children and violence between intimate partners. Let's begin by using the TRENDS data to get some sense of the extent of such abuse and changes in it over time. First, we'll examine substantiated cases of child maltreatment, which includes neglect, physical and sexual abuse, and other forms of mistreatment such as psychological abuse, threats to physically harm, abandonment, and even giving birth to babies who are already drug-addicted.

---

[1] I am drawing heavily on Eitzen and Baca Zinn's (op cit., pages 372–373) approach to defining "child abuse."

[2] See the descriptions in *Child Maltreatment 1999*, U.S. Department of Health and Human Services, Washington D.C.: U.S. Government Printing Office, 2001, page 12. See also Mooney et al., op cit., page 130.

[3] Callie Marie Rennison and Sarah Welchans, *Intimate Partner Violence*, U.S. Department of Justice, Bureau of Justice Statistics: Washington, D.C., 2000, page 1. Some researchers also include ex-boy/girlfriends. Some would also include *threats* to commit violent crimes (cf. Mooney et al., op cit., page 128).

[4] Throughout this exercise, when using the term "assault," both "aggravated" and "simple" assaults are included. That is, assault in which severe injury was inflicted or attempted (usually with a weapon) *and* that in which no weapon was used and serious injury did not result.

➤ *Data File:* **TRENDS**
➤ *Task:* **Historical Trends**
➤ *Variable:* **159) CHILDVICT**

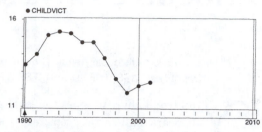

Rate of child maltreatment (mostly neglect, physical and sexual abuse)
per 1,000 children

As we can see, the rate of substantiated cases of child abuse dropped from 1993 to 1999, then increased somewhat to 12.4 per 1,000 children in 2001. Does this give us a "true" understanding of the extent of child abuse and changes in it over time? Maybe, but it's hard to say for sure. Most child abuse is not reported. Moreover, in many unsubstantiated cases, abuse did occur. The actual amount of child abuse is much higher than that of which any recording agency is aware. Still, it is sobering to consider that there were 526,841 confirmed cases of child abuse in the lowest year on this chart, 1999.[5]

One way to try to get at the true extent of child abuse is through using surveys to collect such data. As you can imagine, getting honest answers to questions about this is difficult! Let's consider the National Crime Victimization Survey (NCVS) that we discussed in Exercise 6. By asking respondents about their experience as victims, and about their relationship to the offender, the NCVS is a major source of information about domestic violence. However, while this survey instrument has been improved in recent years to better measure domestic abuse, it is still difficult for NCVS researchers to get full reporting on it.[6] Moreover, only victims over age 12 are included, while murder, abuse resulting in fatalities, and other types of child abuse (such as neglect) are not. Let's see some of what NCVS shows us about the amount of violence (rape and other sexual assaults, robbery, and assault) by parents against their children. All of the victims identified here were over 12 years old and most (but not all) were under 18.

Data File: **TRENDS**
Task: **Historical Trends**
➤ *Variables:* **160) PARVIOL**
161) PARTHREAT

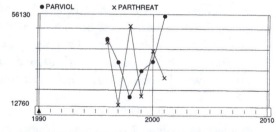

Estimated number of people 12 and over (mostly under 18) threatened
or actually assaulted, robbed, or raped by a parent

The amount of violent crime committed by parents against children generally increased between 1996 and 2001, while threats of the same went down. But there were also lots of fluctuations. In 2001, the

---

[5] *Child Maltreatment 1999*, op cit., page 9.

[6] *National Crime Victimization Survey: Questions About the Redesign*, U.S. Department of Justice, Bureau of Justice Statistics, Washington D.C., 1994, page 1.

NCVS estimated, there were 56,120 such crimes and another 26,000 were threatened. Notice how much smaller the former number is than the numbers of substantiated child abuses we noted earlier. Given how many child victims and types of abuse are excluded from the NCVS data, and how difficult it is to get honest answers about child abuse in these kinds of household surveys, we should not be surprised at these relatively low NCVS numbers.

What about violence between intimate partners? Let's look at some data here, starting with the estimated number of victims of violence (murder from the UCR; robbery, rape, and assault from the NCVS) by intimate partners in recent years.

Data File: **TRENDS**
Task: **Historical Trends**
➤ Variable: **162) #INTIVOL**

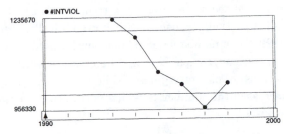

Number of victims of violence (murder, rape, assault, and robbery) by intimate partners

Notice that, like other violent crimes, violence by intimate partners generally declined between 1993 and 1998. Though their figure is almost certainly too low, the Department of Justice estimated the number of such acts at 1,033,670 for 1998. How about just the most serious violent crime—homicide?

Data File: **TRENDS**
Task: **Historical Trends**
➤ Variable: **167) INTMURDER**

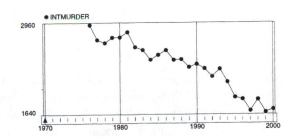

Total number of intimate partner homicides

From 1976 on, the number of intimate homicides dropped. This is especially noteworthy as the size of the population as a whole increased during that period. In 1999, the FBI figured that there were 1,687 such killings in the United States, compared to 2,957 in 1976.

But as we have already noted, a number of different types of relationships (both homosexual and heterosexual) are comprehended in the term "intimate." To get a more precise picture of reality here, let's compare the number of people killed by spouses with those killed by either boyfriends or girlfriends.[7]

---

[7] This latter category includes both same-sex and opposite-sex relationships.

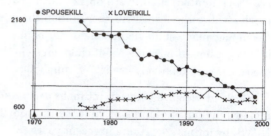

Data File: **TRENDS**
Task: **Historical Trends**
➤ Variables: **172) SPOUSEKILL**
 174) LOVERKILL

Number of people murdered by their spouse, boyfriend, or girlfriend

Here, we see some interesting trends. Between 1976 and 1999 overall, while the number of people killed by their spouses declined dramatically, murder by boyfriends or girlfriends rose slightly. By 1999, these numbers had become much closer, with 836 murdered by a spouse, and 743 by a boyfriend or girlfriend, compared to 2,174 and 662 (respectively) in 1976. This is to be expected. After all, things such as people getting married later, and increasing numbers of people who have been divorced, have increased the number of adults who have boyfriends or girlfriends. Now, what about killings by ex-spouses?

Data File: **TRENDS**
Task: **Historical Trends**
➤ Variable: **173) EXSPSEKILL**

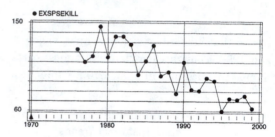

Number of people murdered by their ex-spouse

I don't know about you, but I find it surprising that, despite the increased number of adults who have been divorced and thus have ex-spouses, the number of people murdered by ex-spouses decreased quite a bit between 1976 and 1999 (from 123 to 63, or by about half). This number has also remained much lower than that for killings by spouses or lovers.

How about violence among *teenagers* between boyfriends and girlfriends? Let's turn to the Youth Risk Behavior Survey (YRBS) to take a quick look at high school seniors in 2001.

➤ Data File: **YRBS**
➤ Task: **Univariate**
➤ Primary Variable: **11) STEADYHIT**
➤ View: **Pie**

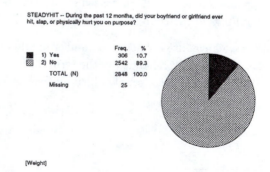

STEADYHIT -- During the past 12 months, did your boyfriend or girlfriend ever hit, slap, or physically hurt you on purpose?

		Freq.	%
■	1) Yes	306	10.7
▨	2) No	2542	89.3
	TOTAL (N)	2848	100.0
	Missing	25	

[Weight]

Investigating Social Problems

We see here that about 11% of seniors said their steady boyfriend or girlfriend has deliberately hit, slapped, or physically hurt them during the past year. Let's see if this trend of violence also extends to forced sex.

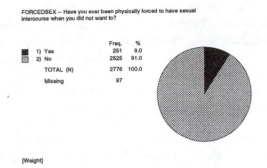

Data File: **YRBS**
Task: **Univariate**
➤ Primary Variable: **12) FORCEDSEX**
➤ View: **Pie**

FORCEDSEX -- Have you ever been physically forced to have sexual intercourse when you did not want to?

		Freq.	%
■	1) Yes	251	9.0
▨	2) No	2525	91.0
	TOTAL (N)	2776	100.0
	Missing	97	

[Weight]

About 9% stated that they had been forced to have sexual intercourse. These percentages are alarming.

Gender differences and dynamics related to them are very important aspects of violence within intimate relationships. Shall we take a look at these last two variables again, this time looking at gender differences among them?

Data File: **YRBS**
➤ Task: **Cross-tabulation**
➤ Row Variable: **11) STEADYHIT**
➤ Column Variable: **1) GENDER**
➤ View: **Tables**
➤ Display: **Column %**

STEADYHIT by GENDER
Weight Variable: WEIGHT
Cramer's V: 0.031

		GENDER			
		Female	Male	Missing	TOTAL
STEADYHIT	Yes	142	164	0	306
		9.8%	11.7%		10.8%
	No	1306	1231	5	2537
		90.2%	88.3%		89.2%
	Missing	14	11	0	25
	TOTAL	1448	1395	5	2843
		100.0%	100.0%		

These results are not what we might expect; males (11.7%) and females (9.8%) are about equally likely to have been hit by their steady boyfriend or girlfriend (V = 0.031). Let's check our second variable now.

Data File: **YRBS**
Task: **Cross-tabulation**
➤ Row Variable: **12) FORCEDSEX**
➤ Column Variable: **1) GENDER**
➤ View: **Tables**
➤ Display: **Column %**

FORCEDSEX by GENDER
Weight Variable: WEIGHT
Cramer's V: 0.112 **

		GENDER			
		Female	Male	Missing	TOTAL
FORCEDSEX	Yes	171	79	1	250
		12.2%	5.8%		9.0%
	No	1234	1288	3	2522
		87.8%	94.2%		91.0%
	Missing	57	40	0	97
	TOTAL	1405	1366	5	2772
		100.0%	100.0%		

The last figure is pretty much what we'd expect. Females (about 12%) are twice as likely as males (about 6%) to say they were forced into sex (V = 0.112**).

On the one hand, the first finding about the relative incidence of violence by or toward men and women among teens reflects findings from other surveys that suggest males and females are each about as likely to strike their partner.[8] While this is important, others, including many feminist scholars, assert that these types of survey questions may not help us to differentiate between levels of violence, with male violence often being much more severe and physically damaging. Also, these social scientists suggest, when females hit their male intimate partners, it is often in self-defense.[9] For example, according to the NCVS, three-quarters of female victims of intimate partner violence between 1992 and 1996 defended themselves.[10]

While we cannot look at the self-defense question much here, we can examine differences in the extent to which males and females are the victims of *serious* violence by their partners. Let's start with the number per 1,000 who have been victims of intimate violence, including rape, murder, robbery, and assault.

➤ *Data File:* **TRENDS**
   ➤ *Task:* **Historical Trends**
➤ *Variables:* **163) INTVIOLFM**
             164) INTVIOLML

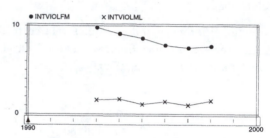

Female victims of violence by intimate partners per 1,000 women and men

As you can clearly see, the rate of female victims of intimate violence has consistently been much higher than that for males. For example, the NCVS estimates that in 1998 about 8 in every 1,000 females were victims of violence by their partners, compared to 1.5 of every 1,000 males. This is quite a difference. Let's look at intimate homicide now.

Data File: **TRENDS**
   Task: **Historical Trends**
➤ *Variables:* **168) INTMURDRFM**
             169) INTMURDRML

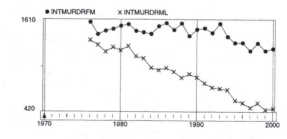

Number of female and male victims of intimate partner homicide

---

[8] See for example Parillo's (op cit., pages 289–290) discussion of findings from the 1996 *National Survey of Families and Households.*

[9] These types of arguments are set forth in Curran and Renzetti, op cit., pages 257–258.

[10] *Violence by Inmates*, U.S. Department of Justice, Bureau of Justice Statistics, Washington D.C., 1998, p. 17.

                                                  Investigating Social Problems

Again, we see many more female than male victims. Moreover, this gap between men and women has been widening. The numbers being killed by intimate partners have been declining much more quickly for males than for females. Overall, our data to this point strongly suggest females are much more likely than males to be the victims of more serious physical violence within intimate relationships.

Now, let's return briefly again to the issue of child abuse. We will start by examining variations in the level of child abuse (all types combined) among American states.

➤ Data File: **STATES**
   ➤ Task: **Mapping**
➤ Variable 1: **80) KIDABUSE00**
     ➤ View: **Map**

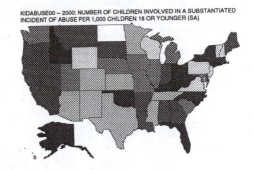

KIDABUSE00 – 2000: NUMBER OF CHILDREN INVOLVED IN A SUBSTANTIATED INCIDENT OF ABUSE PER 1,000 CHILDREN 18 OR YOUNGER (SA)

It's hard to see any clear geographic pattern from this map. So, we'll look at the rankings.

Data File: **STATES**
Task: **Mapping**
Variable 1: **80) KIDABUSE00**
➤ View: **List: Rank**

RANK	CASE NAME	VALUE
1	Alaska	37
2	Kentucky	23
2	Florida	23
2	Idaho	23
5	Connecticut	21
6	Ohio	20
7	North Carolina	19
7	West Virginia	19
7	Oklahoma	19
7	New York	19

Here, we see that in 2000 Alaska had the highest rank here with 37 substantiated incidents of abuse per 1,000 children, while Pennsylvania had the least, with 2. How about child fatalities that occurred as a result of abuse? Let's take a look.

Data File: **STATES**
Task: **Mapping**
➤ Variable 1: **85) CHILDDIE**
   ➤ View: **List: Rank**

RANK	CASE NAME	VALUE
1	West Virginia	4.01
2	Kentucky	3.71
3	Oklahoma	3.70
4	Texas	3.43
5	Arkansas	3.22
5	Indiana	2.92
7	Ohio	2.78
8	Louisiana	2.71
9	Florida	2.44
10	Illinois	2.43

In 2001, the highest rate of child fatalities due to abuse was in West Virginia (4.01). The lowest rates were in California and New Hampshire, where each reported 0.32.

It makes sense to expect that rates of different types of child abuse tend to be positively associated with each other. For example, where there is more physical abuse, there may be more neglect or sexual abuse. Why don't we test this idea?

Data File: **STATES**
Task: **Mapping**
➤ Variable 1: **82) CHILDPHYS**
➤ Variable 2: **83) NEGLECT**
➤ View: **Map**

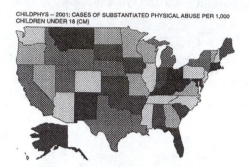

CHILDPHYS -- 2001: CASES OF SUBSTANTIATED PHYSICAL ABUSE PER 1,000 CHILDREN UNDER 18 (CM)

r = 0.624**

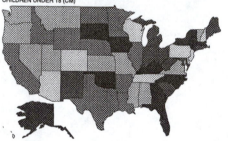

NEGLECT -- 2001: SUBSTANTIATED CASES OF CHILD NEGLECT PER 1,000 CHILDREN UNDER 18 (CM)

It is quite clear just through visual comparison of these maps that states with high rates of substantiated physical abuse of children also tend to discover more child neglect (for example, look at Alaska, Florida, Kentucky, and Massachusetts). The $r = 0.624**$, which is quite strong.

Data File: **STATES**
Task: **Mapping**
Variable 1: **82) CHILDPHYS**
➤ Variable 2: **84) CHSEXABUSE**
➤ View: **Map**

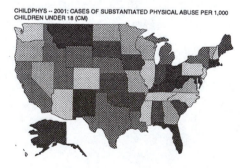

CHILDPHYS -- 2001: CASES OF SUBSTANTIATED PHYSICAL ABUSE PER 1,000 CHILDREN UNDER 18 (CM)

r = 0.461**

Investigating Social Problems

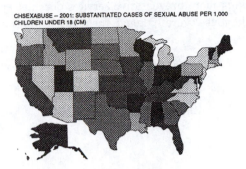

CHSEXABUSE -- 2001: SUBSTANTIATED CASES OF SEXUAL ABUSE PER 1,000 CHILDREN UNDER 18 (CM)

There is a moderate positive correlation between rates of substantiated physical and sexual abuse of children (r = 0.461**). However, we should probably note in the midst of this analysis of state-level, ecological data that there is one "fly" in its "ointment." That is, we are still looking only at levels of abuse detected by agencies. These may not accurately reflect how much abuse is really going on in these states. Such statistics may instead reflect variations in such things as the policies and practices of child welfare agencies, or people's willingness to report abuse to them, more than actual levels of child abuse.

States also vary in how they handle child abuse. For example, states differ in how many families are provided with services to prevent child abuse. They also vary in how often they remove children from parents that they have determined are abusive. Are these actions associated with higher or lower levels of substantiated abuse? Let's see.

Data File: **STATES**
Task: **Mapping**
➤ Variable 1: **80) KIDABUSE00**
➤ Variable 2: **86) ABUSEPREV**
➤ View: **Map**

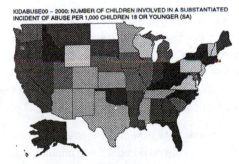

KIDABUSE00 -- 2000: NUMBER OF CHILDREN INVOLVED IN A SUBSTANTIATED INCIDENT OF ABUSE PER 1,000 CHILDREN 18 OR YOUNGER (SA)

r = −0.223

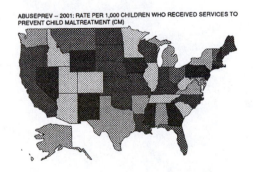

ABUSEPREV -- 2001: RATE PER 1,000 CHILDREN WHO RECEIVED SERVICES TO PREVENT CHILD MALTREATMENT (CM)

Having more preventative services does not appear to be correlated with significantly lower levels of child abuse overall, though the relationship is negative as we might expect (r = –0.223).

Data File: **STATES**
Task: **Mapping**
Variable 1: **80) KIDABUSE00**
➤ *Variable 2:* **87) REMOVEHOME**
➤ *View:* **Map**

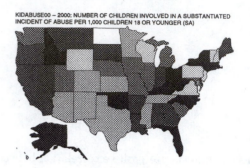

KIDABUSE00 -- 2000: NUMBER OF CHILDREN INVOLVED IN A SUBSTANTIATED INCIDENT OF ABUSE PER 1,000 CHILDREN 18 OR YOUNGER (SA)

r = –0.316*

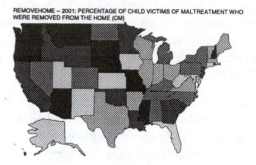

REMOVEHOME -- 2001: PERCENTAGE OF CHILD VICTIMS OF MALTREATMENT WHO WERE REMOVED FROM THE HOME (CM)

However, the more often states remove kids from homes where parents are determined to be abusive, the lower the level of substantiated abuse. This correlation is moderate (r = –0.316*). Is there less abuse reported in states where it is more likely that children will be removed from the home because there really is less abuse occurring in them? Or are people simply less likely to report (or substantiate) child abuse if it is more likely that the parent will lose their child(ren)? Or is there some other reason for this last correlation? What do you think?

Now, of course, it is time for you to explore child abuse and violence between intimate partners on your own. In doing so, you'll learn more about it and also delve into the kinds of factors that may or may not be associated with variations in the occurrence of abuse within intimate relationships.

WORKSHEET

NAME:

COURSE:

DATE:

EXERCISE

12

REVIEW QUESTIONS

Based on the first part of this exercise, answer True or False to the following items:

The psychological mistreatment of children is not normally considered to be a type of "child abuse."   T   F

The term "intimate partner violence" refers to violent crimes against spouses, ex-spouses, boyfriends, and girlfriends.   T   F

In 1999, there were over one million confirmed cases of child abuse in the United States.   T   F

The NCVS does not collect information on *all* types of child abuse.   T   F

In recent years, intimate partner violence overall has been increasing, though intimate partner *homicide* has been decreasing.   T   F

Between 1976 and 1999, the number of people murdered by ex-spouses and intimate partners increased, while the number murdered by spouses decreased.   T   F

Among seniors in the YRBS, females were more likely than males to have been hit in some way by their steady boyfriend or girlfriend.   T   F

Data in this exercise so far suggest that females are more likely than males to be the victims of serious intimate partner violence.   T   F

Alaska had the highest rate of substantiated child abuse cases, but not the highest rate of child fatalities as a result of abuse.   T   F

States with higher rates of physical abuse of children also tend to have higher rates of child neglect and sexual abuse.   T   F

Substantiated child abuse is significantly lower in states where more families receive services to prevent child abuse.   T   F

EXPLORIT QUESTIONS

1. There are social scientists who believe that spanking has negative repercussions on child development. Some would even go so far as to identify it as a form of child abuse. On the other hand, it appears to be a fairly common practice. Why don't we see how Americans generally feel about spanking?

   a. Open the TRENDS data set and carefully examine the variable description for 158) SPANK?.

Exercise 12: Abusive Intimate Relationships   227

b. Look at the Historical Trends chart for 158) SPANK?. Then, answer the following questions about what you see there.

> ➤ *Data File:* **TRENDS**
>   ➤ *Task:* **Historical Trends**
> ➤ *Variable:* **158) SPANK?**

c. Generally, between the mid-1980s and 2002, did the percentage of Americans who supported spanking increase, decrease, or stay about the same?(Circle one.)

                  Increased

                  Decreased

       Stayed About the Same

d. As of 2002, about what percentage of Americans supported spanking? (Write in your answer.)

            _____%

2. Let's look at this same question now in our GSS file, in order to consider what kinds of people are more or less likely to support spanking. Here is our first hypothesis: *the more educated people are, the less likely they will be to support spanking.*

   a. Open the GSS data set.

   b. Cross-tabulate 73) SPANKING with 13) DEGREE. Then, fill in the percentages that support spanking.

> ➤ *Data File:* **GSS**
>   ➤ *Task:* **Cross-tabulation**
> ➤ *Row Variable:* **73) SPANKING**
> ➤ *Column Variable:* **13) DEGREE**
>   ➤ *View:* **Tables**
> ➤ *Display:* **Column %**

	NOT H.S.	H.S.	JR. COL	4 YR DEG	GRAD DEG
AGREE	_____%	_____%	_____%	_____%	_____%

Now, get the Cramer's V and the significance level for these two variables.

c. Record the value of Cramer's V for this table. (Include asterisks, if any.)   V = _____

d. Is the relationship between SPANKING and DEGREE statistically significant? (Circle one.)   Yes   No

e. Was the hypothesis supported? (Circle one.)   Yes   No

f. Was there any educational level at which a majority of of the respondents did *not* support spanking? (Circle one.) Yes   No

3. Let's try this hypothesis: *the older people are, the more likely they will be to support spanking.*

a. Cross-tabulate 73) SPANKING with 1) AGE.Then, fill in the percentages that support spanking.

Data File:	**GSS**
Task:	**Cross-tabulation**
Row Variable:	**73) SPANKING**
➤ *Column Variable:*	**1) AGE**
➤ *View:*	**Tables**
➤ *Display:*	**Column %**

	<30	30–49	50–64	65 AND UP
AGREE	_____%	_____%	_____%	_____%

Now, examine the Cramer's V and the significance level for these two variables.

b. Is the relationship between SPANKING and AGE statistically significant? (Circle one.)   Yes   No

c. Was the hypothesis supported? (Circle one.)   Yes   No

d. Do these results surprise you? Why or why not?

4. Let's turn now to the YRBS to explore violence between teenage boyfriends and girlfriends. It is sometimes said that marital violence is more common in cities than in suburbs or rural areas.[11] Perhaps this is true for teenage dating violence. Let's take a look. Here is our hypothesis: *high school seniors in urban areas will be most likely to have been struck by a dating partner, while those in rural areas will be least likely to have been struck by a dating partner.*

a. Open the YRBS data set.

b. Cross-tabulate 11) STEADYHIT with 5) METRO. Then, fill in the percentages that had been struck by a steady dating partner within the past year.

---

[11] See, for example, Soroka and Bryjak, op cit., page 42.

> ➤ *Data File:* **YRBS**
> ➤ *Task:* **Cross-tabulation**
> ➤ *Row Variable:* **11) STEADYHIT**
> ➤ *Column Variable:* **5) METRO**
> ➤ *View:* **Tables**
> ➤ *Display:* **Column %**

	URBAN	SUBURBAN	RURAL
YES	_____%	_____%	_____%

Now, examine the Cramer's V and the significance level for these two variables.

c. Is the relationship between STEADYHIT and METRO statistically
significant? (Circle one.)   Yes   No

d. Was the hypothesis supported? (Circle one.)   Yes   No

e. Do you think that there was much of a difference between urban and suburban schools in the
degree to which teens had been struck by their steady boyfriend or girlfriend? Explain.

5. Alcohol abuse is commonly implicated in violence within intimate relationships. Could this be true for
high school seniors? Here is our hypothesis: *the more often high school seniors binge drink, the
more likely it will be that they have been struck by their boyfriend or girlfriend.* Of course, we'll stick
with YRBS here. (You looked at this YRBS binge-drinking question before, in Exercise 5.)

a. Cross-tabulate 11) STEADYHIT with 23) RECBINGE. Then, fill in the percentages that had been
struck by a steady dating partner within the past year.

> *Data File:* **GSS**
> *Task:* **Cross-tabulation**
> *Row Variable:* **11) STEADYHIT**
> ➤ *Column Variable:* **23) RECBINGE**
> ➤ *View:* **Tables**
> ➤ *Display:* **Column %**

	NONE	ONE	2–5	6–9	10+
YES	_____%	_____%	_____%	_____%	_____%

Now, examine the Cramer's V and the significance level for these two variables.

b. Is the relationship between STEADYHIT and RECBINGE statistically significant? (Circle one.)

Yes   No

c. Is the relationship between STEADYHIT and RECBINGE weak, moderate, strong, or not significant? (Circle one.)

Weak

Moderate

Strong

Not Significant

d. Was the hypothesis supported? (Circle one.)

Yes   No

e. Do you think that (a) alcohol abuse leads to violence between boyfriends and girlfriends, (b) those who abuse alcohol a lot also just tend to be more violent and would be whether or not they drank too much, or (c) alcohol abuse and intimate violence are not associated with each other? Explain your answer.

6. Perhaps alcohol abuse is also implicated in teens being forced into sexual intercourse. Here is our hypothesis: *the more often high school seniors binge drink, the more likely it will be that they have been forced to have sexual intercourse.*

a. Cross-tabulate 12) FORCEDSEX with 23) RECBINGE. Then, fill in the percentages that had ever been forced to have sex.

> Data File: **YRBS**
> Task: **Cross-tabulation**
> ➤ Row Variable: **12) FORCEDSEX**
> ➤ Column Variable: **23) RECBINGE**
> ➤ View: **Tables**
> ➤ Display: **Column %**

	NONE	ONE	2–5	6–9	10-
YES	_____%	_____%	_____%	_____%	_____%

Now, examine the Cramer's V and the significance level for these two variables.

b. Is the relationship between FORCEDSEX and RECBINGE statistically
    significant? (Circle one.)   Yes   No

c. Is the relationship between FORCEDSEX and RECBINGE weak,
    moderate, strong, or not significant? (Circle one.)   Weak

                                                                      Moderate

                                                                        Strong

                                                                 Not Significant

d. Is the hypothesis supported? (Circle one.)   Yes   No

e. Looking at these results, as well as those from the last question 5, overall, do you think alcohol
    abuse has destructive effects upon the intimate relationships of young people? If so, what are
    they? Explain your answer.

7. While we're on the topic of violence in intimate relationships, let's consider the issue of whether or
    not people typically report such violence to the police. To do so, we'll return briefly to the TRENDS
    data set.

    a. Open the TRENDS data set and carefully examine the variable descriptions for 165) %IVREPFM
        and 166) %IVREPML.

    b. Look at the Historical Trends chart for 165) %IVREPFM and 166) %IVREPML. Then, answer the
        following questions about what you see there.

                    Data File: **TRENDS**
                        Task: **Historical Trends**
               ➤ Variables: **165) %IVREPFM**
                                166) %IVREPML

c. Between 1993 and 1998, did the percentage of females who reported
    violence by intimate partners to the police increase, decrease, or stay
    about the same? (Circle one.)

                                                              Increased

                                                              Decreased

                                                    Stayed About the Same

d. Between 1993 and 1998, did the percentage of males who reported violence
    by intimate partners to the police increase, decrease, or stay about the same?
    (Circle one.)   -   Increased

                                                              Decreased

                                                    Stayed About the Same

e. Are females or males more likely to report violence by intimate partners to the police? If there is a
    difference between genders here, what do you think are the reasons for it?

8. For the last few items, let's turn to STATES again to look further into the sad reality of child abuse.
    First, we'll consider whether or not *states that remove more victims of child abuse from the home will
    have lower rates of <u>fatality from child abuse</u>*. Of course, this will be our hypothesis.

    a. Open the STATES data set.

    b. Does this hypothesis predict a negative or a positive correlation? (Circle one.)   Negative

                                                                                                Positive

    c. Draw two maps, one showing state variations in the rate of child death due to maltreatment, and the
        other showing state variations in the percentage of victims of child abuse who are removed from the
        home. When you have done so, look at Pearson's *r*.

            ➤ *Data File:* **STATES**
                ➤ *Task:* **Mapping**
            ➤ *Variable 1:* **85) CHILDDIE**
            ➤ *Variable 2:* **87) REMOVEHOME**
                ➤ *View:* **Maps**

    d. Provide Pearson's *r* (including asterisks, if any, and the direction sign, if any).   *r* = _____

    e. Is this correlation significant *and* negative, significant *and* positive,
        or *not* significant? (Circle one.)
                                                            Significant *and* Negative

                                                            Significant *and* Positive

                                                                    Not Significant

f.   Is this correlation weak, moderate, strong, or not significant? (Circle one.)

                                                 Weak

                                            Moderate

                                            Strong

                                     Not Significant

g. Was the hypothesis supported? (Circle one.)   Yes   No

h. What do you think? What are the reasons you did, or did not, have a significant correlation here?

9.   We saw earlier that removing victims from the home is associated with lower rates of substantiated cases of child abuse overall. Is this true for specific types of child abuse? Here is our next hypothesis: *states that remove more victims of child abuse from the home will have lower rates of substantiated physical abuse of children.*

    a. Draw two maps, one showing state variations in the rate of substantiated physical abuse of children, and the other showing state variations in the percentage of victims of child maltreatment who are removed from the home. When you have done so, look at Pearson's *r*.

>   *Data File:* **STATES**
>   *Task:* **Mapping**
> ➤ *Variable 1:* **82) CHILDPHYS**
> ➤ *Variable 2:* **87) REMOVEHOME**
>   ➤ *View:* **Maps**

Examine Pearson's *r*.

    b. Is this correlation significant *and* negative, significant *and* positive, or *not* significant? (Circle one.)

                                          Significant *and* Negative

                                          Significant *and* Positive

                                          Not Significant

c. Is this correlation weak, moderate, strong, or not significant? (Circle one.)

Weak

Moderate

Strong

Not Significant

d. Was the hypothesis supported? (Circle one.)

Yes   No

e. What do you think? What are the reasons you did, or did not, have a significant correlation here?

10. Another hypothesis: *states that remove more victims of child abuse from the home will have lower rates of substantiated child neglect.*

a. Draw two maps, one showing state variations in the rate of substantiated child neglect, and the other showing state variations in the percentage of victims of child maltreatment who are removed from the home. When you have done so, look at Pearson's *r*.

> Data File: **STATES**
> Task: **Mapping**
> ➤ Variable 1: **83) NEGLECT**
> ➤ Variable 2: **87) REMOVEHOME**
> ➤ View: **Maps**

Examine Pearson's *r*.

b. Is this correlation significant *and* negative, significant *and* positive, or *not* significant? (Circle one.)

Significant *and* Negative

Significant *and* Positive

Not Significant

c. Is this correlation weak, moderate, strong, or not significant? (Circle one.)

Weak

Moderate

Strong

Not Significant

d. Was the hypothesis supported? (Circle one.) Yes No

11. Our final hypothesis: *states that remove more victims of child abuse from the home will have lower rates of substantiated sexual abuse of children.*

a. Draw two maps, one showing state variations in the rate of substantiated sexual abuse of children, and the other showing state variations in the percentage of victims of child maltreatment who are removed from the home. When you have done so, look at Pearson's *r*.

> Data File: **STATES**
> Task: **Mapping**
> ➤ Variable 1: **84) CHSEXABUSE**
> ➤ Variable 2: **87) REMOVEHOME**
> ➤ View: **Maps**

Examine Pearson's *r*.

b. Is this correlation significant *and* negative, significant *and* positive, or *not* significant? (Circle one.)

Significant *and* Negative

Significant *and* Positive

Not Significant

c. Is this correlation weak, moderate, strong, or not significant? (Circle one.)

Weak

Moderate

Strong

Not Significant

d. Was the hypothesis supported? (Circle one.) Yes No

12. Look at the correlations for questions 9–11. Do you think that removing victims of child maltreatment from the home reduces child abuse, or just decreases the *extent to which child abuse is reported to authorities*, neither, or both? Explain your answer.

POPULATION PROBLEMS

Tasks: Cross-tabulation, Historical Trends, Mapping, Scatterplot
Data Files: GSS, TRENDS, STATES, COUNTRIES

There is widespread agreement among sociologists that issues associated with population growth constitute a major set of social problems. For example, there is a great deal of concern about the continued rapid growth in the world's population overall. Scholars especially tend to worry about increases in the number of people in poorer, developing countries that do not have the means to care for the needs of their growing populations.

Yet among scientists who deal with population issues, there are many important, unsettled controversies. How many people can our planet support? (The latter has to do with ***carrying capacity***, that is, the number that can be sustained within a given area.) Do more people inevitably mean strained resources and too much pollution? Or can shortages and ecological threats associated with rising populations be overcome with things like better planning, distribution of resources, economic growth, and technology? What are the main factors that lead to population growth, stabilization, or decline? What types of social policies would best facilitate desired population changes? What would constitute an equitable distribution of resources among the peoples of the world, and how could this best be achieved? Some scholars even argue that, for some nations (including many in Europe such as Italy, Russia, and Germany) current trends of ***population decline*** may lead to problems in the future.[1] They contend that *decreases* in the number of people within nations can lead to problems such as labor shortages, economic decline, and the kinds of challenges associated with rising proportions of elderly people that we discussed in Exercise 11. One thing is certain. Social problems related to population, and debates about them, will likely remain active, complex, and fascinating for many years.

In this exercise, we cannot address all of these issues, and we certainly won't resolve any of these major controversies! But I do want you to learn about basic concepts, facts, and relationships that will help you to better understand these population problems and debates. We will look at variations in population size and growth in the United States and internationally, across place and time. We will consider some of the factors that appear to be associated with such changes in the number of people. In the process, we will also examine the main factors that directly affect population growth: how many babies are born (***fertility***); how many people die (***mortality***; which is in turn related to ***life expectancy***; that is, how long people can be expected to live on average); and *migration*, that is, the number moving in (***immigration***) or out (***emigration***) of an area.[2] Let's begin by looking at the United States.

---

[1] See, for example, Soroka and Bryjak, op cit., pages 369–376.

[2] See, for example, Kendall, op cit., pages 318–320.

➤ Data File: **TRENDS**
➤ Task: **Historical Trends**
➤ Variable: **135) USPOPULAT**

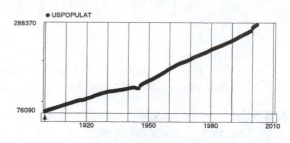

United States population in thousands

Notice the steady rise of the American population during the past century from a bit over 76,090,000 in 1900 to roughly 288,369,000 in 2002. Of course, this has also meant increases in population density, that is, in the number of people per square mile of land.

Data File: **TRENDS**
Task: **Historical Trends**
➤ Variable: **136) USPOPDENSE**

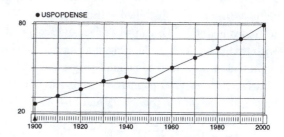

United States population per square mile of land

The drop between 1940 and 1950 is because from 1950 on, Alaska and Hawaii were included. Other than that, U.S. population density rose throughout the 20th century. As the old pioneer Daniel Boone would have said, there's less "elbow room" these days.

In Exercise 11, we saw that birth rates generally fell in the 20th century. But we also saw a number of things that helped to increase population size during this period, such as the Baby Boom between 1946 and about 1964, and steadily rising life expectancies. Let's consider a factor strongly related to rising life expectancies, namely, shifts in death rates.

Data File: **TRENDS**
Task: **Historical Trends**
➤ Variable: **140) DEATH RATE**

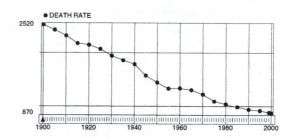

Age-adjusted deaths per 100,000 people, United States

As you can see, the death rate fell throughout the past century. The death rate in 2000 was roughly one-third the death rate in 1900. In addition to the decline in death rates, immigration has helped to expand the United States population in the past century.

Investigating Social Problems

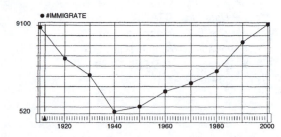

Data File: **TRENDS**
Task: **Historical Trends**
➤ *Variable:* **141) #IMMIGRATE**

Number (in thousands) immigrating into the United States during the previous 10 years

The immigration figures each represent the number of immigrants (in thousands) who came in during ten-year periods ending on the designated date.[3] Here, we see immigration numbers falling up to the year 1940 (from about 8,795,000 between 1901 and 1910, to only 528,000 from 1931 to 1940), before rising again to roughly 9,095,000 from 1991 to 2000.

Unlike the U.S. population, of course, *world* population has not been influenced by immigration! (So far as we know, no one is migrating to the Earth from other planets!) However, driven by falling death rates and, in many nations, high birth rates, the world's population also rose dramatically during the 20th century. Let's take a look.

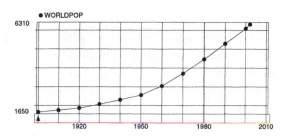

Data File: **TRENDS**
Task: **Historical Trends**
➤ *Variable:* **138) WORLDPOP**

Population of the world in millions

Here, we see a very steady rise. United Nations estimates put the figure at 1,650,000,000 in 1900. By 2002, the number had multiplied dramatically to about a whopping 6,307,000,000.

Let's consider population distribution. We'll look first at the United States, focusing on population density and growth between 1990 and 2000. We'll do both maps together.

---

[3] With the exception of the last figure, which represents only 1991–98.

➤ *Data File:* **STATES**
  ➤ *Task:* **Mapping**
➤ *Variable 1:* **3) POP$GRO**
➤ *Variable 2:* **4) DENSITY 00**
  ➤ *View:* **Maps**

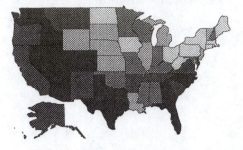

POP%GRO -- 1990-2000: PERCENT GROWTH IN RESIDENT POPULATION (SA)

r = −0.260*

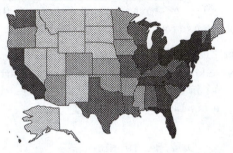

DENSITY 00 -- 2000: POPULATION PER SQUARE MILE (CENSUS)

The most crowded states are east of the Mississippi (except for California), especially the Northeast states. However, the biggest population *growth* has been in the West and South. In fact, the crowded states in the Northeast (dark in the lower map) are growing most slowly. There is a significant, though mild, negative correlation between density and population growth ($r = −0.260*$). Now let's look at the same variables to consider *international* population distribution.

➤ *Data File:* **COUNTRIES**
  ➤ *Task:* **Mapping**
➤ *Variable 1:* **5) POP GROWTH**
➤ *Variable 2:* **3) DENSITY**
  ➤ *View:* **Maps**

POP GROWTH -- CURRENT ANNUAL POPULATION GROWTH RATE (TWF, 2001)

r = 0.150*

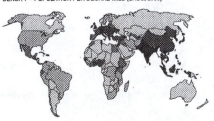

DENSITY -- POPULATION PER SQUARE MILE (SAUS, 2000)

Investigating Social Problems

Notice that while the most crowded nations are in places like Europe (dark color on the lower map), the biggest population growth areas are in places like Africa and parts of the Middle East. Still, here there is a slightly positive correlation between density and growth rates ($r = 0.150*$). Staying with COUNTRIES, let's look now at the correlation of factors such as migration, birth rates and death rates with population growth.

<table>
<tr><td align="right">Data File:</td><td>COUNTRIES</td></tr>
<tr><td align="right">➤ Task:</td><td>Scatterplot</td></tr>
<tr><td align="right">➤ Dependent Variable:</td><td>5) POP GROWTH</td></tr>
<tr><td align="right">➤ Independent Variable:</td><td>6) NETMIGRT</td></tr>
<tr><td align="right">➤ View:</td><td>Reg. Line</td></tr>
</table>

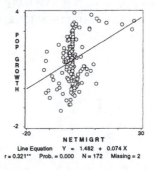

Line Equation   Y = 1.482 + 0.074 X
r = 0.321**   Prob. = 0.000   N = 172   Missing = 2

Net migration (that is, the balance between those moving into a nation and those moving out of it) is positively associated with population growth ($r = 0.321**$).

<table>
<tr><td align="right">Data File:</td><td>COUNTRIES</td></tr>
<tr><td align="right">Task:</td><td>Scatterplot</td></tr>
<tr><td align="right">Dependent Variable:</td><td>5) POP GROWTH</td></tr>
<tr><td align="right">➤ Independent Variable:</td><td>7) BIRTH RATE</td></tr>
<tr><td align="right">➤ View:</td><td>Reg. Line</td></tr>
</table>

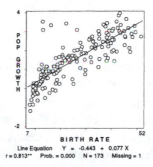

Line Equation   Y = -0.443 + 0.077 X
r = 0.813**   Prob. = 0.000   N = 173   Missing = 1

Birth rates are also positively associated with population growth, and quite strongly ($r = 0.813**$).

<table>
<tr><td align="right">Data File:</td><td>COUNTRIES</td></tr>
<tr><td align="right">Task:</td><td>Scatterplot</td></tr>
<tr><td align="right">Dependent Variable:</td><td>5) POP GROWTH</td></tr>
<tr><td align="right">➤ Independent Variable:</td><td>15) DEATH RATE</td></tr>
<tr><td align="right">➤ View:</td><td>Reg. Line</td></tr>
</table>

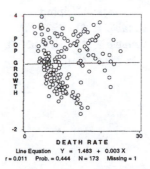

Line Equation   Y = 1.483 + 0.003 X
r = 0.011   Prob. = 0.444   N = 173   Missing = 1

However, death rates are not statistically correlated with decreasing populations or with less population growth ($r = 0.011$). This is because many countries that have high death rates also have high birth rates that offset their negative impact. This is clear if we compare maps of both rates.

Data File: **COUNTRIES**
➤ Task: **Mapping**
➤ Variable 1: **7) BIRTH RATE**
➤ Variable 2: **15) DEATH RATE**
➤ Views: **Map**

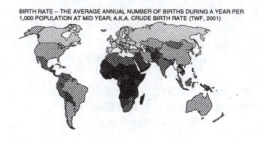

BIRTH RATE -- THE AVERAGE ANNUAL NUMBER OF BIRTHS DURING A YEAR PER 1,000 POPULATION AT MID YEAR; A.K.A. CRUDE BIRTH RATE (TWF, 2001)

$r = 0.445**$

DEATH RATE -- THE AVERAGE ANNUAL NUMBER OF DEATHS DURING A YEAR PER 1,000 POPULATION AT MIDYEAR; A.K.A. CRUDE DEATH RATE (TWF, 2001)

If you compare the maps closely, you can see that many nations in Africa and places like Afghanistan (which is just to the "left" and "north" of India and Pakistan, as you may have learned from the media since September 11, 2001) have high death and birth rates (i.e., dark on both maps). In fact, there is a *positive* correlation between these two variables ($r = 0.445**$). This should not surprise us. In many nations, people have large numbers of children partly because they want to offset the effects of rampant death, especially among babies. Let's consider this, focusing now on fertility rates (i.e., the number of babies born to the average woman).

Data File: **COUNTRIES**
Task: **Mapping**
➤ Variable 1: **8) FERTILITY**
➤ Variable 2: **10) INF. MORTL**
➤ View: **Maps**

FERTILITY -- AVERAGE NUMBER OF CHILDREN BORN TO EACH WOMAN (TWF, 2001)

$r = 0.811**$

INF. MORTL -- NUMBER OF INFANT DEATHS PER 1,000 BIRTHS (TWF, 2001)

As you can see, there is a very powerful correlation between these two variables ($r = 0.811**$). Where higher proportions of babies die, fertility tends to be much higher.[4] And both tend to be extremely high in Africa and the Middle East. While we have these maps open, let's take a closer look at this by looking at the rankings for both variables.

Data File: **COUNTRIES**
Task: **Mapping**
Variable 1: **8) FERTILITY**
Variable 2: **10) INF. MORTL**
➤ *Views:* **List: Rank**

RANK	CASE NAME	VALUE
1	Somalia	7.2
2	Niger	7.2
3	Ethiopia	7.1
4	Yemen	7.1
5	Uganda	7.0

RANK	CASE NAME	VALUE
1	Angola	195.78
2	Afghanistan	149.28
3	Sierra Leone	148.66
4	Mozambique	139.86
5	Liberia	134.63

Notice how many of the highest ranked nations are in Africa and the Middle East. As you can see, the highest fertilities are in Somalia and Niger (an average of 7.2 babies per woman in each). These two nations also have very high infant mortality rates (ranked #8 and #9, respectively). In each, close to 125 babies die for every 1,000 who are born (or over 12%)! In Angola, close to 20% of all babies die (roughly 196 per every 1,000 births), and women there average 6.5 babies each.

Fertility is clearly associated with population growth and size, and it is controllable. Let's consider the association of family planning beliefs and practices and fertility rates.

---

[4] Of course, it may be that babies who are born into larger and/or more rapidly growing families may be less likely than other babies to survive, especially in poorer nations.

Data File: **COUNTRIES**
➤ *Task:* **Scatterplot**
➤ *Dependent Variable:* **8) FERTILITY**
➤ *Independent Variable:* **9) LARGE FAML**
➤ *View:* **Reg. Line**

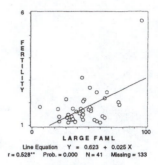

Line Equation   Y = 0.623 + 0.025 X
r = 0.528**   Prob. = 0.000   N = 41   Missing = 133

Not surprisingly, where people value larger families, fertility rates tend to be higher ($r = 0.528^{**}$).

Data File: **COUNTRIES**
Task: **Scatterplot**
Dependent Variable: **8) FERTILITY**
➤ *Independent Variable:* **12) CONTRACEPT**
➤ *View:* **Reg. Line**

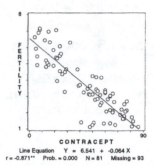

Line Equation   Y = 6.541 + -0.064 X
r = -0.871**   Prob. = 0.000   N = 81   Missing = 93

Again we get our expected result: where the percentage of women using contraception increases, fertility rates fall ($r = 0.871^{**}$).

It is often said that religion commonly promotes larger family sizes. How is fertility related to the degree to which people are religiously active?

Data File: **COUNTRIES**
Task: **Scatterplot**
Dependent Variable: **8) FERTILITY**
➤ *Independent Variable:* **73) CH.ATTEND**
➤ *View:* **Reg. Line**

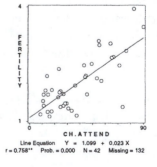

Line Equation   Y = 1.099 + 0.023 X
r = 0.758**   Prob. = 0.000   N = 42   Missing = 132

It appears that the more religiously active people are, the higher the fertility rate tends to be ($r = 0.758^{**}$). What do you think are the reasons for this very powerful correlation?

A well-known theory that seeks to explain population shifts—Kingsley Davis' ***demographic transition theory***—predicts that while modernization initially brings on population *expansion*, it eventually leads to population *stabilization* (**ZPG**, or "zero population growth"). When nations first modernize, their death rates fall while birth rates remain high. Thus, their populations grow. But as modernization progresses, births also begin dropping. Changes such as lower infant and child mortality, and less need for children as farm labor, mean that many people in modern nations feel that it is not in their advantage to have large numbers of babies. Low death rates are balanced by low birth rates, and the population stabilizes.[5]

We already saw something that supported the demographic transition idea, namely, that fertility rates decreased as infant mortality rates became lower. When we looked at modernization in Exercise 8, we saw that it was associated with things like less reliance on agriculture but growth in the service sector of the economy. These things ought to be, in turn, tied to lower fertility and less population growth. Let's find out.

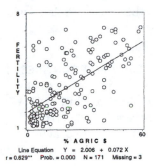

> Data File: **COUNTRIES**
> Task: **Scatterplot**
> Dependent Variable: **8) FERTILITY**
> ➤ Independent Variable: **27) % AGRIC $**
> ➤ View: **Reg. Line**

The more nations' economies depend on agriculture, the higher their fertility tends to be ($r = 0.629**$). Now look at fertility rates in relation to the size of the service sector.

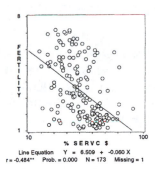

> Data File: **COUNTRIES**
> Task: **Scatterplot**
> Dependent Variable: **8) FERTILITY**
> ➤ Independent Variable: **29) % SERVC $**
> ➤ View: **Reg. Line**

This result is consistent with Davis' theory. The larger service sectors are associated with *lower* fertility ($r = -0.484**$).

---

[5] I am grateful for the clear, succinct discussion of this in Stark, op cit., pages 528–538. Davis' original theory was laid out in "The World Demographic Transition," *Annals of the American Academy of Political and Social Sciences*, Vol. 237, pages 1–11, 1945.

Data File: **COUNTRIES**
Task: **Scatterplot**
➤ Dependent Variable: **5) POP GROWTH**
➤ Independent Variable: **29) % SERVC $**
➤ View: **Reg. Line**

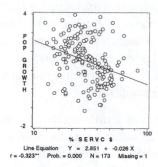

Finally, yes, a large service sector is also associated with lower population growth ($r = -0.323**$).

In Exercise 8, we pointed out that modernization is associated with higher literacy and more wealth. Are both of these also correlated with less fertility, which would be consistent with demographic transition theory?[6]

Data File: **COUNTRIES**
Task: **Scatterplot**
➤ Dependent Variable: **8) FERTILITY**
➤ Independent Variable: **32) LITERACY**
➤ View: **Reg. Line**

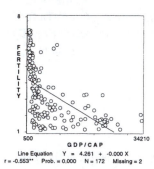

Yes, fertility tends to decline precipitously with higher levels of literacy ($r = -0.797**$).

Data File: **COUNTRIES**
Task: **Scatterplot**
Dependent Variable: **8) FERTILITY**
➤ Independent Variable: **25) GDP/CAP**
➤ View: **Reg. Line**

Fertility also declines with higher wealth ($r = -0.553**$). The jury may still be out as to whether or not modernization will reduce the extremely high fertility we have seen in many less developed nations in Africa, the Middle East, and elsewhere.[7] But so far, this theory is supported by what has happened in

---

[6] Stark, op cit., pages 530–531.

[7] See, for example, ibid., pages 536–537 versus Kendall, op cit., page 322.

today's developed, advanced nations. Now it's time to work through some of this on your own. In the worksheets to follow, you'll have more opportunity to use the COUNTRIES and STATES data sets, as well as do some cross-tabulation with the GSS. In other words, your turn!

REVIEW QUESTIONS

Based on the first part of this exercise, answer True or False to the following items:

Almost all social scientists agree that while population increase is a problem, population decrease never is.	T	F
Changes in fertility rates, death rates, and migration can all lead to changes in population size.	T	F
Immigration to the United States fell steadily through the 20th century.	T	F
In the United States, on average, populations in crowded states are growing more slowly than those in less densely populated states.	T	F
The world population is now over 8 billion people.	T	F
In our COUNTRIES data set, higher death rates are statistically associated with lower population growth and with decreases in population size.	T	F
Among nations, on average, women have more babies where there are higher death and infant mortality rates.	T	F
African nations tend to have high fertility rates, sometimes slightly higher than 7 babies per woman.	T	F
Nations that have greater percentages of women who use contraceptives also tend to have lower fertility rates.	T	F
Among nations, fertility rates appear to be unrelated to the percentage of people who attend church regularly.	T	F
Demographic transition theory argues that, as nations modernize, their fertility rates will eventually fall.	T	F
Larger service sectors and higher literacy rates are both associated with lower fertility rates.	T	F

EXPLORIT QUESTIONS

1. We saw earlier in this exercise that in countries where people want larger families, the fertility rates tend to be higher. Now, let's consider what proportion of people in the United States want larger families. We'll turn to the GSS to do so, and start by finding out whether or not the elderly are more likely than younger people to want larger families. We'll define "larger families" as "three or more children."

    a. Open the GSS data set and carefully examine the variable description for 89) IDEAL#KIDS.

b. Cross-tabulate 89) IDEAL#KIDS with 1) AGE. Then, fill in the percentages that consider three or more children, and zero children to one child, to be ideal.

> Data File: **GSS**
>> Task: **Cross-tabulation**
> Row Variable: **89) IDEAL#KIDS**
> Column Variable: **1) AGE**
>> View: **Tables**
>> Display: **Column %**

	<30	30–49	50–64	65 AND UP
0–1	_____%	_____%	_____%	_____%
3+	_____%	_____%	_____%	_____%

Now, get the Cramer's V and the significance level for these two variables.

c. Record the value of Cramer's V for this table. (Include asterisks, if any.)   V = _____

d. Is the relationship between AGE and IDEAL#KIDS statistically significant? (Circle one.)

Yes   No

e. Is the relationship between AGE and IDEAL#KIDS weak, moderate, strong, or not significant? (Circle one.)

Weak

Moderate

Strong

Not Significant

f. Fill in the blanks: The group aged _____ is *most* likely to consider three or more children to be the ideal number, while the group aged _____ is *least* likely to want such a large family.

_____

_____

g. Fill in the blanks: The group aged _____ is *most* likely to consider 0 to 1 to be the ideal number of children, while the group aged _____ is *least* likely to want no children or only one child.

_____

_____

h. Assuming that the information in this last table accurately reflects the ideals of the American public, do you expect that births will increase, decrease, or remain about the same over the next decade or so? Justify your answer with specifics from this last table.

2. We saw earlier that countries in which people attend church regularly tend to have higher fertility rates than countries in which people do not. Could it be that, among Americans, *those who attend church regularly will be more likely to desire large families*? We'll test this idea, with the latter statement serving as our hypothesis.

    a. Cross-tabulate 89) IDEAL#KIDS with 26) ATTEND. Then, fill in the percentages that consider three or more children to be ideal.

    > Data File: **GSS**
    > Task: **Cross-tabulation**
    > Row Variable: **89) IDEAL#KIDS**
    > ➤ Column Variable: **26) ATTEND**
    > ➤ View: **Tables**
    > ➤ Display: **Column %**

	NEV/SELDOM	MONTHLY	WKLY+
3+	_____%	_____%	_____%

    Now, examine the Cramer's V and the significance level for these two variables.

    b. Is the relationship between ATTEND and IDEAL#KIDS statistically significant? (Circle one.)   Yes   No

    c. Is the relationship between ATTEND and IDEAL#KIDS weak, moderate, strong, or not significant? (Circle one.)

    Weak

    Moderate

    Strong

    Not Significant

    d. Was the hypothesis supported? (Circle one.)   Yes   No

3. What about education? Here is our hypothesis: *the more educated Americans are, the less likely they will be to desire large families.*

    a. Cross-tabulate 89) IDEAL#KIDS with 13) DEGREE. Then, fill in the percentages that consider three or more children to be ideal.

    > Data File: **GSS**
    > Task: **Cross-tabulation**
    > Row Variable: **89) IDEAL#KIDS**
    > ➤ Column Variable: **13) DEGREE**
    > ➤ View: **Tables**
    > ➤ Display: **Column %**

	NOT H.S.	H.S.	JR.COL.	4 YR DEG	GRAD DEG
3+	_____%	_____%	_____%	_____%	_____%

Now, examine the Cramer's V and the significance level for these two variables.

b. Is the relationship between DEGREE and IDEAL#KIDS statistically significant? (Circle one.)

Yes   No

c. Is the relationship between DEGREE and IDEAL#KIDS weak, moderate, strong, or not significant? (Circle one.)

Weak

Moderate

Strong

Not Significant

d. Was the hypothesis supported? (Circle one.)

Yes   No

e. Is there much of a difference here between those with different levels of college education? Explain, drawing on the table percentages.

4. People often say that Roman Catholics, due to their official church doctrine, are more likely than those of other religious groups to prefer larger families. Here is our hypothesis: *Catholics will be more likely to prefer large families than people from other religious groups.*

a. Cross-tabulate 89) IDEAL#KIDS with 25) RELIGION. Then, fill in the percentages that consider three or more children to be ideal.

Data File: **GSS**
Task: **Cross-tabulation**
Row Variable: **89) IDEAL#KIDS**
➤ Column Variable: **25) RELIGION**
➤ View: **Tables**
➤ Display: **Column %**

	PROTESTANT	CATHOLIC	JEWISH	NONE
3+	_____%	_____%	_____%	_____%

Now, examine the Cramer's V and the significance level for these two variables.

b. Is the relationship between RELIGION and IDEAL#KIDS statistically significant? (Circle one.)

Yes   No

c. Is the relationship between RELIGION and IDEAL#KIDS weak, moderate, strong, or not significant? (Circle one.)

Weak

Moderate

Strong

Not Significant

d. Was the hypothesis supported? (Circle one.)

Yes   No

5. Are Roman Catholics actually more likely to have larger families? Here is our hypothesis: *Catholics will be more likely to have large families than people from all other religious groups.*

a. Cross-tabulate 10) #CHILDREN with 25) RELIGION. Then, fill in the percentages that have 3 to 4, and more than 4, children. Compare, especially, Protestant versus Catholic.

Data File: **GSS**
Task: **Cross-tabulation**
➤ Row Variable: **10) #CHILDREN**
➤ Column Variable: **25) RELIGION**
➤ View: **Tables**
➤ Display: **Column %**

	PROTESTANT	CATHOLIC	JEWISH	NONE
3–4	_____%	_____%	_____%	_____%
>4	_____%	_____%	_____%	_____%

Now, examine the Cramer's V and the significance level for these two variables.

b. Is the relationship between RELIGION and #CHILDREN statistically significant? (Circle one.)

Yes   No

c. Was the hypothesis supported? (Circle one.)

Yes

No

Not Clear

d. Carefully compare the results of this last table with the results of the table in question 4. Do the findings shown in these two tables appear to be consistent with each other? If not, *in what way(s)* are they inconsistent and what do you think the reasons are for the inconsistency(ies)?

6. We saw earlier that nations with more immigration than emigration (i.e., higher net migration) tended to experience higher rates of population growth. Let's see if this is true for American states. We'll look first at domestic migration, that is, migration in and out of the state from other parts of the United States. Here is our hypothesis: *among states, the higher the net domestic immigration relative to emigration, the higher the rate of population growth will tend to be.*

a. Open the STATES data set and carefully examine the variable description for 19) NDM 90–99.

b. Construct a scatterplot that represents the association between 3) POP%GRO and 19) NDM 90–99.

> *Data File:* **STATES**
> *Task:* **Scatterplot**
> *Dependent Variable:* **3) POP%GRO**
> *Independent Variable:* **19) NDM 90–99**
> *View:* **Reg. Line**

c. Provide Pearson's *r* (including asterisks, if any, and the direction sign, if any)   *r* = _____

d. Is this correlation significant *and* negative, significant *and* positive, or *not* significant? (Circle one.)

Significant *and* Negative

Significant *and* Positive

Not Significant

e. Is this correlation weak, moderate, strong, or not significant? (Circle one.)

Weak

Moderate

Strong

Not Significant

f. Is the hypothesis supported? (Circle one.)

Yes   No

7. Now let's look at international migration, that is, migration in and out of the state from outside the United States. Here is our hypothesis: *among states, the higher the net international immigration relative to emigration, the higher the rate of population growth will tend to be.*

    a. Carefully examine the variable description for 20) NIM 90–99.

    b. Construct a scatterplot that represents the association between 3) POP%GRO and 20) NIM 90–99.

    > Data File: **STATES**
    > Task: **Scatterplot**
    > ➤ Dependent Variable: **3) POP%GRO**
    > ➤ Independent Variable: **20) NIM 90–99**
    > ➤ View: **Reg. Line**

    Examine Pearson's *r*.

    c. Is this correlation significant *and* negative, significant *and* positive, or *not* significant? (Circle one.)

    Significant *and* Negative

    Significant *and* Positive

    Not Significant

    d. Is this correlation weak, moderate, strong, or not significant? (Circle one.)

    Weak

    Moderate

    Strong

    Not Significant

    e. Is the hypothesis supported? (Circle one.)   Yes   No

    f. Are the results of this last scatterplot similar to the results of the scatterplot in question 6? If not, what do you think are the reasons why, among American states, international migration did not have the same effect on population growth, as did domestic migration?

8. We saw earlier that among nations, higher literacy was associated with lower fertility. We also looked at the relationship of education to desired family size among GSS respondents in question 3. Let's consider whether or not high school dropout rates are associated with fertility rates among states. Here is our hypothesis: *among states, the greater the percentage of high school dropouts, the greater the fertility rate will tend to be.*

   a. Carefully examine the variable descriptions for 27) FERTIL00 88) HS DROP 00

   b. Construct a scatterplot that represents the association between 27) FERTIL00 and 88) HS DROP 00.

   > Data File: **STATES**
   > Task: **Scatterplot**
   > ➤ Dependent Variable: **27) FERTIL00**
   > ➤ Independent Variable: **88) HS DROP 00**
   > ➤ View: **Reg. Line**

   Examine Pearson's *r*.

   c. Is this correlation significant *and* negative, significant *and* positive, or *not* significant? (Circle one.)

   Significant *and* Negative

   Significant *and* Positive

   Not Significant

   d. Is the hypothesis supported? (Circle one.)   Yes   No

   e. Did these results surprise you? Why or why not?

9. Here is another hypothesis: *among states, the greater the percentage of college graduates, the lower the fertility rate will tend to be.*

   a. Carefully examine the variable description for 89) COLL GR 00.

   b. Construct a scatterplot that represents the association between 27) FERTIL00 and 89) COLL GR 00.

   > Data File: **STATES**
   > Task: **Scatterplot**
   > Dependent Variable: **27) FERTIL00**
   > ➤ Independent Variable: **89) COLL GR 00**
   > ➤ View: **Reg. Line**

Examine Pearson's *r*.

c. Is this correlation significant *and* negative, significant *and* positive, or *not* significant? (Circle one.)

Significant *and* Negative

Significant *and* Positive

Not Significant

d. Is the hypothesis supported? (Circle one.)

Yes   No

e. Did these results surprise you? Why or why not?

PHYSICAL HEALTH AND HEALTH CARE

Tasks: Historical Trends, Mapping, Cross-tabulation, Univariate, Scatterplot
Data Files: TRENDS, COUNTRIES, STATES, YRBS, ELECTION, GSS

In the mid-1980s I was fresh out of graduate school and beginning my first full-time job as a professional sociologist. My new position was as an applied social researcher for a consulting firm that studied health and health care issues as these related to corporate and government policies and management systems. Diving right in, I found myself taking a "crash course" in pressing national and international social problems related to physical health and medical care. I was amazed at just how enormous, and growing, these difficulties were. It was quite clear that solving them would be unbelievably challenging, not only in terms of finding "technical solutions," but also in dealing with many political and moral quandaries.

The issues we studied then are still with us today (and, in some ways, getting worse). They remain centers of a great deal of attention, concern, and controversy. What were they? Well, most of our attention was focused, in one way or another, on the *finances* of health care. For example, I put together many presentations on skyrocketing American health care costs. Looking at inequality in access to medical care, and its effects on the health of the disadvantaged here and overseas, occupied a great deal of my time as well. Particularly troubling to me was the number of people in the United States who had no health insurance or who (like "*John Q*" in the 2002 movie of that name) did not have *adequate* coverage. There were also other things that negatively impacted the health of disadvantaged people in America and across the world, such as poor sanitation, nutrition, and prenatal care, to name just a few. Finally, our company was interested in the connection between lifestyles and health *and* corporate and government policies and practices that might encourage healthier ways of living.

In this exercise, I'd like to revisit these issues of physical health and health care with you. Why don't we start with trends in American health care costs? We'll look first at per capita expenditures on health care in dollars.

➤ *Data File:* **TRENDS**
  ➤ *Task:* **Historical Trends**
➤ *Variable:* **181) HEAL$/CAP**

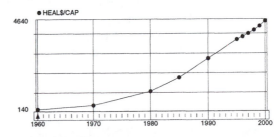

Total health expenditures per capita, United States

As you can see, the term "skyrocketing" is not exaggerated to describe increases in health care spending per capita. By 2000, annual per person spending on this was $4,637, compared to $143 in 1960. This increase is well beyond regular inflation rates. Let's get a closer look at this by examining per capita expenditures as a percentage of gross domestic product (GDP).

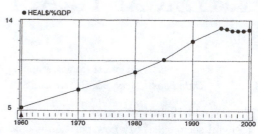

Data File: **TRENDS**
Task: **Historical Trends**
➤ Variable: **182) HEAL$/%GDP**

Total health expenditures as a percentage of gross domestic product,
United States

As this graph makes clear, U.S. medical care has also occupied a rapidly increasing percentage of its GDP, from 5.1% in 1960 to 13.2% in 2000. So, how do American costs compare internationally? Let's view rankings in the COUNTRIES data set to contrast the United States to other developed nations.

➤ Data File: **COUNTRIES**
➤ Task: **Mapping**
➤ Variable 1: **76) HLTH$/CAP**
➤ View: **List: Rank**

RANK	CASE NAME	VALUE
1	United States	4180
2	Switzerland	2739
3	Germany	2488
4	Norway	2467
5	Canada	2391
6	Iceland	2358
7	Luxembourg	2327
8	Belgium	2172
9	Denmark	2141
10	France	2102

Look at the top 20 countries here in order to get an idea where the United States stands relative to some other developed nations.[1] The United States clearly spent the most on health care in 1998, 65% higher than even the second ranked Switzerland ($4,180 versus $2,739)!

How much has America's higher spending been associated with better health, compared to these other developed nations? To get an idea, let's also look at average life expectancies.

Data File: **COUNTRIES**
Task: **Mapping**
Variable 1: **76) HLTH$/CAP**
➤ Variable 2: **16) LIFE EXPCT**
➤ Views: **List: Rank**

RANK	CASE NAME	VALUE
1	United States	4180
2	Switzerland	2739
3	Germany	2488
4	Norway	2467
5	Canada	2391

RANK	CASE NAME	VALUE
1	Japan	80.7
2	Australia	79.8
3	Switzerland	79.6
4	Sweden	79.6
5	Canada	79.4

---

[1] Notice the 1998 estimate for the United States differs very slightly from that in the TRENDS data set. This is a different source (the *United Nations Human Development Report*) for this number.

Investigating Social Problems

Comparing the top-ranked nations on both health care spending and life expectancy is instructive. It is certainly clear that, among countries generally, greater investments in medical care are associated with longer life expectancy ($r = 0.632$**). However, it also seems that the higher "price tag" of health in America has not brought it better health than other modernized, developed nations that spend much less on medical care per capita. Notice, for example, that the United States ranks 17th in life expectancy, while the two nations with the longest average life spans (Japan and Australia) each spent less than half of what the U.S. did ($1,844 and $1,980, respectively).

Scroll down to the bottom of both of these rankings, however, and you can look at one aspect of another problem we are exploring in this exercise, namely, *inequality* in physical health and medical care. The discrepancy between the "have" and "have-not" nations here is incredible and sad. In Tanzania, the U.S. equivalent of $15 per person was spent on medical care in 1998! In Niger, which had health care expenditures of $20 per person, the average life expectancy is only a little over 41 years. Zambia, with the lowest average life expectancy at 37.2 years, spent only $52 per capita on medical care in 1998.

I suppose we should expect wealthier nations to have more physicians than poorer nations as well. Let's take a look. We'll continue to use rankings to explore this in depth.

Data File: **COUNTRIES**
Task: **Mapping**
➤ Variable 1: **25) GDP/CAP**
➤ Variable 2: **74) DOCTORS**
➤ Views: **List: Rank**

RANK	CASE NAME	VALUE
1	Luxembourg	34200
2	United States	33900
3	Singapore	27800
4	Switzerland	27100
5	Norway	25100

RANK	CASE NAME	VALUE
1	Italy	554
2	Belarus	443
3	Georgia	436
4	Spain	424
5	Russia	421

Obviously, the richer nations are, the higher their relative number of physicians tends to be *(r = 0.537**)*. Notice what you see by scrolling to the *bottom* of the DOCTORS list. The 24 lowest ranked nations each have fewer than 10 physicians for every 100,000 citizens!

We saw earlier in this workbook that the poorer nations we are discussing here (many of which are in Africa) disproportionately suffer from things like poor nutrition, as well as high death, maternal mortality, and infant mortality rates.[2] How do these disadvantaged nations fare in areas that are clearly related to public health, such as adequate sanitation and drinking water? We'll continue listing ranks to look closely at the most disadvantaged nations.

---

[2] See Exercises 8 and 13.

Data File: **COUNTRIES**
Task: **Mapping**
Variable 1: **25) GDP/CAP**
➤ *Variable 2:* **78) GOODWATER**
➤ *Views:* **List: Rank**

RANK	CASE NAME	VALUE
1	Luxembourg	34200
2	United States	33900
3	Singapore	27800
4	Switzerland	27100
5	Norway	25100

RANK	CASE NAME	VALUE
1	Lebanon	100
1	Norway	100
1	Canada	100
1	Slovak Republic	100
1	Bulgaria	100

It isn't surprising to find that adequate water becomes more available as national wealth increases ($r = 0.519**$). Scroll to the bottom of the GOODWATER list. Less than 30% of the populations in Ethiopia, Chad, and Sierra Leone have access to adequate drinking water. Does this trend continue with access to sanitation? Let's find out.

Data File: **COUNTRIES**
Task: **Mapping**
Variable 1: **25) GDP/CAP**
➤ *Variable 2:* **77) SANITATION**
➤ *Views:* **List: Rank**

RANK	CASE NAME	VALUE
1	Luxembourg	34200
2	United States	33900
3	Singapore	27800
4	Switzerland	27100
5	Norway	25100

RANK	CASE NAME	VALUE
1	Sweden	100
1	Canada	100
1	Slovak Republic	100
1	Turkmenistan	100
1	Switzerland	100

It certainly does! Adequate sanitation is definitely lacking in poorer countries ($r = 0.483**$). Scroll to the bottom of the SANITATION list to view the results. Do you notice there are 31 countries in which more than half the population does not have decent sanitation?

Such shameful disparities exist in the United States as well. And one big problem, as we have already mentioned, is the millions of people without medical insurance. Let's explore this, beginning with TRENDS.

➤ *Data File:* **TRENDS**
➤ *Task:* **Historical Trends**
➤ *Variable:* **183) UNINSURED#**

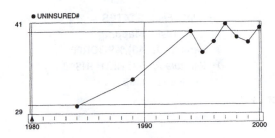

Number of Americans, in millions, who are under 65 years of age and without health care coverage

The *number* of those without medical insurance rose in the time period graphed, from about 29,800,000 in 1984 to a high of 41,000,000 in 1997, before falling slightly to roughly 40,500,000 in 2000.

Data File: **TRENDS**
Task: **Historical Trends**
➤ *Variable:* **184) UNINSURED%**

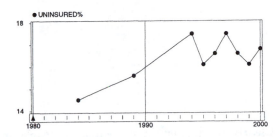

Percent of population under 65 years of age without health care coverage

The *percentages* of uninsured Americans followed a similar trend, from 14.3% in 1984 to highs of 17.4% in 1994 and 1997, and then down to 16.8% in 2000.

No matter which way you look at it, many millions of Americans have no medical insurance. And the uninsured are disproportionately poor. Let's take a look.

Data File: **TRENDS**
Task: **Historical Trends**
➤ *Variable:* **185) UNINSPOOR**
 186) UNINSRICH

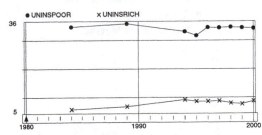

Percent of those under poverty level and percent of those with household incomes two times greater than the poverty level or higher, all under 65 years of age without health coverage

Wow—look at that "insurance gap"! Poor Americans under age 65 are much more likely to be uninsured than those whose income is at least two times higher than the official poverty level. In 2000, the poor were about 4 times more likely than the wealthier folk to be uninsured—8.7% versus 34.2%, respectively. Now let's see how this looks among the states.

➤ *Data File:* **STATES**
  ➤ *Task:* **Mapping**
➤ *Variable 1:* **48) %POOR00**
➤ *Variable 2:* **92) HLTH INS00**
  ➤ *Views:* **Map**

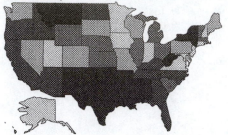

%POOR00 -- 2000: PERCENT BELOW POVERTY LEVEL (CENSUS CPS, BASED ON 1999-2000 AVERAGE)

r = 0.669**

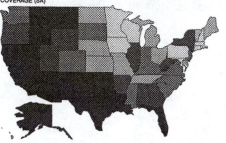

HLTH INS00 -- 2000: PERCENT OF PERSONS WITHOUT HEALTH INSURANCE COVERAGE (SA)

Clearly, the higher the percentage of people in states that are poor, the greater the proportion of persons without medical insurance ($r = 0.669**$). For example, use your mouse to click on number-one-ranked New Mexico.

Data File: **STATES**
  Task: **Mapping**
Variable 1: **48) %POOR00**
➤ *Variable 2:* **92) HLTH INS00**
  ➤ *Views:* **Map**
  ➤ *Display:* **New Mexico**

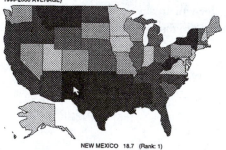

%POOR00 -- 2000: PERCENT BELOW POVERTY LEVEL (CENSUS CPS, BASED ON 1999-2000 AVERAGE)

NEW MEXICO 18.7 (Rank: 1)

r = 0.669**

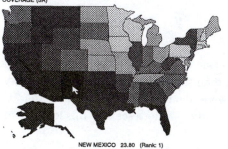

HLTH INS00 -- 2000: PERCENT OF PERSONS WITHOUT HEALTH INSURANCE COVERAGE (SA)

NEW MEXICO 23.80 (Rank: 1)

Investigating Social Problems

Now you can see that in the year 2000, 18.7% of New Mexico's population was poor and 23.8% (roughly one out of four) were uninsured.

As we saw earlier, among nations, the poorer they were the fewer doctors they had relative to population size. Why don't we look at roughly the same thing here, namely, whether or not wealthier states have a higher rate of physicians than poorer states?

<table>
<tr><td align="right">Data File:</td><td>STATES</td></tr>
<tr><td align="right">Task:</td><td>Mapping</td></tr>
<tr><td align="right">➤ Variable 1:</td><td>29) PER CAP$00</td></tr>
<tr><td align="right">➤ Variable 2:</td><td>91) DOCTORS 99</td></tr>
<tr><td align="right">➤ Views:</td><td>Map</td></tr>
</table>

PER CAP$00 – 2000: PER CAPITA MONEY INCOME (CENSUS:C2SS)

r = 0.677**

DOCTORS 99 – 1999: MEDICAL DOCTORS PER 100,000 POPULATION (SA)

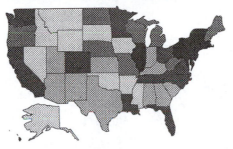

The higher the average per capita income, the more physicians there are per 100,000 people ($r = 0.677$**). Poorer states really are at a disadvantage here. Is the wealth of states also related to health outcomes, such as death rates?

<table>
<tr><td align="right">Data File:</td><td>STATES</td></tr>
<tr><td align="right">Task:</td><td>Mapping</td></tr>
<tr><td align="right">Variable 1:</td><td>29) PER CAP$00</td></tr>
<tr><td align="right">➤ Variable 2:</td><td>22) DEATH 99</td></tr>
<tr><td align="right">➤ Views:</td><td>Map</td></tr>
</table>

PER CAP$00 – 2000: PER CAPITA MONEY INCOME (CENSUS:C2SS)

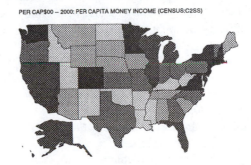

r = –0.353**

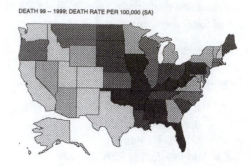

DEATH 99 -- 1999: DEATH RATE PER 100,000 (SA)

As per capita income increases, death rates decrease ($r = -0.353**$). Of course, this means that the reverse is also true: states with lower per capita incomes have higher death rates.

We have seen how inequality in physical health and access to health care shows up in rates and geographic comparisons. Now, let's consider whether or not, and how, these inequities show up in different experiences of disadvantaged individuals versus those who are better off. We'll start with your ELECTION data set.

➤ *Data File:* **ELECTION**
➤ *Task:* **Cross-tabulation**
➤ *Row Variable:* **63) MED DELAY**
➤ *Column Variable:* **5) FAMINCOME**
➤ *View:* **Tables**
➤ *Display:* **Column %**

MED DELAY by FAMINCOME
Cramer's V: 0.263 **

MED DELAY	FAMINCOME				
	< $25,000	$25K-64.9K	$65,000 +	Missing	TOTAL
Yes	101	105	37	35	243
	46.8%	32.6%	15.2%		31.1%
No	115	217	207	110	539
	53.2%	67.4%	84.8%		68.9%
Missing	549	762	534	316	2161
TOTAL	216	322	244	461	782
	100.0%	100.0%	100.0%		

As you can see, respondents from poorer families were much more likely than those from wealthier families to indicate that they had put off medical or dental treatment in the past year for lack of funds ($V = 0.263**$). About 47% of those with family incomes less than $25,000 did so, compared to roughly 15% of respondents at $65,000 or above. Now let's move on to the GSS.

➤ *Data File:* **GSS**
➤ *Task:* **Cross-tabulation**
➤ *Row Variable:* **90) HEALTH**
➤ *Column Variable:* **16) $FAMRANK**
➤ *View:* **Tables**
➤ *Display:* **Column %**

HEALTH by $FAMRANK
Cramer's V: 0.192 **

HEALTH	$FAMRANK				
	Below	Average	Above	Missing	TOTAL
Excellent	177	486	303	304	966
	18.8%	31.2%	42.4%		30.0%
Good	418	772	332	435	1522
	44.4%	49.5%	46.5%		47.3%
Fair	236	246	66	168	548
	25.1%	15.8%	9.2%		17.0%
Poor	111	55	13	49	179
	11.8%	3.5%	1.8%		5.6%
Missing	264	441	226	480	1411
TOTAL	942	1559	714	1436	3215
	100.0%	100.0%	100.0%		

Investigating Social Problems

Notice how income is significantly related to self-perceived health (V = 0.192**). Roughly 12% of those whose family income was below average rated their own health as "poor," and about another 25% said their health was only "fair." For those with above average incomes, those figures were about 2% and 9% respectively. Meanwhile, 42% of those in the above average group said their health was "excellent," compared to about 31% of those of average income and roughly 19% of those of below average income.

Finally, let's turn briefly to the issue of health and personal behavior. We'll return to STATES to consider the association between cigarette smoking and death rates.

➤ Data File: **STATES**
➤ Task: **Mapping**
➤ Variable 1: **39) CIGARET00**
➤ Variable 2: **22) DEATH 99**
➤ Views: **Map**

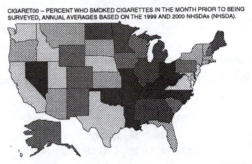

CIGARET00 -- PERCENT WHO SMOKED CIGARETTES IN THE MONTH PRIOR TO BEING SURVEYED, ANNUAL AVERAGES BASED ON THE 1999 AND 2000 NHSDAs (NHSDA).

r = 0.596**

DEATH 99 -- 1999: DEATH RATE PER 100,000 (SA)

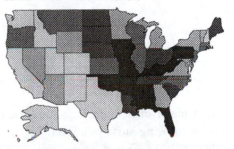

There is a strong correlation between these two variables (r = 0.596**). How about the association between cigarette use and a specific cause of death, namely, heart disease?

Data File: **STATES**
Task: **Mapping**
Variable 1: **39) CIGARET00**
➤ Variable 2: **94) HEART DT99**
➤ Views: **Map**

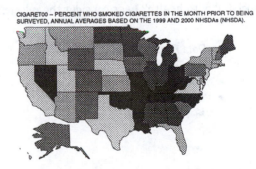

CIGARET00 -- PERCENT WHO SMOKED CIGARETTES IN THE MONTH PRIOR TO BEING SURVEYED, ANNUAL AVERAGES BASED ON THE 1999 AND 2000 NHSDAs (NHSDA).

r = 0.556**

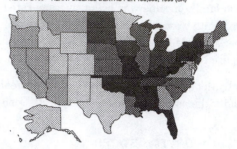

HEART DT99 -- HEART DISEASE DEATHS PER 100,000, 1999 (SA)

Where there is more cigarette smoking there is more heart disease ($r = 0.556**$). Now, before we close out our look at smoking, let's look at state rankings in current cigarette use.

Data File: **STATES**
Task: **Mapping**
Variable 1: **39) CIGARET00**
➤ View: **List: Rank**

RANK	CASE NAME	VALUE
1	Kentucky	32.5
2	West Virginia	30.5
3	Missouri	29.1
4	Ohio	29.1
5	Nevada	29.1
6	Oklahoma	28.5
7	Arkansas	28.5
8	Tennessee	28.2
9	North Carolina	28.1
10	Louisiana	27.6

Kentucky, a major tobacco-growing state, leads the way with 32.5% having smoked cigarettes in the month prior to being surveyed. West Virginia ranks second with slightly greater than 30%. Last is Utah, where only 17.4% had smoked in the previous month. What is the percentage of current smokers for your home state?

Studies keep pointing out that, despite new diets and exercise programs being presented in popular magazines every week, the percentage of Americans who are overweight keeps increasing. How is this associated with health? Let's consider the relationship between obesity and death rates.

Data File: **STATES**
Task: **Mapping**
➤ Variable 1: **90) % FAT 99**
➤ Variable 2: **22) DEATH 99**
➤ Views: **Map**

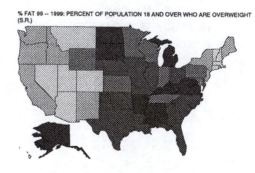

% FAT 99 -- 1999: PERCENT OF POPULATION 18 AND OVER WHO ARE OVERWEIGHT (S.R.)

$r = 0.412**$

Investigating Social Problems

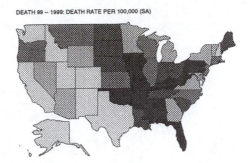

DEATH 99 -- 1999: DEATH RATE PER 100,000 (SA)

The relationship here is significant and positive ($r = 0.412^{**}$). States with higher rates of obesity do have higher death rates. But what types of related health problems may play a role here? Heart disease is a primary cause of death in this country. Let's see if states with higher obesity rates also have higher rates of heart disease.

Data File: **STATES**
Task: **Mapping**
Variable 1: **90) % FAT 99**
➤ Variable 2: **94) HEART DT99**
➤ Views: **Map**

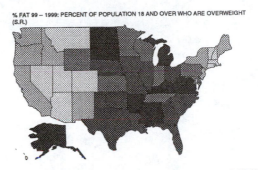

% FAT 99 -- 1999: PERCENT OF POPULATION 18 AND OVER WHO ARE OVERWEIGHT (S.R.)

$r = 0.437^{**}$

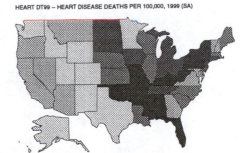

HEART DT99 -- HEART DISEASE DEATHS PER 100,000, 1999 (SA)

Again we find a moderately strong positive correlation ($r = 0.437^{**}$). As we expected, obesity is associated with health problems.

We've only scratched the surface with regard to social problems related to physical health and health care. Time to explore this a bit more on your own.

REVIEW QUESTIONS

Based on the first part of this exercise, answer True or False to the following items:

American health care costs, both in per capita figures and as a percentage of GDP, have risen a great deal since 1960.   T   F

In recent years, the United States has spent less per capita on health care than have other developed nations.   T   F

In 1998, many African countries spent less than $100 per capita on health care, and had average life expectancies of less than 50 years.   T   F

People in poorer countries have almost as much access to physicians as those in wealthier countries.   T   F

Poorer countries often suffer from shortages of adequate drinking water and decent sanitation.   T   F

By the year 2000, about one third of all Americans did not have health care insurance.   T   F

It appears that being without health insurance is almost as much a problem for people who are well-off as for those who are poor.   T   F

Poorer states have higher death rates than wealthier states.   T   F

Poor people are more likely than those who are well off to indicate that they have delayed medical treatment for lack of funds.   T   F

Poor people are not more likely than wealthier people to state that they are in bad health.   T   F

States where more people smoke cigarettes have higher rates of death due to heart disease.   T   F

States with greater percentages of overweight people have higher death rates.   T   F

EXPLORIT QUESTIONS

1. We have seen that cigarette smoking is associated with extremely negative health outcomes. Thus, it appears reasonable that we should be concerned about the degree to which younger people begin smoking. Let's take a look at smoking among high school seniors.

    a. Open the YRBS data set and carefully examine the variable description for 18) AGE1STCIG.

    b. Look at the pie chart and percentages for AGE1STCIG.

> *Data File:* **YRBS**
> *Task:* **Univariate**
> *Primary Variable:* **18) AGE1STCIG**
> *View:* **Pie**

c. What percentage of seniors had never smoked? _____%

d. Subtracting the last number from 100, we see that the percentage of seniors
who had smoked is approximately (Circle one.)

50%

60%

35%

75%

e. Now, let's just consider those seniors who have smoked cigarettes. We'll do this by excluding those who have never smoked from the analysis.

> *Data File:* **YRBS**
> *Task:* **Univariate**
> *Primary Variable:* **18) AGE1STCIG**
> *Subset Variable:* **18) AGE1STCIG**
> *Subset Category:* **Exclude: Nev Smoked**
> *View:* **Pie**

Be sure that, after selecting "Nev Smoked" as your subset category, you choose the [Exclude] option. Then click [OK] and continue as usual.

f. What percentage of seniors who had smoked did so for the first time by age 12? _____%

g. What percentage of seniors who had smoked did so for the first time between ages 13 and 16? _____%

h. Assuming that this YRBS data are representative of American high school seniors generally, does underage smoking appear to be rare or common among American young people these days? Justify your answer using percentages from the above two charts.

2. Let's look at the association between the age at which young people began smoking cigarettes and *how often* they do so. Again, we will focus only on those who have smoked.

    a. Carefully examine the variable description for 19) RECSMOKE.

    b. Cross-tabulate 19) RECSMOKE with 18) AGE1STCIG. Then, fill in the percentages of those who smoked only infrequently (1–5 days), and of those who did so every day, in the month prior to being surveyed.

Data File:	**YRBS**
➤ Task:	**Cross-tabulation**
➤ Row Variable:	**19) RECSMOKE**
➤ Column Variable:	**18) AGE1STCIG**
➤ Subset Variable:	**18) AGE1STCIG**
➤ Subset Category:	**Exclude: Nev Smoked**
➤ View:	**Tables**
➤ Display:	**Column %**

	12 OR LESS	13–16	17+
1–5	_____%	_____%	_____%
ALL 30	_____%	_____%	_____%

Now, get the Cramer's V and the significance level for these two variables.

c. Record the value of Cramer's V for this table. (Include asterisks, if any.)   V = _____

d. Is the relationship between AGE1STCIG and RECSMOKE statistically significant? (Circle one.)   Yes   No

e. Is the relationship between AGE1STCIG and RECSMOKE weak, moderate, strong, or not significant? (Circle one.)

                                                                        Weak

                                                                        Moderate

                                                                        Strong

                                                                        Not Significant

f. Consider the following proposal: "The longer we can delay young people's first experience with smoking a cigarette, the less likely they will be to become regular, daily smokers." Is this proposal supported by the above cross-tabulation? Why or why not? Be specific.

3. Since we're on the topic of cigarette smoking, let's examine some trends in this unhealthy behavior. We'll start with high school seniors.

    a. Open the TRENDS data set and carefully examine the variable description for 28) EVCIG12GR.

    b. Look at the Historical Trends chart for 28) EVCIG12GR. Print it also. Then, answer the following questions about what you see there.

        ➤ *Data File:* **TRENDS**
          ➤ *Task:* **Historical Trends**
        ➤ *Variable:* **28) EVCIG12GR**

    c. Generally, between the mid-1970s and 2002, did the percentage of high school seniors had ever smoked increase, decrease, or stay about the same? (Circle one.)

                                                                      Increased

                                                                      Decreased

                                                         Stayed About the Same

    d. Fill in the blanks: Looking at the numbers on the chart's vertical line on the   _____
        left, we can see that at the *highest* point the percentage of seniors who had
        ever smoked was about _____%, and that at the *lowest* point this percent-   _____
        age was about _____%. Thus the total range of variation in the percentage
        of seniors who had ever smoked during this period was about _____%.   _____
        (Hint: To get this last number, subtract the low point from the high point.)

    e. The lowest percentage was in the year _____.   _____

    f. Carefully examine the variable description for 29) DLYCIG12GR.

    g. Look at the Historical Trends chart for 29) DLYCIG12GR. Print it also. Then, answer the following questions about what you see there.

        ➤ *Data File:* **TRENDS**
          ➤ *Task:* **Historical Trends**
        ➤ *Variable:* **29) DLYCIG12GR**

    h. Generally, between the mid-1970s and 2002, did the percentage of high school seniors who had smoked every day during the month prior to being surveyed increase, decrease, or stay about the same? (Circle one.)

                                                                      Increased

                                                                      Decreased

                                                         Stayed About the Same

i. Fill in the blanks: Looking at the numbers on the chart's vertical line on the   _____
left, we can see that at the *highest* point the percentage of seniors who had
smoked every day for the past month was about _____%, and that at   _____
the *lowest* point this percentage was about _____%. Thus the total range
of variation in the percentage of seniors who had smoked daily for the past   _____
month during this period was about _____%.

j. The lowest percentage was in the year _____.   _____

k. Considering both of these trend charts, briefly describe what happened between 1990 and 2002
with regard to smoking among high school seniors.

4. Now, let's look at a trend in smoking among American adults generally.

    a. Carefully examine the variable description for 42) CIGARETTE.

    b. Look at the Historical Trends chart for 42) CIGARETTE. Then, answer the following questions
about what you see there.

>   *Data File:* **TRENDS**
>   *Task:* **Historical Trends**
> ➤ *Variable:* **42) CIGARETTE**

    c. Fill in the blanks: Looking at the numbers on the chart's vertical line on the   _____%
left, we can see that at the *highest* point the percentage of Americans who
currently smoked was about _____% and this was in the year _____.   _____
At the *lowest* point this percentage was about _____% and this was in the
year _____. Thus the total range of variation in the percentage of Americans   _____%
who currently smoked during this time period was about _____%.
                                                              _____%

    d. Create one trend chart that shows both the variables 29) DLYCIG12GR and
42) CIGARETTE. Look at it carefully. Have the patterns of smoking among
high school seniors, and American adults, since the mid 1970s been similar,
or not? (Circle one.)   Very Similar

                                                                 Somewhat Similar

                                                               Not At All Similar

5. We have already seen that among American states, cigarette smoking is associated with higher death rates. Could this be true among nations as well?

    a. Open the COUNTRIES data set.

    b. Carefully examine the variable description for 62) CIGARETTES.

    c. Construct a scatterplot that represents the association between 62) CIGARETTES and 15) DEATH RATE.

        ➤ Data File: **COUNTRIES**
        ➤ Task: **Scatterplot**
        ➤ Dependent Variable: **15) DEATH RATE**
        ➤ Independent Variable: **62) CIGARETTES**
        ➤ View: **Reg. Line**

    d. Provide Pearson's r (including asterisks, if any, and the direction sign, if any). $r =$ _____

    e. Is this correlation significant *and* negative, significant *and* positive, or *not* significant? (Circle one.)

        Significant *and* Negative

        Significant *and* Positive

        Not Significant

    f. Among nations, as cigarette consumption increased, the death rate (Circle one.)

        Decreased a Lot

        Decreased a Little

        Neither Increased nor Decreased

        Increased a Little

        Increased a Lot

    g. How does this finding compare with the association that we saw between cigarette smoking and death rates when we looked at American states earlier in this exercise? (Circle one.)

        Similar

        Not At All Similar

        Opposite

6. If you analyzed the data properly in the last question 5, you probably found the results a bit puzzling. Here, it is helpful to remember something that we talked about in Exercise 3. That is, a correlation may exist only because both of the "associated" variables are actually correlated with some other variable(s). That is, the correlation may be spurious. It is important to consider this possibility, especially when confronted by a correlation that is inconsistent with other things that we know to be true. Could it be that there is something that is associated with both *lower* death rates and *higher* cigarette consumption, which may help to shed light on this puzzling correlation between them? Let's look.

a. Construct a scatterplot that represents the association between 25) GDP/CAP and 15) DEATH RATE.

            Data File: **COUNTRIES**
            Task: **Scatterplot**
   Dependent Variable: **15) DEATH RATE**
➤ *Independent Variable:* **25) GDP/CAP**
          ➤ *View:* **Reg. Line**

b. Provide Pearson's r (including asterisks, if any, and the direction sign, if any). $r =$ _____

c. On average, wealthier countries have death rates that are _____ death rates in poorer countries. (Circle the one answer that best fills in this blank.)

                                          lower than

                                         higher than

                                         similar to

d. Now, construct a scatterplot that represents the association between 25) GDP/CAP and 62) CIGARETTES.

            Data File: **COUNTRIES**
            Task: **Scatterplot**
➤ *Dependent Variable:* **62) CIGARETTES**
➤ *Independent Variable:* **25) GDP/CAP**
          ➤ *View:* **Reg. Line**

e. Provide Pearson's r (including asterisks, if any, and the direction sign, if any). $r =$ _____

f. On average, people in wealthier countries appear to consume _____ people in poorer countries. (Circle the one answer that best fills in this blank.)

                                      more cigarettes than

                                    fewer cigarettes than

                         about the same number of cigarettes as

g. Consider the correlation between death rates and cigarette consumption that you obtained in question 5. Is it possible that this puzzling finding can be explained by taking into consideration the influences of wealth upon both death rates and cigarette consumption? Why or why not? Draw on the two correlations you obtained in parts of a–f above in constructing your answer.

7. Let's return now to the issue of social class disparities in access to health care. We saw trend information that revealed the poor are less likely to be insured. Now, let's see if this disparity shows up in survey data, even when government-provided health insurance such as Medicaid and Medicare is taken into account.

a. Open the GSS data set and carefully examine the variable description for 93) HLTHINSR.

b. Cross-tabulate 93) HLTHINSR with 16) $FAMRANK. Then, fill in the percentages that have no medical insurance.

         ➤ Data File: **GSS**
            ➤ Task: **Cross-tabulation**
      ➤ Row Variable: **93) HLTHINSR**
   ➤ Column Variable: **16) $FAMRANK**
            ➤ View: **Tables**
          ➤ Display: **Column %**

	BELOW	AVERAGE	ABOVE
NO	_____%	_____%	_____%

Now, get the Cramer's V and the significance level for these two variables.

c. Record the value of Cramer's V for this table. (Include asterisks, if any.)   V = _____

d. Is the relationship between $FAMRANK and HLTHINSR statistically significant? (Circle one.)   Yes   No

e. Is the relationship between $FAMRANK and HLTHINSR weak, moderate, strong, or not significant? (Circle one.)

                                                Weak

                                           Moderate

                                            Strong

                               Not Significant

f. GSS respondents of below average family income were _____ those with above average family income to have no medical insurance. (Circle the one answer that best fills in this blank.)

                                            less likely than

                                          equally likely as

                                 about three times as likely as

                              about twelve times as likely as

8. It makes sense, as conflict theories would assert, that the wealthier people are, the more likely they will accept the "status quo" with regard to our current health care system and vice versa. Let's test this hypothesis: *the lower respondents' family income, the more they will believe that it is "unjust" that rich people can buy better health care than poorer people.*

    a. Carefully examine the variable description for 92) RICH HLTH.

    b. Cross-tabulate 92) RICH HLTH with 16) $FAMRANK. Then, fill in the percentages of respondents in each income category who say that such disparity in ability to purchase better health care is "unjust."

        > | | |
        > |---:|:---|
        > | Data File: | **GSS** |
        > | Task: | **Cross-tabulation** |
        > | ➤ Row Variable: | **92) RICH HLTH** |
        > | ➤ Column Variable: | **16) $FAMRANK** |
        > | ➤ View: | **Tables** |
        > | ➤ Display: | **Column %** |

	BELOW	AVERAGE	ABOVE
UNJUST	_____%	_____%	_____%

    Now, examine the Cramer's V and the significance level for these two variables.

    c. Is the relationship between $FAMRANK and RICH HLTH statistically significant? (Circle one.)　　　　　　　　　　　　　Yes　　No

    d. Is the relationship between $FAMRANK and RICH HLTH weak, moderate, strong, or not significant? (Circle one.)

    　　　　　　　　　　　　　　　　　　　　　　　　Weak

    　　　　　　　　　　　　　　　　　　　　　　　Moderate

    　　　　　　　　　　　　　　　　　　　　　　　　Strong

    　　　　　　　　　　　　　　　　　　　　Not Significant

    e. Was the hypothesis supported? (Circle one.)　　　　　　Yes　　No

    f. Do these results surprise you? Why or why not?

9. Finally, following up on the cross-tabulation in question 8, let's test this hypothesis: *the lower respondents' family income, the more they will believe that government spending on health care is "too little."*

   a. Carefully examine the variable description for 91) GOVTHEALTH.

   b. Cross-tabulate 91) GOVTHEALTH with 16) $FAMRANK. Then, fill in the percentages of respondents in each income category who say that government spending on health care is "too little."

Data File:	**GSS**
Task:	**Cross-tabulation**
➤ Row Variable:	**91) GOVTHEALTH**
➤ Column Variable:	**16) $FAMRANK**
➤ View:	**Tables**
➤ Display:	**Column %**

	BELOW	AVERAGE	ABOVE
TOO LITTLE	_____%	_____%	_____%

Now, examine the Cramer's V and the significance level for these two variables.

   c. Is the relationship between $FAMRANK and GOVTHEALTH statistically significant? (Circle one.)   Yes   No

   d. Is the relationship between $FAMRANK and GOVTHEALTH weak, moderate, strong, or not significant? (Circle one.)

   Weak

   Moderate

   Strong

   Not Significant

   e. Was the hypothesis supported? (Circle one.)   Yes   No

   f. Did the majority of respondents, regardless of family income, feel that the government was spending "too little" on health care? (Circle one.)   Yes   No

   g. Approximately what percentage felt that the government was spending "too much" on health care? (Hint: Look at the "Totals" column.)

   15%

   8%

   5%

   23%

ENVIRONMENTAL PROBLEMS

Tasks: Mapping, Cross-tabulation, Univariate, Scatterplot
Data Files: COUNTRIES, ELECTION, GSS

Rivers and lakes with fish that can't be safely eaten and water that is no longer even suitable for swimming. Places where the elderly and sick are often instructed to avoid going outdoors because the air is not clean. Areas where rain containing "abnormally high sulfuric and nitric acid content" (***acid rain***)[1] falls from the sky, contaminating land and water, and harming animals, fish, and plants.[2] Various types of wastes, pesticides, and fertilizers contaminating the ground, leaching into our water, and making their way into our bodies, and those of many animals, by numerous routes. Office workers breathing second-hand cigarette smoke and fumes from carpets, cleaning products, and office supplies.[3] What do all these things have in common? They are all environmental pollution caused by human beings, threatening not only our own health, but often also the well-being of our planet.

Some years ago, my wife Kathy and I pulled together an environmental education curriculum for grades kindergarten through eleven entitled *Kids Can Change the World*. The work was done under contract with the Anhauser-Busch Corporation for SeaWorld, and was distributed in the form of a computer program to schools around the country. At the height of completing this project, our living room was stacked high with books and articles about the environment, the relationship of various organisms (including people) to it (***ecology***),[4] and pollution. The more we read, the more we were overwhelmed both with the complexity and beauty of natural systems and with the many ways in which humans were harming the latter. We were also struck by the variety of people's reactions to environmental issues and threats. Responses took place at levels ranging from individual and community action to state, federal and international policy. And of course, people differed greatly in their support for and views about different measures intended to safeguard and/or restore the environment. For example, some wanted governments to enact more environmental regulations and actions, whereas others felt that such policies threatened human welfare by eliminating jobs, raising taxes, and decreasing business freedoms and opportunities.

In this exercise we will examine some data that, like the material on sanitation and usable water that we looked at in the previous exercise, allow us to compare degrees of some forms of pollution among nations, and to consider factors that increase or decrease them. Then, we will consider various opinions among the American people about environmental issues and movements, and how these vary across different groups of people.

One major area of controversy in recent years has been ***global warming***. This is something that most scientists who specialize in the study of climate and related issues believe is taking place.[5] These specialists

---

[1] *American Heritage Dictionary*, op cit.

[2] Mooney et al., op cit., page 428.

[3] Ibid., pages 425–427.

[4] *American Heritage Dictionary*, op cit.

[5] Though to be fair, I must point out that agreement on this by specialists is hardly unanimous at this time.

believe that as carbon dioxide levels rise in the atmosphere, heat is trapped close to the surface of the earth (the **greenhouse effect**), and so average temperatures rise. Over time, such warming of just a few degrees could melt polar ice, leading to catastrophic problems. Sources of this carbon dioxide include the fuels we humans burn, not only those based on fossil fuels (oil and coal, for example), but also wood, peat, straw, and so on.[6]

All of this means, of course, that it is important for scientists to study levels of carbon dioxide emissions. International comparisons of these levels are key to understanding where the problems are most severe in order to address them most effectively. However, too often nations are compared in terms of their total emissions, without taking into account differences in the size of their populations. As I pointed out in Exercise 3, using percentages and rates in comparative research allows us to meaningfully contrast units of different size. Let's use a kind of rate now as we compare countries in terms of how many metric tons of carbon dioxide they emitted in 1999 for each person in their nation.

➤ *Data File:* **COUNTRIES**
➤ *Task:* **Mapping**
➤ *Variable 1:* **80) CO2/CAP**
➤ *View:* **List: Rank**

RANK	CASE NAME	VALUE
1	Qatar	66.7
2	United Arab Emirates	34.5
3	Kuwait	28.9
4	Bahrain	25.5
5	Singapore	23.4
6	United States	20.1
7	Luxembourg	18.9
8	Brunei	17.5
9	Australia	17.3
10	Trinidad & Tobago	17.2

As you can see, although the United States ranks very high here, there are five countries with higher carbon dioxide emissions per capita. Notice that in the highest ranked nation, Qatar, about 67 metric tons of carbon dioxide are released for each person. The United States' level is about 20 tons and is higher than that of any other Western country.

What about the emission of carbon dioxide through burning fossil fuels or making cement (both of which are associated with modern development)? Let's take a look at the percentage of carbon dioxide released by humans that comes from these two sources.

Data File: **COUNTRIES**
Task: **Mapping**
➤ *Variable 1:* **81) CO2%**
➤ *View:* **List: Rank**

RANK	CASE NAME	VALUE
1	United States	22.6
2	China	13.9
3	Russia	5.9
4	Japan	4.8
5	India	4.2
6	Germany	3.4
7	United Kingdom	2.2
8	Canada	2.0
9	South Korea	1.8
10	Italy	1.7

---

[6] I utilized Kornblum and Julian's (op cit., pages 508–509) excellent synopsis of global warming here; see also Eitzen and Baca Zinn, op cit., pages 90–91; and Mooney et al., op cit, pages 428–429.

Now we see that in 1997 the United States had the dubious distinction of being the "leader," with about 23% of human-generated carbon dioxide emissions coming from burning fossil fuels or making cement. This means that Americans could bring down their overall carbon dioxide emissions quite a bit by cutting back on their use of fossil fuels. If you go much further down the list, you can see that Qatar, which had the highest per capita carbon dioxide emissions overall, produces very little of this pollution through the use of fossil fuels or cement (0.2%).

People think of electricity as "clean." But producing it creates pollution in many ways, such as power plants heating up rivers and lakes that they discharge water into (which has many detrimental effects on plant and animal life) or burning fuel. Why don't we compare nations' per capita usage of electricity?

Data File: **COUNTRIES**
Task: **Mapping**
➤ Variable 1: **79) ELECTRIC**
➤ View: **List: Rank**

RANK	CASE NAME	VALUE
1	Norway	24607
2	Iceland	20150
3	Canada	15071
4	Finland	14129
5	Sweden	13955
6	Qatar	13912
7	Kuwait	13800
8	Luxembourg	12400
9	United States	11832
10	United Arab Emirates	9892

The highest ranked nations are cold places like Norway, Finland, and Iceland. The United States ranks 9th—every year 11,832 kilowatt-hours are used per person in this country.

Technological and economic development, including increases in industrial production, is often linked to greater pollution.[7] This would include releasing more carbon dioxide and using more electricity. Thus, we should expect that agriculture-dependent nations should have lower per capita carbon dioxide emissions and electricity usage than "modernized" nations whose economies rely heavily on manufacturing and the provision of services.[8] Let's see if this is so.

Data File: **COUNTRIES**
➤ Task: **Scatterplot**
➤ Dependent Variable: **80) CO2/CAP**
➤ Independent Variable: **27) % AGRIC $**
➤ View: **Reg. Line**

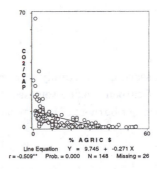

Line Equation Y = 9.745 + -0.271 X
r = -0.509**   Prob. = 0.000   N = 148   Missing = 26

---

[7] Cf. ibid., pages 441–442; Kendall, op cit., pages 328–330; Sullivan, op cit., pages 438–441.

[8] You may recall that we described and contrasted agricultural, industrial, and service economies in Exercise 8.

The first part of our hypothesis appears to be supported here. Among nations, the greater the percentage of the GDP that is derived from agriculture, the lower the per capita emission of carbon dioxide ($r = -0.509**$). Now let's check the second part of our hypothesis and see if agriculture-dependent economies also use less electricity.

Data File: **COUNTRIES**
Task: **Scatterplot**
➤ *Dependent Variable:* **79) ELECTRIC**
➤ *Independent Variable:* **27) % AGRIC $**
➤ *View:* **Reg. Line**

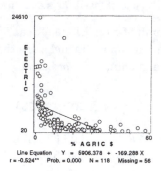

Sure enough, lower usage of electricity ($r = -0.524**$) is related to a greater percentage of the GDP being derived from agriculture.

Despite the kind of benefits of modernization and its affluence that we have identified elsewhere in this workbook, it does seem to carry a price in terms of pollution. For example, Mooney et al., citing Lori Hunter, assert that "a positive linear correlation has been established between per capita income and national carbon dioxide emissions."[9] Let's test this idea.

Data File: **COUNTRIES**
Task: **Scatterplot**
➤ *Dependent Variable:* **80) CO2/CAP**
➤ *Independent Variable:* **25) GDP/CAP**
➤ *View:* **Reg. Line**

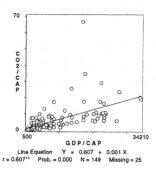

Hunter's assertion is certainly supported here ($r = 0.607**$). With increased affluence come increased amounts of carbon dioxide released. Consider, for example, how the relative number of automobiles, which are major burners of fossil fuels, increases with wealth.

---

[9] See op cit., page 441, citing Lori M. Hunter, 2001, *The Environmental Implications of Population Dynamics*, Santa Monica, Calif.: Rand Corporation.

Investigating Social Problems

Data File: **COUNTRIES**
Task: **Scatterplot**
➤ Dependent Variable: **30) AUTO**
➤ Independent Variable: **25) GDP/CAP**
➤ View: **Reg. Line**

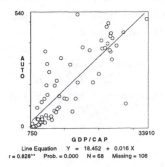

Line Equation   Y = 18.452 + 0.016 X
r = 0.828**   Prob. = 0.000   N = 68   Missing = 106

This correlation is positive and about as powerful as we could imagine ($r = 0.828**$). Car ownership increases dramatically with wealth. Use your mouse to click on the dot at the upper right corner of the graph to see U.S. values. The Y number shows that there are about 513 cars for every 1,000 persons in America. This is a little more than 1 car for every 2 people.

What do Americans think about environmental issues and policies? Would they like to see more government actions and spending designed to clean up and protect the environment? Are they willing to see such policies enacted even if it would require paying higher taxes and prices or cut into their standard of living generally? Let's open the GSS and start this examination by looking at how adequate the respondents believe government spending is on the environment.

➤ Data File: **GSS**
➤ Task: **Univariate**
➤ Primary Variable: **107) GVT ENV $**
➤ View: **Pie**

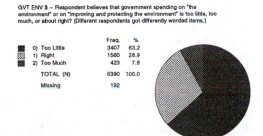

GVT ENV $ – Respondent believes that government spending on "the environment" or on "improving and protecting the environment" is too little, too much, or about right? (Different respondents got differently worded items.)

		Freq.	%
■	0) Too Little	3407	63.2
▨	1) Right	1560	28.9
▦	2) Too Much	423	7.8
	TOTAL (N)	5390	100.0
	Missing	192	

Well over half of respondents (63.2%) believe the government spends "too little" improving and protecting the environment. Does this mean these same respondents would be willing to pay much higher taxes if the money went to protect the environment?

Data File: **GSS**
Task: **Univariate**
➤ Primary Variable: **97) GREEN TAX?**
➤ View: **Pie**

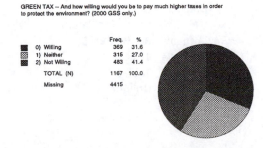

GREEN TAX -- And how willing would you be to pay much higher taxes in order to protect the environment? (2000 GSS only.)

		Freq.	%
■	0) Willing	369	31.6
▨	1) Neither	315	27.0
▦	2) Not Willing	483	41.4
	TOTAL (N)	1167	100.0
	Missing	4415	

Apparently not. Less than a third of respondents (31.6%) would be willing to pay much higher taxes and more than 41% are *un*willing. Would respondents be more willing to pay much higher prices to protect the environment?

Data File: **GSS**
Task: **Univariate**
➤ Primary Variable: **96) GREEN $$**
➤ View: **Pie**

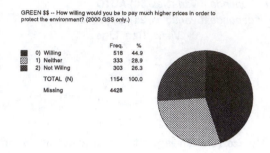

GREEN $$ -- How willing would you be to pay much higher prices in order to protect the environment? (2000 GSS only.)

		Freq.	%
■	0) Willing	518	44.9
▨	1) Neither	333	28.9
▩	2) Not Willing	303	26.3
	TOTAL (N)	1154	100.0
	Missing	4428	

Less than half are willing, but 45% of respondents indicated a willingness to pay much higher prices. Does this translate into accepting a cut in the standard of living?

Data File: **GSS**
Task: **Univariate**
➤ Primary Variable: **98) GREEN CUTS**
➤ View: **Pie**

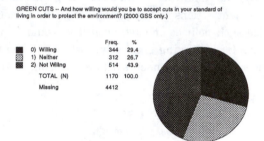

GREEN CUTS -- And how willing would you be to accept cuts in your standard of living in order to protect the environment? (2000 GSS only.)

		Freq.	%
■	0) Willing	344	29.4
▨	1) Neither	312	26.7
▩	2) Not Willing	514	43.9
	TOTAL (N)	1170	100.0
	Missing	4412	

No, only 29% are willing to accept a cut in their standard of living while 44% are definitely not. The American public appears to be giving mixed messages about the environment. Confusing, isn't it?

It appears that where the "rubber meets the road" in how much a person wants to see the environment protected is whether or not he or she is willing to experience some personal loss in order to achieve that protection. Given the way that reality is often portrayed in the media, we might also expect that younger people will display more concern about the environment than those who are older. Let's find out if there are these kinds of age differences in the willingness to pay higher prices and to suffer reductions in one's standard of living in order to protect the environment.

Data File: **GSS**
➤ Task: **Cross-tabulation**
➤ Row Variable: **96) GREEN $$**
➤ Column Variable: **1) AGE**
➤ View: **Tables**
➤ Display: **Column %**

GREEN $$ by AGE
Cramer's V: 0.033

		AGE					
		<30	30-49	50-64	65 and Up	Missing	TOTAL
GREEN $$	Willing	100	232	106	79	1	517
		45.2%	46.0%	43.6%	42.7%		44.8%
	Neither	67	146	66	54	0	333
		30.3%	29.0%	27.2%	29.2%		28.9%
	Not Willing	54	126	71	52	0	303
		24.4%	25.0%	29.2%	28.1%		26.3%
	Missing	835	1875	912	785	21	4428
	TOTAL	221	504	243	185	22	1153
		100.0%	100.0%	100.0%	100.0%		

Investigating Social Problems

Here we see no difference between age groups at all (V = 0.033) although again we see that, in every age group, most respondents did *not* say that they were definitely willing to pay higher prices for the sake of the environment.

Data File: **GSS**
Task: **Cross-tabulation**
➤ Row Variable: **98) GREEN CUTS**
➤ Column Variable: **1) AGE**
➤ View: **Tables**
➤ Display: **Column %**

GREEN CUTS   by   AGE
Cramer's V: 0.079 *

		AGE					
		<30	30-49	50-64	65 and Up	Missing	TOTAL
GREEN CUTS	Willing	59	169	74	42	0	344
		27.2%	32.9%	30.1%	21.9%		29.4%
	Neither	67	137	53	54	1	311
		30.9%	26.7%	21.5%	28.1%		26.6%
	Not Willng	91	208	119	96	0	514
		41.9%	40.5%	48.4%	50.0%		44.0%
	Missing	839	1865	909	778	21	4412
	TOTAL	217	514	246	192	22	1169
		100.0%	100.0%	100.0%	100.0%		

When it comes to a willingness to accept reductions in living standards, though there are significant differences between the age groups (V = 0.079*), these are relatively weak and mixed. For example, more of those 30 to 49 (33%) and 50 to 64 (30%) years of age are willing to experience such losses than are those under 30 (27%), though those 65 and older are least likely to accept this kind of change to protect the environment (roughly 22%).

What kind of difference might education make in such views? We might expect that, given the exposure to environmental issues and threats that one typically receives in school, a willingness to pay higher prices and experience reduced standards of living in order to protect the environment will increase with the amount of education. Let's check.

Data File: **GSS**
Task: **Cross-tabulation**
➤ Row Variable: **96) GREEN $$**
➤ Column Variable: **13) DEGREE**
➤ View: **Tables**
➤ Display: **Column %**

GREEN $$ by   DEGREE
Cramer's V: 0.111 **

		DEGREE						
		Not H.S.	H.S.	Jr. Col	4 Yr Deg	Grad Deg	Missing	TOTAL
GREEN $$	Willing	87	237	35	103	54	2	516
		47.5%	40.0%	41.7%	50.5%	62.8%		44.9%
	Neither	39	192	31	53	17	1	332
		21.3%	32.4%	36.9%	26.0%	19.8%		28.9%
	Not Willng	57	163	18	48	15	2	301
		31.1%	27.5%	21.4%	23.5%	17.4%		26.2%
	Missing	656	2394	324	674	362	18	4428
	TOTAL	183	592	84	204	86	23	1149
		100.0%	100.0%	100.0%	100.0%	100.0%		

People of different educational levels vary significantly in their willingness to pay higher prices to protect the environment (V = 0.111**). Certainly, those who have not finished high school (47.5%) are more likely to say they would pay higher prices than those who have completed high school (40%) or junior college (42%). But such willingness is higher among college graduates (50.5%) and especially rises among those with graduate degrees (63%). High school dropouts were most likely *not* to be willing to pay higher prices to protect the environment (31%), while those with graduate degrees were the least likely to feel this way (about 17%).

Data File: **GSS**
Task: **Cross-tabulation**
➤ Row Variable: **98) GREEN CUTS**
➤ Column Variable: **13) DEGREE**
➤ View: **Tables**
➤ Display: **Column %**

GREEN CUTS by DEGREE
Cramer's V: 0.084 *

		DEGREE						
		Not H.S.	H.S.	Jr. Col.	4 Yr Deg	Grad Deg	Missing	TOTAL
GREEN CUTS	Willing	58	162	26	59	35	4	340
		31.5%	26.7%	31.3%	28.6%	41.2%		29.2%
	Neither	36	165	27	62	21	1	311
		19.6%	27.2%	32.5%	30.1%	24.7%		26.7%
	Not Willing	90	279	30	85	29	1	513
		48.9%	46.0%	36.1%	41.3%	34.1%		44.1%
	Missing	655	2380	325	672	363	17	4412
	TOTAL	184	606	83	206	85	23	1164
		100.0%	100.0%	100.0%	100.0%	100.0%		

On the issue of cuts in standards of living the picture is very similar, though the differences between educational levels are pretty small (V = 0.084*). The percentages of those who stated they are willing to accept such losses doesn't change much from high school dropouts (31.5%) through the college educated (28.6%), though those with graduate degrees are clearly more likely to say they are disposed to do so (41%). But the percentages of those who say they are definitely *not* willing to drop their standard of living to protect the environment falls clearly as educational level rises, moving from 49% of those without high school diplomas to only 34% of those with graduate degrees.

In popular discussions of environmental issues, we often see debates about "jobs versus environmental protection." Let's switch to ELECTION to look at responses to an item that specifically addresses this issue.

➤ Data File: **ELECTION**
➤ Task: **Univariate**
➤ Primary Variable: **66) JOBENV**
➤ View: **Pie**

JOBENV -- Did respondent feel that it was more important to protect the environment even if it costs some jobs, or that maintaining jobs and the standard of living was more important.

		Freq.	%
■	1) Envir	660	72.1
▨	2) Jobs	255	27.9
	TOTAL (N)	915	100.0
	Missing	2173	

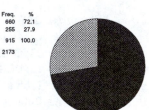

Here, we see a large majority that favors protecting the environment even if it costs some jobs (about 72%). How might views on this vary by educational level? Might the less educated feel differently from the more educated? Why don't we find out?

➤ Data File: **ELECTION**
➤ Task: **Cross-tabulation**
➤ Row Variable: **66) JOBENV**
➤ Column Variable: **4) EDUCATION**
➤ View: **Tables**
➤ Display: **Column %**

JOBENV by EDUCATION
Cramer's V: 0.189 **

		EDUCATION					
		No HS	HS Deg	College	Adv Degree	Missing	TOTAL
JOBENV	Envir	49	179	344	88	0	660
		53.8%	67.3%	75.1%	88.0%		72.1%
	Jobs	42	87	114	12	0	255
		46.2%	32.7%	24.9%	12.0%		27.9%
	Missing	258	639	1039	225	12	2173
	TOTAL	91	266	458	100	12	915
		100.0%	100.0%	100.0%	100.0%		

Investigating Social Problems

The relationship between educational level and views on this issue is pretty strong (V = 0.189**). Certainly, a majority within each age group places the environment ahead of maintaining jobs. But the less educated are more likely to place jobs and the standard of living ahead of protecting the environment (moving from about 46% among high school dropouts to roughly 25% among college graduates and just 12% among those with advanced degrees).

Finally, one big area of controversy in the area of environmental policy has to do with the extent to which businesses need to be regulated. Let's consider this.

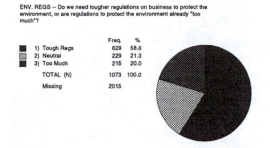

> Data File: **ELECTION**
> ➤ Task: **Univariate**
> ➤ Primary Variable: **67) ENV. REGS**
> ➤ View: **Pie**

ENV. REGS -- Do we need tougher regulations on business to protect the environment, or are regulations to protect the environment already "too much"?

		Freq.	%
▪	1) Tough Regs	629	58.6
▨	2) Neutral	229	21.3
▨	3) Too Much	215	20.0
	TOTAL (N)	1073	100.0
	Missing	2015	

Clearly, most respondents support tougher regulations on business to protect the environment. But I suppose we might expect big differences here by political affiliation, with Republicans being a lot less willing than Democrats to support such regulations.

> Data File: **ELECTION**
> ➤ Task: **Cross-tabulation**
> ➤ Row Variable: **67) ENV. REGS**
> ➤ Column Variable: **20) PARTY AFIL**
> ➤ View: **Tables**
> ➤ Display: **Column %**

ENV. REGS by PARTY AFIL
Cramer's V: 0.159 **

		PARTY AFIL				
		Republican	Democrat	Independ	Missing	TOTAL
ENV. REGS	Tough Regs	123	263	187	56	573
		42.4%	67.6%	62.3%		58.5%
	Neutral	76	70	58	25	204
		26.2%	18.0%	19.3%		20.8%
	Too Much	91	56	55	13	202
		31.4%	14.4%	18.3%		20.6%
	Missing	497	709	536	273	2015
	TOTAL	290	389	300	367	979
		100.0%	100.0%	100.0%		

Party affiliation makes a big difference (V = 0.159**). While about 68% of Democrats, and 62% of Independents support tougher regulations on businesses to protect the environment, only about 42% of Republicans do. And roughly 31% of Republicans believe that existing regulations are "too much," compared to about 14% of Democrats and 18% of Independents.

Well, there's still plenty more to look at and analyze. But it's your turn.

REVIEW QUESTIONS

Based on the first part of this exercise, answer True or False to the following items:

It is thought that the greenhouse effect is caused by an overabundance of oxygen in the atmosphere.	T	F
Per capita carbon dioxide emissions are higher in the United States than in any other country.	T	F
The percentage of human-generated carbon dioxide that is produced by fossil fuels and making cement is higher in the United States than in any other country.	T	F
Per capita electrical usage and carbon dioxide emissions are lower in countries with economies that are more dependent upon agriculture.	T	F
Among nations, per capita carbon dioxide emissions are positively correlated with affluence.	T	F
On every GSS measure we looked at, most Americans indicated that they were willing to suffer some personal loss in order to improve the protection of the environment.	T	F
The younger Americans are, the higher the percentages that are willing to suffer some personal loss to protect the environment.	T	F
The less educated Americans are, the more likely they are to say that they are *not* willing to pay higher prices or experience drops in their standard of living to protect the environment.	T	F
Most Americans feel the environment should be protected even if it costs some jobs.	T	F
Contrary to popular belief, Republicans are just as likely as Democrats to support tougher regulations on businesses to protect the environment.	T	F

EXPLORIT QUESTIONS

1. We have already seen that agricultural (and thus more rural) nations have lower carbon dioxide emissions per capita then more modernized nations. And we can easily see that lots of things associated with city life (like automobile traffic and industry) would increase carbon dioxide output. It makes sense, then, that among countries the larger the percentage living in urban areas, the greater the per capita carbon dioxide emissions. Let's test this hypothesis.

    a. Open the COUNTRIES data set and carefully examine the variable description for 4) URBAN.

b. Construct a scatterplot that represents the association between 4) URBAN and 80) CO2/CAP.

> ➤ *Data File:* **COUNTRIES**
> ➤ *Task:* **Scatterplot**
> ➤ *Dependent Variable:* **80) CO2/CAP**
> ➤ *Independent Variable:* **4) URBAN**
> ➤ *View:* **Reg. Line**

c. Provide Pearson's *r* (including asterisks, if any, and the direction sign, if any).   *r* = _____

d. Is this correlation significant *and* negative, significant *and* positive,
or *not* significant? (Circle one.)

                                      Significant *and* Negative

                                      Significant *and* Positive

                                      Not Significant

e. Is this correlation weak, moderate, strong, or not significant? (Circle one.)   Weak

                                        Moderate

                                        Strong

                                      Not Significant

f. Is the hypothesis supported? (Circle one.)   Yes   No

2. As we saw in Exercise 8, in post-industrial countries such as the United States and others that are among the most modern and wealthy, a high percentage of the economy is based on "services." This is associated with developing and using a great deal of electronic technology such as computers. However, industrial production need not be associated with such high use of electricity. If this is true, then we might expect that *the percentage of the gross domestic product (GDP) that is accounted for by the service sector will be positively associated with per capita electricity consumption. However, the percentage of the GDP that is accounted for by industry will not be as positively associated with per capita electricity use and, in fact, may not be associated with greater per capita electricity consumption at all.* Let's find out.

a. Construct a scatterplot that represents the association between 29) % SERVC $ and 79) ELECTRIC.

> *Data File:* **COUNTRIES**
> *Task:* **Scatterplot**
> ➤ *Dependent Variable:* **79) ELECTRIC**
> ➤ *Independent Variable:* **29) % SERVC $**
> ➤ *View:* **Reg. Line**

Examine Pearson's *r*.

b. Is this last correlation significant *and* negative, significant *and* positive, or *not* significant? (Circle one.)

Significant *and* Negative

Significant *and* Positive

Not Significant

c. Now, construct a scatterplot that represents the association between 28) % INDUS $ and 79) ELECTRIC.

Data File:	**COUNTRIES**
Task:	**Scatterplot**
Dependent Variable:	**79) ELECTRIC**
➤ Independent Variable:	**28) % INDUS $**
➤ View:	**Reg. Line**

Examine Pearson's *r*.

d. Is this last correlation significant *and* negative, significant *and* positive, or *not* significant? (Circle one.)

Significant *and* Negative

Significant *and* Positive

Not Significant

e. Look again at our idea (in italics above) about the differences in electrical consumption of industrial versus post-industrial countries. Do these last two scatterplots support this idea? Explain.

3. When I think of the most wealthy, modern countries today, I picture a lot of things that burn fossil fuels (like cars) and miles of concrete buildings and streets. So I suppose that these (again, generally post-industrial, service-oriented) countries may release more carbon dioxide emissions from using fossil fuels and cement than will countries whose economies depend more on straight industry. Thus, we might expect that *the percentage of the gross domestic product (GDP) accounted for by the service sector will be positively associated with the percentage of human-generated carbon dioxide emissions produced by burning fossil fuels and making cement. However, the percentage of the GDP accounted for by industry will not be as positively associated, or may not be associated at all, with this latter variable.*

a. Construct a scatterplot that represents the association between 29) % SERVC $ and 81) CO2%.

> Data File: **COUNTRIES**
> Task: **Scatterplot**
> ➤ Dependent Variable: **81) CO2%**
> ➤ Independent Variable: **29) % SERVC $**
> ➤ View: **Reg. Line**

Examine Pearson's *r*.

b. Among nations, as the percentage of the GDP accounted for by the service sector increased, the percentage of human-generated carbon dioxide emissions produced by fossil fuels and cement: (Circle one.)

Decreased a Lot

Decreased a Little

Neither Increased nor Decreased

Increased a Little

Increased a Lot

c. Construct a scatterplot that represents the association between 28) % INDUS $ and 81) CO2%.

> Data File: **COUNTRIES**
> Task: **Scatterplot**
> Dependent Variable: **81) CO2%**
> ➤ Independent Variable: **28) % INDUS $**
> ➤ View: **Reg. Line**

Examine Pearson's *r*.

d. Among nations, as the percentage of the GDP accounted for by the industrial sector increased, the percentage of human-generated carbon dioxide emissions produced by fossil fuels and cement: (Circle one.)

Decreased a Lot

Decreased a Little

Neither Increased nor Decreased

Increased a Little

Increased a Lot

e. Look again at our idea (in italics above) about the differences in the percentage of human-generated carbon dioxide emissions coming from fossil fuels and cement in industrial versus post-industrial countries. Do these last two scatterplots support this idea? Explain.

4. For obvious reasons, we might expect people who are currently unemployed and/or laid off to be more concerned with maintaining jobs and standard of living than with protecting the environment. Here's our hypothesis: *those who are currently unemployed will be more likely than others to favor maintaining jobs and standard of living over protecting the environment.*

   a. Open the ELECTION data set and carefully examine the variable description for 13) LAID OFF.

   b. Cross-tabulate 66) JOBENV with 13) LAID OFF. Then, fill in the percentages that feel that maintaining jobs and standard of living are more important than protecting the environment.

   > ➤ *Data File:* **ELECTION**
   > ➤ *Task:* **Cross-tabulation**
   > ➤ *Row Variable:* **66) JOBENV**
   > ➤ *Column Variable:* **13) LAID OFF**
   > ➤ *View:* **Tables**
   > ➤ *Display:* **Column %**

	YES	**NO**
JOBS	_____%	_____%

   Now, get the Cramer's V and the significance level for these two variables.

   c. Record the value of Cramer's V for this table. (Include asterisks, if any.)   V = _____

   d. Is the relationship between LAID OFF and JOBENV statistically significant? (Circle one.)   Yes   No

   e. Was the hypothesis supported? (Circle one.)   Yes   No

5. How do people of different income levels feel about environmental protection? Let's explore this question by looking at a few items.

   a. Cross-tabulate 65) ENVIRON$ with 5) FAMINCOME. Then, fill in the percentages that feel federal spending on the environment should be increased and decreased.

   > *Data File:* **ELECTION**
   > *Task:* **Cross-tabulation**
   > ➤ *Row Variable:* **65) ENVIRON$**
   > ➤ *Column Variable:* **5) FAMINCOME**
   > ➤ *View:* **Tables**
   > ➤ *Display:* **Column %**

	<$25,000	$25K–64.9K	$65,000+
INCREASED	_____%	_____%	_____%
DECREASED	_____%	_____%	_____%

Now examine the value of Cramer's V for this table.

b. Cross-tabulate 66) JOBENV with 5) FAMINCOME. Then, fill in the percentages in the table below.

> Data File: **ELECTION**
> Task: **Cross-tabulation**
> ➤ Row Variable: **66) JOBENV**
> ➤ Column Variable: **5) FAMINCOME**
> ➤ View: **Tables**
> ➤ Display: **Column %**

	<$25,000	$25K–64.9K	$65,000+
ENVIR	_____%	_____%	_____%
JOBS	_____%	_____%	_____%

Now examine the value of Cramer's V for this table.

c. Cross-tabulate 67) ENV. REGS with 5) FAMINCOME. Then, fill in the percentages that feel that tougher business regulations are needed and that current regulations are already too much.

> Data File: **ELECTION**
> Task: **Cross-tabulation**
> ➤ Row Variable: **67) ENV. REGS**
> ➤ Column Variable: **5) FAMINCOME**
> ➤ View: **Tables**
> ➤ Display: **Column %**

	<$25,000	$25K–64.9K	$65,000+
TOUGH REGS	_____%	_____%	_____%
TOO MUCH	_____%	_____%	_____%

Now examine the value of Cramer's V for this table.

   d. Which of the following variables was significantly associated with
       family income? (Circle *each* that applies.)

ENVIRON$

JOBENV

ENV. REGS

Not Significant

   e. Consider income groups that were significantly less supportive of environmental protection on
       any of the above items (if any). What do you think might be the reason(s) why this income group
       is less supportive of either (1) increased government spending on the environment, or (2) envi-
       ronmental policy that costs jobs, or (3) increased regulations on business?

6.   One thing that can be both fascinating and frustrating for researchers doing surveys is the extent to
     which people can appear, at least on the surface, to be logically inconsistent in the responses they
     give. This is often the case with people who want the government to do something, but don't want to
     pay higher taxes to fund the actions they want! Why don't we consider whether or not this is apparent
     in answers to two of the environmental items in the GSS?

   a. Open the GSS data set.

   b. Cross-tabulate 97) GREEN TAX with 107) GVT ENV $.

            ➤ *Data File:* **GSS**
                ➤ *Task:* **Cross-tabulation**
          ➤ *Row Variable:* **97) GREEN TAX**
       ➤ *Column Variable:* **107) GVT ENV $**
                ➤ *View:* **Tables**
             ➤ *Display:* **Column %**

   c. Fill in the blanks: Of those who said that the government was spending "too little" _____%
       to improve or protect the environment, the percentage that was not willing to pay
       much higher taxes in order to protect the environment was _____%, while the   _____%
       percentage that definitely was willing to pay higher taxes to protect the environ-
       ment was only _____%.

d. Look closely at the wording of GSS variables 107) GVT ENV $ and 97) GREEN TAX. Then, consider those respondents who said that the government was spending too little on the environment, but who also said that they were not willing to pay much higher taxes in order to protect the environment. Do you think that these respondents were being logically inconsistent? Why or why not?

7. While people are certainly not always as logically consistent as we would like them to be, we can often use their responses to some survey items to predict which answers they will be more likely to give on other survey items. Let's see, for example, if the following hypothesis is supported: *the more respondents say that they trust information from environmental groups, the less likely they will be to say that claims about environmental threats are exaggerated.*

a. Carefully examine the variable descriptions for 103) INFO GREEN and 101) GREEN EXAG.

b. Cross-tabulate 101) GREEN EXAG with 103) INFO GREEN. Then, fill in the percentages that "agree" and "disagree" that claims about environmental threats are often exaggerated.

Data File:	**GSS**
Task:	**Cross-tabulation**
➤ Row Variable:	**101) GREEN EXAG**
➤ Column Variable:	**103) INFO GREEN**
➤ View:	**Tables**
➤ Display:	**Column %**

	ALOT	**SOME**	**NOT MUCH**
AGREE	_____%	_____%	_____%
DISAGREE	_____%	_____%	_____%

Now, examine the Cramer's V and the significance level for these two variables.

c. Is the relationship between INFO GREEN and GREEN EXAG statistically significant? (Circle one.)   Yes   No

d. Is the relationship between INFO GREEN and GREEN EXAG weak, moderate, strong, or not significant? (Circle one.)

Weak

Moderate

Strong

Not Significant

e. Was the hypothesis supported? (Circle one.)

Yes   No

f. Some respondents who thought that information about pollution from environmental groups could be trusted "a lot" also agreed that many of the claims about environmental threats were exaggerated. Do you think that these respondents were being logically inconsistent? Why or why not?

8. In this exercise, we dealt with the greenhouse effect and carbon dioxide emissions that are thought to contribute to this. Let's see what percentage of the public agrees with most climatologists that the greenhouse effect is a real environmental threat.

a. Carefully examine the variable description for 105) TEMP.ENVIR.

b. Look at the percentages in GSS that considered the greenhouse effect to be dangerous for the environment. Then, fill in those percentages below.

> Data File: **GSS**
> ➤ Task: **Univariate**
> ➤ Primary Variable: **105) TEMP.ENVIR**
> ➤ View: **Pie**

Extr./Very: _____%

Smewht Dng: _____%

9. Finally, concerns about the greenhouse effect and other issues where the actions of some countries may have negative environmental impact on the planet as a whole have led many to feel that countries ought to be involved in international agreements to deal with environmental problems. Let's see what percentage of the public agrees that the United States should enter such agreements.

a. Carefully examine the description for 102) GREEN INTL.

b. Look at the percentage in GSS that agree America and other countries should have to follow international environmental agreements. Then, fill in that percentage below.

> Data File: **GSS**
> Task: **Univariate**
> ➤ Primary Variable: **102) GREEN INTL**
> ➤ View: **Pie**

Agree: _____%

APPENDIX: VARIABLE NAMES AND SOURCES

Note for MicroCase Users: These data files may be used with the MicroCase Analysis System. If you are moving variables from these files into other MicroCase files, or vice versa, you may need to reorder the cases. Also note that files that have been modified in MicroCase will not function properly in Student ExplorIt.

◆ DATA FILE: COUNTRIES ◆

1) COUNTRY
2) POPULATION
3) DENSITY
4) URBAN
5) POP GROWTH
6) NETMIGRT
7) BIRTH RATE
8) FERTILITY
9) LARGE FAML
10) INF. MORTL
11) MOM MORTAL
12) CONTRACEPT
13) ABORTION
14) ABORT LEGL
15) DEATH RATE
16) LIFE EXPCT
17) SEX RATIO
18) ECON DEVEL
19) QUAL. LIFE
20) CALORIES
21) PUB EDUCAT
22) $ RICH 10%
23) INEQUALITY
24) GDP GROWTH
25) GDP/CAP
26) UNEMPLYRT
27) % AGRIC $

28) % INDUS $
29) % SERVC $
30) AUTO
31) TELPH
32) LITERACY
33) TLVSN
34) PRIM/TOT
35) FEM.PROF.
36) FEM.MANAGE
37) FEM.OFFICE
38) %FEM.LEGIS
39) %FEM.HEADS
40) %WKR WOMEN
41) M/F EDUC.
42) GEM
43) WORK MOM?
44) HOME&KIDS
45) ASSAULT 97
46) MURDER 97
47) RAPE 97
48) ROBBERY 97
49) BURGLARY97
50) THEFT 97
51) POLICE
52) PRISONERS
53) CAP PUNISH
54) CIRRHOSIS

55) SUICIDE
56) AIDS
57) DRUGS
58) ALCOHOL
59) SPIRITS
60) BEER DRINK
61) WINE DRINK
62) CIGARETTES
63) SMOKE DOPE
64) REVOLUTION
65) LEFT/RIGHT
66) %TURNOUT
67) DEMOCRACY
68) ANTI-FORGN
69) RACISM
70) ANTI-SEM.
71) ANTI-MUSLM
72) REL.PERSON
73) CH.ATTEND
74) DOCTORS
75) PUB HLTH$
76) HLTH$/CAP
77) SANITATION
78) GOODWATER
79) ELECTRIC
80) CO_2/CAP
81) CO_2%

◆ DATA FILE: ELECTION ◆

1) REGION
2) GENDER
3) AGE
4) EDUCATION
5) FAMINCOME
6) PERS INCOM

7) CLASS
8) RACE
9) HISPANIC
10) MARITAL
11) CHILDREN
12) WORK FT

13) LAID OFF
14) OCCUPATION
15) UNION
16) CHATTEND
17) CHATTFREQ
18) RELIGID

◆ DATA FILE: ELECTION (Cont'd) ◆

19) BORN AGAIN
20) PARTY AFIL
21) POLVIEW
22) BIGPROB
23) GOVPROB
24) PRTYPROB
25) DOMPROB
26) FORPROB
27) GFUNPROB
28) RACEPROB
29) CRIMEPROB
30) POORPROB
31) HEALTHPROB
32) ENVIRPROB
33) DRUGPROB
34) WOMENPROB
35) FAMILY VAL

36) USE FORCE
37) EQUALITY
38) GOV MEDDLE
39) GOVVSFM
40) ISOLATION
41) GAY ADOPT
42) GAYMIL SUP
43) GAY THERM
44) CRIME RATE
45) CRIME$
46) DEATH PEN
47) GUNS SUP
48) CRIMESOL
49) AFFIRM.ACT
50) HELP BLK?
51) WORK UP
52) ASIA THERM

53) HISP THERM
54) WH THERM
55) BL THERM
56) WOM INFL
57) FEM THERM
58) WLIB THERM
59) WOMEN EQL
60) SOCSEC SP
61) AGED THERM
62) VOLUNTR
63) MED DELAY
64) ENVR THERM
65) ENVIRON$
66) JOBENV
67) ENV. REGS

◆ DATA FILE: GSS ◆

1) AGE
2) GENDER
3) RACE
4) HISPANIC
5) REGION
6) HOME@16
7) HOME NOW
8) MARITAL
9) EVER DIV?
10) #CHILDREN
11) #SIB
12) FAM@16
13) DEGREE
14) PAR DEGREE
15) CLASS?
16) $FAMRANK
17) OWN INCOME
18) FULL TIME?
19) UNEMPLOYED
20) PRESTIGE
21) HIPRESTIGE
22) PAR HIPRST
23) R.FUND/LIB
24) R.FUND@16
25) RELIGION
26) ATTEND

27) PREM.SEX
28) TEEN SEX?
29) SEX ED
30) TEEN BC OK
31) HOMO.SEX
32) SX.PRTNRS
33) SEX FREQ.
34) SEXSINCE18
35) CONDOM
36) OTHERSEX
37) SEXOFSEX5
38) SEXOFSEXYR
39) GRASS?
40) EXECUTE?
41) GUN LAW?
42) COURTS?
43) CRIME$
44) FEAR WALK
45) VOTE96
46) PRES96
47) VOTE00
48) PRES00
49) EQUALIZE$
50) POL. VIEW
51) HAPPY?
52) MISTRUST

53) WORK IF $$
54) INTERMAR.?
55) AFFRM.ACT
56) RACE PUSH
57) MARRY BLK
58) MARRY ASN
59) MARRY HSP
60) MARRY WHT
61) LIVE BLACK
62) LIVE HISP
63) LIVE ASIAN
64) LIVE WHITE
65) RACE DIF
66) REV.DISCRM
67) WHITE WORK
68) JEW WORK
69) BLACK WORK
70) ASIAN WORK
71) HISP. WORK
72) KIDS SOL
73) SPANKING
74) ABORT RAPE
75) ABORT HLTH
76) ABORT SING
77) ABORT ANY
78) WIFE@HOME

79) MEN BETTER
80) PRESCH.WRK
81) MOTH.WORK
82) LIVE W KID
83) NEWSPAPER
84) WATCH TV
85) SOC.KIN
86) SOC.NEIGH
87) SOC.FRIEND
88) SAT.$

89) IDEAL#KIDS
90) HEALTH
91) GOVTHEALTH
92) RICH HLTH
93) HLTHINSR
94) ENV. WORRY
95) ECON.HARM
96) GREEN $$
97) GREEN TAX
98) GREEN CUTS

99) PUB.DECIDE
100) BUS.DECIDE
101) GREEN EXAG
102) GREEN INTL
103) INFO GREEN
104) INDUS.ENV.
105) TEMP.ENVIR
106) CARS ENVIR
107) GVT ENV $

◆ DATA FILE: STATES ◆

1) STATE NAME
2) POP 2002
3) POP%GRO
4) DENSITY 00
5) %RURAL00
6) SEX RAT.00
7) SEX RAT.90
8) SEX RAT.40
9) %WHITE00
10) %BLACK00
11) %AMER.IN00
12) %ASIAN/P00
13) %HISP.00
14) %WHITE90
15) %BLACK90
16) %AMER.IN90
17) %HISPANC90
18) IMMIGRNT00
19) NDM 90–99
20) NIM 90–99
21) BIRTHS 00
22) DEATH 99
23) INFMRT 99
24) WINFMRT99
25) BINFMRT99
26) WBINFMRT99
27) FERTIL00
28) MED.FAM$00
29) PER CAP$00
30) DRUG ED 90
31) BEER 97
32) WINE 95

33) CAR SBA 98
34) CAR HBA 98
35) ALCOHOL 89
36) SPIRITS 84
37) COKEUSER90
38) BINGE00
39) CIGARET00
40) COKE00
41) ILCTDRG00
42) POT00
43) DIVORCE 01
44) DIVORCE 89
45) F HEAD/C00
46) F HEAD/C90
47) F.HEAD P89
48) %POOR00
49) %POOR89
50) BLK POOR89
51) WHT POOR89
52) UNEMP 01
53) %FEM LAB40
54) %FEM MD 95
55) %FEM.LAB90
56) VIOLCRIM01
57) PROPCRIM01
58) MURDER01
59) RAPE01
60) ROBBERY01
61) ASSAULT01
62) BURGLARY01
63) LARCENY01
64) CARTHEFT01

65) %SMHOUSE00
66) SUICIDE 99
67) SUICIDE 80
68) SHRINKS 80
69) SHRINKS 95
70) SHRINKS 90
71) PSYTODAY96
72) %BAD MH
73) $ MENTAL97
74) % CHNG MH$
75) ALZHEIMERS
76) MENT RES00
77) MENT HS00
78) %65 & OVER
79) NURSING HM
80) KIDABUSE00
81) FAMARRST00
82) CHILDPHYS
83) NEGLECT
84) CHSEXABUSE
85) CHILDDIE
86) ABUSEPREV
87) REMOVEHOME
88) HS DROP 00
89) COLL GR 00
90) % FAT 99
91) DOCTORS 99
92) HLTH INS00
93) CHLD INS00
94) HEART DT99

1) Date	49) COKE1825	97) SUICIDE514
2) ENVIR $	50) COKE2634	98) SUICID1524
3) DEFENSE $	51) COKE35+	99) SUICID2544
4) WELF $	52) GRASS	100) SUICID4564
5) HEALTH $	53) GRASS12?	101) SUICIDE65+
6) BLACK $	54) COKE12?	102) SUICID6574
7) DRUG $	55) #VIOLNCVS	103) SUICID7584
8) CRIME $	56) #VIOLUCR	104) SUICID85+
9) EDUCATE $	57) VIOLUCR	105) RATERESMH
10) TEENSEX	58) VIOL1215	106) RTEN-RESMH
11) SEXGRD9	59) VIOL1619	107) EXPENSE MH
12) SEXGRD12	60) VIOL2024	108) RATE MH
13) SEXBY13	61) VIOL2534	109) #TREAT MH
14) TEENSX4+	62) VIOL3549	110) % MHT RES
15) TNSEXACTV	63) VIOL5064	111) % MHT N-RS
16) SEXACTVGR9	64) VIOL65+	112) #PSYCHOL
17) SEXACVGR12	65) VIOLWH	113) #MH STAFF
18) TNCONDOM	66) VIOLBL	114) %NOT HAPPY
19) TNPILL	67) VIOLML	115) %BADMH17
20) AIDSED	68) VIOLFM	116) %BADMH830
21) TEENBC	69) MURDER	117) %POOR
22) TEENPILL	70) UCRMURDER	118) %POORCHLD
23) TEENCONDOM	71) UCRRAPE	119) %POORWH
24) PREGRATE14	72) NCVSRAPE	120) %POORBL
25) PREGRT1517	73) UCRROB	121) %POORHS
26) PREGRT1819	74) NCVSROB	122) %POORFH/CH
27) TEENPREG	75) UCRASSAULT	123) RACE PUSH
28) EVCIG12GR	76) NCVSASSLT	124) RACE SEG
29) DLYCIG12GR	77) PROPUCR	125) VOTE BLK
30) EVPOT12GR	78) PROPNCVS	126) RACE DIF
31) EVINH12GR	79) UCRBURGL	127) %FEM PRES
32) EVHAL12GR	80) NCVSBURGL	128) %M F.PRES
33) EVHER12GR	81) UCRTHEFT	129) %F F.PRES
34) EVCOKE12GR	82) NCVSTHEFT	130) F.LAB SING
35) EVNRC12GR	83) UCRCARTHFT	131) F.LAB. MAR
36) EVAMP12GR	84) NCVSCRTHFT	132) MOM LABOR
37) EVSED12GR	85) #PRISONERS	133) WIFE@HOME
38) EVTRQ12GR	86) #DEATHROW	134) WIFE WORK
39) EVILL12GR	87) %DEATHROWB	135) USPOPULAT
40) EVDRNK12GR	88) #EXECUTED	136) USPOPDENSE
41) BINGE12GR	89) SUPPEXEC	137) %USPOPCHNG
42) CIGARETTE	90) SUICIDE RT	138) WORLDPOP
43) POT1825	91) SUICIDE ML	139) BIRTH RATE
44) POT2634	92) SUICIDE FM	140) DEATH RATE
45) POT35+	93) SUICIDE WM	141) #IMMIGRATE
46) BINGE1825	94) SUICIDE WF	142) IMMIGRATE
47) BINGE2634	95) SUICIDE BM	143) LIFE EXP
48) BINGE35+	96) SUICIDE BF	144) LIFE EXP65

◆ DATA FILE: TRENDS cont'd ◆

145) LIFE EXP85
146) #65&UP
147) %65&UP
148) %85&UP
149) MEDIAN AGE
150) WORK@70
151) NURS HM65
152) NURS HM75
153) NURS HM85
154) NURS HMML
155) NURS HMFM
156) NURS HMWH
157) NURS HMBL
158) SPANK?
159) CHILDVICT

160) PARVIOL
161) PARTHREAT
162) #INTVIOL
163) INTVIOLFM
164) INTVIOLML
165) %IVREPFM
166) %IVREPML
167) INTMURDER
168) INTMURDRFM
169) INTMURDRML
170) WHITE MVF
171) BLACK MVF
172) SPOUSEKILL
173) EXSPSEKILL
174) LOVERKILL

175) %SPSEKILL
176) %EXSPEKILL
177) %LOVERKILL
178) DOCTOR RTE
179) MED$/POP
180) HEAL$/POP
181) HEAL$/CAP
182) HEAL$/%GDP
183) UNINSURED#
184) UNINSURED%
185) UNINSPOOR
186) UNINSRICH
187) UNINSHISP
188) UNINSWHT
189) UNINSBLACK

◆ DATA FILE: YRBS ◆

1) GENDER
2) RACE
3) WEIGHT
4) REGION
5) METRO
6) RDWDRK
7) DRVDRK
8) WEAPSCHL
9) SAFESCHL
10) THREATWEAP
11) STEADYHIT
12) FORCEDSEX
13) SAD

14) CDRSUICIDE
15) PLNSUICIDE
16) TRYSUICIDE
17) DOCSUICIDE
18) AGE1STCIG
19) RECSMOKE
20) HWMNYCIGS
21) EVDRINK
22) AGEDRINK
23) RECBINGE
24) HWMNYMARIJ
25) AGE1STMARJ
26) HWMNYCOC

27) HWMNYSNIFF
28) HWMNYHERO
29) HWMNYMETH
30) EVERSEX
31) AGE1STSEX
32) SEX#PPL
33) RECSEX#PPL
34) PREVPREG
35) PREGNANT
36) DESCWEIGHT
37) VOMITDIET

SOURCES

STATES

The data in the STATES file are from a variety of sources. In most cases, they are the most recent statistics available when this manuscript went to press. The description of each variable includes one of the following abbreviations to indicate the source.

BRFSS: Behavior Risk Factor Surveillance System, National Center for Chronic Disease Prevention & Health Promotion, Centers for Disease Control and Prevention, U.S. Department of Health & Human Services.

CENSUS: U.S. Census Bureau, Department of Commerce, Washington D.C.

CM: Child Maltreatment 2001, U.S. Department of Health and Human Services, Administration on Children, Youth, and Families, Washington D.C. 2003.

HCSR: Health Care State Rankings (Morgan Quitno, Lawrence, KS) for the indicated year.

HUS: Health United States, National Center for Health Statistics, Department of Health and Human Services, Washington D.C.

INS: Immigration & Naturalization Service.

NCHS: National Center for Health Statistics, Department of Health and Human Services.

NHSDA: National Household Survey on Drug Abuse, Substance Abuse and Mental Health Services Administration, U.S. Department of Health and Human Services.

UCR: *Uniform Crime Reports* (latest version, unless otherwise noted), Federal Bureau of Investigation, Department of Justice, Washington D.C.

SA: *Statistical Abstract of the United States* (latest version, unless otherwise noted), published annually by the U.S. Department of Commerce.

USA Today, Gannett Newspapers, (indicated date).

VS: Vital Statistics, U.S. Bureau of the Census.

COUNTRIES

The data in the COUNTRIES file are also from a variety of sources. In most cases, they are the most recent statistics available when this manuscript went to press. The description of each variable includes one of the following abbreviations to indicate the source.

FITW: *Freedom in the World,* published annually by Freedom House.

HDR: *Human Development Report*, published annually by the United Nations Development Program.

IBWR: *Illustrated Book of World Rankings*, 2001.

IDB: *International Data Base*, U.S. Bureau of the Census.

IP: *International Profile: Alcohol and Other Drugs*, published by the Alcoholism and Drug Addiction Research Foundation (Toronto), 1994.

KIDRON & SEGAL: *State of the World Atlas*, 5th ed., London: Penguin, 1995.

NBWR: *The New Book of World Rankings*, 3rd ed., Facts on File, 1991.

SAUS: *Statistical Abstract of the United States*, published annually by the U.S. Department of Commerce.

TWF: *The World Factbook*, published annually by the Central Intelligence Agency.

TWW: *The World's Women*, published by the United Nations, 1995.

UNCRIME: United Nations. THE SIXTH UNITED NATIONS SURVEY OF CRIME TRENDS AND OPERATIONS OF CRIMINAL JUSTICE SYSTEMS, 1997 (Computer files). Vienna, Austria: Crime Prevention and Criminal Justice Branch, United Nations Office at Vienna.

UNSY: *United Nations Statistical Yearbook*, United Nations.

WVS: World Values Study Group. WORLD VALUES SURVEY, 1981–1984, 1990–1993 and 1995–1997 (Computer files). ICPSR version. Ann Arbor, MI: Institute for Social Research (producer). Ann Arbor, MI: Inter-university Consortium for Political and Social Research (distributor).

TRENDS

The data in the TRENDS file are also from a variety of sources. Years included utilize the most recent statistics available when this manuscript went to press. The description of each variable includes one of the following abbreviations to indicate the source.

AGI: The Alan Guttmacher Institute, New York, NY.

BJS: Bureau of Justice Statistics, Department of Justice, Washington D.C.

BRFSS: Behavior Risk Factor Surveillance System, National Center for Chronic Disease Prevention and Health Promotion, Centers for Disease Control and Prevention, U.S. Department of Health and Human Services.

Census: U.S. Census Bureau, U.S. Department of Commerce.

CM: Child Maltreatment 1999.

CPS: Current Population Survey, U.S. Census Bureau, Department of Commerce.

FBI: Federal Bureau of Investigation, Department of Justice.

GSS: General Social Survey, 1972 through 2002, National Opinion Research Corporation, University of Chicago.

HSUS: *Historical Abstracts of the United States, Colonial Times to 1970*, published by the U.S. Department of Commerce.

IPV: *Bureau of Justice Statistics Special Report: Intimate Partner Violence,* Callie Marie Rennison and Sarah Welchans, Bureau of Justice Statistics, Washington D.C., 2000.

MFS: The Monitoring the Future Study, The University of Michigan. (Data obtained from http://monitoringthefuture.org)

MH2000: *Mental Health, United States, 2000.* 2001. Ronald W. Manderscheid and Marilyn J. Henderson, Center for Mental Health Services, Substance Abuse and Mental Health Services Adminsitration, U.S. Department of Health and Human Services, Rockville, MD.

NCHS: National Center for Health Statistics, Hyattsville, MD. (Much of this is from Health United States, 2001 or 2002)

NCVS: National Crime Victimization Survey, Bureau of Justice Statistics, Department of Justice, Washington D.C.

NHIS: National Health Interview Survey, National Center for Health Statistics, Hyattsville, MD. Data pulled from Health United States, 2001.

NHSDA: National Household Survey on Drug Abuse, Substance Abuse and Mental Health Services Administration, Department of Health and Human Services.

SA: *Statistical Abstract of the United States,* published annually by the U.S. Department of Commerce.

UCR: *Uniform Crime Reports,* Federal Bureau of Investigation (FBI), Department of Justice, Washington D.C. UCR rates are expressed in "per 100,000."

VI: *Violence by Intimates,* Bureau of Justice Statistics, Washington D.C., 1998.

Vital Statistics: National Center for Health Statistics, Hyattsville, MD.

YRBS: Youth Risk Behavior Surveillance System, Centers for Disease Control and Prevention, National Center for Chronic Disease Prevention and Health Promotion (CDC), Atlanta, GA.

YRBS

These data are from a survey of high school students titled "Youth Risk Behavior Surveillance System Survey," conducted annually by the Division of Adolescent and School Health, National Center for Chronic Disease Prevention and Health Promotion, Centers for Disease Control and Prevention (CDC). This particular file includes only high school seniors in the year 2001.

Here is contact information to learn more about this valuable survey:
2001 YRBS — Division of Adolescent and School Health
National Center for Chronic Disease Prevention and Health Promotion
Centers for Disease Control and Prevention (CDC)
Mailstop K-33
4770 Buford Highway, NE
Atlanta, Georgia 30341-3717
Phone: (770) 488-6161
E-mail: healthyyouth@cdc.gov

GSS

These data are based on a merged file of 2000 and 2002 General Social Surveys conducted by the National Opinion Research Center (NORC), University of Chicago. Principal Investigators: James A. Davis and Tom W. Smith. This project has been sponsored by the National Science Foundation.

ELECTION

These data are based on a merged file of 1998 and 2000 American National Election Studies surveys. The 1998 study was conducted by the Center for Political Studies of the Institute for Social Research, under the general direction of Principal Investigators Virginia Sapiro and Steven Rosenstone. The 2000 study was conducted under the general direction of Principal Investigators Nancy Burns and Donald R. Kinder. These are the twenty-fifth and twenty-sixth in a series of studies of American national elections produced by the Center for Political Studies and the Survey Research Center. They are the eleventh and twelfth such studies to be conducted under the auspices of National Science Foundation Grants providing long-term support for the National Election Studies.